The Lively
Rhetoric

The Lively Rhetoric

READINGS
ANALYSES
ARGUMENTS

Alexander Scharbach

Ralph H. Singleton

PORTLAND STATE COLLEGE

Holt, Rinehart and Winston, Inc.
New York   Chicago   San Francisco
Atlanta   Dallas

To young men and women everywhere,
whose influence will determine the future.

Preface for Instructors

To INCLUDE only recent articles and essays which present challenges that college freshmen of the late 1960s will enjoy has been our prime guide in shaping *The Lively Rhetoric*. Each of the 32 short, dramatic selections, furthermore, not only exemplifies some aspect of composition or rhetoric, but also has an analytical commentary accompanying it to show in detail the special features that the selection embodies—features and techniques the students can apply to their own class writing. Above all, we feel that freshmen need a wide variety of down-to-earth writing assignment topics based on possible reactions to the issues found in the essays. How well we have succeeded in these purposes you alone can judge.

The five categories making up the content divisions may appear traditional enough in their general subject matter: Campus Life and Education, Mores and Morals, National Issues and the Campus, Issues in Science, and Issues in Literature and Art. But authors like Philip Wylie, James Baldwin, Art Buchwald, Norman Cousins, Loren Eiseley, John Updike, Ernest Hemingway, and Wright Morris make those familiar fields of interest exciting with their critical and outspoken views. Their representative selections provide a wide range of tone and attitude: humor, irony, analytical report, reflection, jeremiad, and all shades of persuasion. The "story" photograph accompanying each of the part openings sets the tone for that section.

Each of the five parts of the book also concentrates on presenting one set of the elements of composition and rhetoric: Purpose and Organization; Development by Details; Logic, Argument, and Persuasion; Paragraphs and Their Sentences; and Style. Each part has an introduction which defines and explains all the terms and techniques specifically exemplified in the selections which follow and which the accompanying commentaries discuss in detail. We believe this method of explanation-with-example followed by full-length illustration and its explication will make the skills and techniques so presented clear and understandable to even the "slow" student. In addition, students will find assistance in the marginal comments and the outline that accompany the first selection of each part.

Two assignment sections follow each commentary. Under the heading of "What Does It Say?" students are led to a simple study of the semantics of the piece. The "What Do You Think?" portion contains the kind of writing assignments wherein all students can find topics within the range of their immediate knowledge and firsthand experience. We constantly stress that students should order their own facts and ideas to support generalizations about which they have strong convictions. The articles from which the assignments stem should cause these reactions. A glance at the table of Contents will suggest the "lively" kind of issues the student will want to voice his views on, but we hope to help make those views well tempered with reason as well as effectively expressed.

For their gracious part in the preparation of *The Lively Rhetoric,* we wish to thank especially Professor Richard Beal of Boston University, whose critical suggestions and comments were invaluable throughout; also the English Language Editor of Holt, Rinehart and Winston, Phillip Leininger, and his staff for their assistance and encouragement. We thank also our colleagues of the Portland State College English Department who encouraged us in the innovations we have tried to incorporate in that most important and often most exasperating course, Freshman Composition.

We hereby also acknowledge with gratitude the authors, publishers, and photographers who have granted us permission to use their works.

Portland, Oregon
January 1968

A.S.

R.H.S.

Preface
for
Students

Ours is the age of the salesman. Television hucksters, political leaders at all levels, clergymen, and even our friends constantly assure us they know best what is good for us. Every minute someone is trying to influence our thinking or open our billfolds. The mass media of television, radio, newspapers, and magazines bombard us with constant "messages." Signboards, neon tubes, loudspeakers vie with one another to capture our attention. From all sides comes this concerted effort to convince us of something, make us do what someone wants us to do.

In short, we can say that we live in an age of rhetoric. For rhetoric is the art of persuasion. And if we would protect ourselves from this barrage of words and sounds and pictures aimed at leveling our defenses, we should learn something about this art ourselves so that we can reach sound and valid decisions—choose wisely and, in turn, become effective persuaders for what we believe is sound and worthwhile.

Let's not fool ourselves. We, as well as others, are constantly explaining or arguing as we try to persuade others to see things as we do. Whenever we discuss a topic or warmly defend an idea that we cherish, we are employing rhetoric. Rhetoric is an ancient art. The Greeks called a public speaker a *rhetor*, because their skilled orators were schooled in all the arts of persuasion.

There never has been a time when the ability to explain, to persuade was a more desirable asset than it is now. You will find in this book a wide range of articles selected from the skilled persuaders engaged in today's arena. Here are many topics arousing controversy on many subjects—subjects on which you most likely have definite opinions of your own. To help you formulate your own ideas, to help you express them adequately and effectively, is the purpose of this book.

No one expects you to become a highly efficient writer in a few days. You need to learn certain principles and methods, and to learn them in a systematic order. You need practice—a good deal of practice—under careful guidance and direction. You will find the help you need in the carefully planned arrangement of this book, in addition to a goodly number of lively articles that will stimulate your thinking.

Read, think, write, and rewrite. These are the guidelines of this book, just as they have obviously been the guidelines of the writers represented here, and surely also of your instructor.

A.S.
R.H.S.

Portland, Oregon
January 1968

Contents

Part 3   NATIONAL ISSUES AND THE CAMPUS

Logic, Argument, and Persuasion   113

Part 4   ISSUES AND SCIENCE

Paragraphs and Their Sentences   169

Part 5   ISSUES IN LITERATURE AND ART

Style   203

Rhetorical Contents

ANALYSIS

DEFINITION

ARGUMENTATION

REPORT

INFORMAL ESSAY

CHARACTER DESCRIPTION

EXPOSITORY NARRATION

The Lively
Rhetoric

1. Do you consider these students as making up a representative group? Why or why not?   2.   Do you see yourself as possibly a typical member of this group? Why or why not?

Photo by Mark Kauffman, LIFE Magazine © Time Inc.

Part 1

CAMPUS LIFE AND EDUCATION

Purpose

and

Organization

SOMEONE IS out there beyond the sound of your voice. You want to tell him something, but the only way to reach him is by putting words on a sheet of paper in such a way that he will understand you and, you hope, respond favorably to you.

Anyone who writes an article for publication finds himself in just such a position. He has something to tell us, his readers, whom he has never met. He may want to point out some overlooked fact, warn us of some danger, or urge us to pursue some course of action. He may even wish us to agree with him as he attacks a commonly accepted idea or the actions of a prominent person. Whatever the purpose, in order to attract and hold our attention, a writer must have a definite *point of view*—a clearly defined attitude toward his subject matter and readers.

If an article is to appear in print, it must meet the composition standards of a discerning editor. The seven essays in this section have received such editorial approval, and you will find in them and in the commentary following each of them some of the basic skills of good writing that you will want to make your own.

To start, Steven Kelman's "You Force Kids to Rebel" shows the function of the three fundamental parts of every composition. In general, the purpose

3

of the *introduction* is to arouse interest by its opening remarks; it often includes the *generalization* or *thesis*—a statement of the aims of the author. Following the introduction comes the *body,* which adequately develops and supports that generalization, or statement of purpose, with carefully chosen facts and ideas. Finally, the *conclusion* leaves the reader with some dramatic impression or fact closely related to the purpose of the essay.

In a way, as a student writer, you also have a body of demanding readers (your classmates) and a "discerning editor" (your instructor). Your editor is one who is eager to help you attain a satisfactory degree of professional proficiency. He would like you to emulate the authors of these articles and adopt the many time-tested devices for holding reader attention and making adequate explanations that they have learned from others.

What are some of these basic elements and skills of good writing? Besides *point of view* and the three fundamental parts of any composition which we have already discussed, the essays in this section show us examples, first of all, of *unity.* Whatever you choose to call it—"consistency" or "sticking to the subject"—unity means giving the reader only the full and detailed information that helps support the basic thesis or purpose of the author. If, for example, a writer makes the general statement "It's the teen-age magazines that make teen-agers hip," he could illustrate his topic by mentioning which magazines the thirty million teen-agers in the U.S. read and on which specific products that are advertised in these magazines the young people spend close to $12 billion every year to make themselves feel "hip." (Of course, this term itself will need some defining.) It is the principle of unity which would forbid including here any lengthy reference to adult magazines except perhaps by way of comparison or contrast.

For clarity and ease in reading, a writer also strives to find a suitable *order,* or *sequence,* for his supporting facts and ideas. Not unlike the planners of supermarkets who arrange for products to be on display in such a fashion that the housewife can quickly find what she is looking for, the writer realizes that most people appreciate time-saving order and organization.

Usually, the writer has the choice of two kinds of structural order: deductive or inductive. The main generalization may be placed in the introduction, or beginning paragraphs of the essay, and then followed with the various particulars or details that support it. (This is called the *deductive order.*) Or the details may be placed first, leading up to the generalization which would appear at the conclusion of the essay. (This is called the *inductive order.*)

Within the framework of either of these structural orders, you have the possibility of arranging the material in a variety of sequences, choosing the one that seems most natural for what you have to say. If you are explaining a process, such as "how to handle a blind date," or giving the grim details of some event such as "the airplane trip I would not like to repeat," you might find a *chronological* sequence helpful, for it enables one to show what happens first and then what follows according to the order of time. If you choose a topic like "why I lost my best summer job," you would do well to adopt some form of *cause and effect* sequence to reveal the various reasons—personal or otherwise—that combined to bring about the painful result. If you are explaining something difficult for the average reader to grasp, you might start with what is *familiar* and work *toward* what is less familiar. In discussing most topics, the experienced writer tries to arrange his paragraph ideas so that they follow one another in an order of increasing importance—*climactic* order, or in an order of decreasing importance—*anticlimactic* order.

Emphasis is yet another element of good writing. In one sense it is closely linked with *order,* because it is acknowledged that the first and last items to engage our attention are the ones that strike us most forcibly. But emphasis is also a matter of *proportion.* That which is most significant should be given the most detailed treatment. The reverse, of course, is also true; one should never give a disproportionate amount of space to an insignificant matter or a minor exception to a principle under discussion.

Gradually as you learn these principles of effective expression, and the others in the sections to follow, you will begin to feel more sure of yourself, more confident that you know what you want to do when you sit down to write. And this assurance, you will discover, brings many benefits and much personal satisfaction.

YOU
FORCE KIDS
TO REBEL

STEVEN KELMAN

ON BOTH high-school and college campuses, the official statements about almost any subject are so widely distrusted nowadays that citing them is the best way to have yourself marked as a dupe or a simpleton. Adults might understand how serious this problem is if they'd listen to the words of the songs of somebody like Bob Dylan. His most popular songs are talking about skepticism, about what's really going on in the world as compared to what we're being taught is going on in the world. *When we take a look for ourselves, the facts we see are so different from what we've been taught that we have no choice but to turn into rebels or at least skeptics.*

Kids grow up "tryin'a be so good"—in the words of one Dylan song. When we fall from this "good" innocence it's like going through an earthquake; the ground under you just isn't solid any more. And it's a quick jump from saying to yourself, "What they taught me is a lie," to saying, "So they must be liars." The

Reprinted from *Saturday Evening Post*, November 19, 1966, by permission of the author.

feeling is that the adult Establishment is phony or self-interested, composed of people you can't trust.

Most parents don't want to accept this explanation. It's said that we're know-it-alls, though we're really know-nothings, and it's said that an affluent society produces spoiled brats who have no sense of values and no appreciation of all the things being done for them.

A prevailing criticism of youth

There are a number of facts that show this isn't true. For instance, philosophy courses in almost every college are in unprecedented demand (as I just discovered when I unsuccessfully tried to get into one with a "limited" enrollment of 325). At Harvard, where I am now, the Phillips Brooks House, which does all sorts of social service and community-assistance projects, is the largest organization on campus.

The criticism unjustified

Perhaps the most popular theory for the kids' rebellion is that the "conflict of generations" is inevitable, and that we will "outgrow it." However, even if some sort of reaction of young people against their parents is inevitable, the revolt is now taking a particular form—skepticism. It took the same form, by the way, in 19th-century Russia. When youth gets skeptical, I submit, it does not indicate that anything is wrong with youth, but rather that something is wrong with adults.

Another source of criticism

And that "something" is the way you usually look at and react to what's going on in the world. "Hypocrisy" is a big word with us, and it's a mortal sin in our moral code, dooming the sinner to our version of hell—permanent eclipse of any moral influence he might have on us.

Hypocrisy behind these attacks

If kids were taught that the world is flat, any reasonably sane person would expect us to revolt against those responsible for teaching that particular "fact." So what else but skepticism and revolt should anybody expect from us when we are being taught a view of the world which is little more sophisticated than the flat-earth theory?

Repetition of thesis in more specific terms

It all starts in first grade. There we are treated to a candy-cane world where all the children in the textbooks are white tots living in suburbia with a dog running around the lawn. When suburban kids find out about slums, they're apt to get skeptical. When slum

BODY
Unreal teaching about slums

kids are taught about a world that has nothing to do with the world in which they live, they have to do the same. A song which has been a hit among students is a parody—perhaps unconscious—of those first-grade primers:

> Little boxes on the hillside.
> Little boxes made of ticky-tacky,
> Little boxes, little boxes, little boxes
> All the same.
> There's a green one, and a pink one,
> And a blue one, and a yellow one,
> And they're all made out of ticky-tacky,
> And they all look just the same.*

Unreal teaching about love and sex

Many of us come to realize just how unreal the classroom world is when our thoughts turn to boy-girl relationships. No teen-ager can escape knowing that love and sex are part of the real world.

So how does society's agent, the school, present this part of reality? It ignores it. For instance, one biology teacher I heard about treated his students to the obscene spectacle of his own sniggering while he described sexual reproduction in algae. Health teachers reduce puberty to a section of an inane chart on "stages of human development." When we find out the facts and feel the emotions, how can anyone expect us not to be skeptical about an adult world which tries to act as if none of this existed? And the moral code that we have developed, "sex with love," seems to us to be more logical than anything you've put up.

Unreal attitude toward literature

The whole idea the school seems to try to get across is that if you don't teach it to us, it doesn't exist. This can sometimes go to extreme length. In junior high school we had a thing called a "Reading Record Card." This was supposed to be a list (and brief discussion) of all the books you had read each year. But "all the books" actually meant all the books that were in the school library. And when students protested against the refusal to allow listing of books like *1984* and *The Grapes of Wrath*, we were treated like people in China who try to whisper that Mao Tse-tung is

---

* *Little Boxes,* words and music by Malvina Reynolds. Copyright © 1962 by Schroder Music Co., Berkeley, Calif. Used by permission.

not the only recognized writer in the world. And what are we taught about literature? We are often required to memorize such details as "What color was Ivanhoe's horse?" and "What hotel did Gatsby and the Buchanans meet in?" rather than talking about how a book means something in helping us to figure out ourselves or other people. So kids often give up the classics. One kid told me that he feared becoming a writer because of what high-school English teachers would do to his books.

And how about student government? I was active in it during high school, but the majority attitude of indifference was a pretty good instinctive reaction. In most schools the "governments" must restrict themselves to planning social extravaganzas. When they try to do something—as when ours voted to fast for a lunch in sympathy with the people of India—the administration vetoed our plans. You say that we should act responsibly, and when we try to, you act as if youthful hordes were trying to take over the school. Is the world like that?

Unreal attitude toward student government

It sometimes seems to us that myths are peddled to us about *everything* we are taught. For example, the quaint myth of the American family farm—enshrined in numerous references in our courses—obscures the reality of giant agricultural industries and underpaid migrant labor. The history of American cities as it is generally presented comes to a screeching halt at the turn of the century. American history textbooks I've seen are at least 30 years behind the latest historical investigations. Thus one widely used junior-high history text states that the sole purpose of American intervention in Latin America in the early part of the century was to "lend a helping hand" to the people by building roads, bridges and hospitals. This is a little hard to believe. More than one kid I know has reacted by taking the position that our only motive in Latin America was financial greed. From my experience, American history courses generally produce more anti-Americanism than understanding of history.

Substitution of myths for reality

And what about the presentation of the one problem which concerns kids most of all—race? Well, one junior-high-school civics book devotes a total of four

Inadequate discussion of racial problems

paragraphs to the history of the Negro in the United States. The last hundred years of Negro history are summed up like this:

> During the War Between the States, all Negro slaves were set free. Since then American Negroes have gone through a difficult period of adjustment to new ways of life. They have made remarkable progress in a short time.

Summary and contrast
with reality

Now, when we leave such textbooks and look at the world, it is entirely natural that we think someone has been trying to put something over on us. Our world includes Watts and also suburbia, grape pickers as well as family farms, Latin Americans whose memories of American troops often center on the two-bit dictators the troops installed rather than the roads they built. And why would you teach us unreality if you didn't accept it?

Inanity of texts on
communism

A sort of "textbook case" (if the pun is acceptable) of codified obscuritanism being peddled under the guise of education is the high-school courses designed to teach us about Communism. In the world presented in most "Communism" courses, "Democracy" and "Communism" fight each other out on a wooden stage. After going through one of these courses, it takes someone with a vivid imagination to realize that these things are ideas millions of people around the world are living and sometimes dying for. The "Comparison Charts" commonly used are of varying lengths (the one in J. Edgar Hoover's high-school guide, *A Study of Communism,* takes the prize, filling up eight pages of text). They are designed to contrast the beliefs of Communism *vs.* Freedom in such fields as government, economics, education, morality, etc. Considering the debates which have gone on about such fundamental questions, it should come as no shock that these "contrasts" can seem ludicrous. Take this example from Hoover's book:

> COMMUNISM: There is a total disregard for the inherent dignity of the individual.
> FREEDOM: There is a deep and abiding respect for the inherent dignity and worth of the individual.

Most students who are paying attention to this react by murmuring, "You must be putting me on," or a less polite variant. For we know that in this world nothing is so simple. And we only have to look at the pictures of the Alabama police dogs to know that things are not simple at all. So a lot of kids react by concluding that there's no difference between "Communism" and "Freedom" in this respect. And if we try to argue, we get Hoover thrown back at our face.

Almost every "Communism" course repeats an account of Marxism. When it centers on doctrines like "dialectical materialism," which even Communists have trouble understanding, the course usually turns into a farce. Afterward we often get the accompanying horror images. One widely used film states that the only three non-Communist countries in the West are Spain, Switzerland and America! In an attempt to get down to what is presumed to be our level, one text shows a cartoon of an Oriental-looking Lenin, left hand on a cannon, leading regimented lines of darkly colored robot people against others who, huddled in small groups around the base of the Statue of Liberty, are riding in a car, watching TV, debating, and mowing a lawn. Most of us think that such things insult our intelligence.

As we go through school, we are subjected to lots more of this evidence that the real world and the world being taught us aren't the same. Of course, some of us never rebel. They will form the shock troops of the older generation and in our vocabulary are "finks." Or, they will just "cop out" to boredom.

But for the others, an overdose of unreality, just like an overdose of anything else, can produce crazy results—even a sickness. Flirtations with things like LSD and "pot" are merely escaping reality, not trying to refuse to adapt to it. It is, for example, a tragedy that anti-Communism is becoming a dirty word on the American campus. It is also a tragedy that the political activism of a generation concerned with the world is in danger of being wasted in the pursuit of semi-anarchist dreams. And the refusal to believe anything people in authority say is only a reaction to the fact that last time we believed we were deceived.

Unrealistic teaching about communism

Student reaction to oversimplified information

Reaction to anti-communistic propaganda

Consequent waste of rebellion

CONCLUSION
Solution offered

What can be done to prevent this revolt against the future? Actually, what is really needed is a revamping of the way we are taught. One suggestion might be to drop our fetish with "objectivity" in subjects toward which we are not objective. Politics are not objective. Love is not objective. People are not objective. Instead of objectivity, the guiding word in our schools should be democracy—which is, as far as I can tell, the prevailing philosophy in our country. Democracy means trusting us to make up our minds. Using democracy in a course about Communism, for example, could mean matching a text that defends a free society with one defending Communism. To the nervous Nellies who recoil, I ask, "Don't you think that the case for Democracy is the better one?" Don't you realize that in the Vietnam war we are given absurd analogies to European history and opponents tend to view the Viet Cong as 20th-century versions of Robin Hood?

Repetition of thesis idea

These are only random examples. The point is this: Adults often like to pretend the real world doesn't exist. Kids can't. We might want to *escape* from it, but we can't *forget* about it. And we know the difference between the world we're taught and the world we experience. And if we blame you for trying to put something over on us, it's only because we're taught what, alas, most Americans seem to think. If the school is trying to turn its back on reality, it only represents an America that's doing the same thing. And that's what really worries us.

OUTLINE

Generalization: "When we take a look for ourselves, the facts we see are so different from what we've been taught that we have no choice but to turn into rebels or at least skeptics."

   I. Young people must rebel against the unrealities they are taught.
     A. At an early age they become skeptical of misinformation about slums.
     B. They see the unrealities and shortcomings in classroom references to love and sex.
     C. They suffer from unreal approaches to literature.

II. As students they rebel against school attitudes toward government.
    A. Their own student government initiatives are vetoed.
    B. They find that myths are substituted for historical realities in history and social science classes.
    C. Textbook discussions of racial problems are inadequate.
III. Students note the contrasts between the unreality of textbook views of world problems and history and the facts of everyday events.
    A. They see through the inanities of textbooks treating of communism.
    B. They are critical of anti-communistic propaganda films and cartoons.
IV. Students react to these unrealities in various ways.
    A. Some never rebel and become "finks," like their elders.
    B. Some turn to drugs to escape reality.
    C. Some refuse to believe any adult in authority.

COMMENTARY

This essay by Steven Kelman, a student at Harvard University, displays the important qualities of *unity* and *order*. As the outline and the marginal comments show, the basic generalization, stated in plain, direct terms, receives adequate support. Kelman attacks various practices and attitudes in elementary and high-school teaching which he considers dangerously unrealistic, and he makes several suggestions to remedy them.

Notice how specific he is. Instead of merely making a number of vague, general statements, he is detailed about what he thinks is wrong. One after the other, he takes up and pinpoints the unrealities of urban life, sex, literature, race, and communism as these are taught in the schools. Then he lists the tragic results growing out of such faulty education. To drive home his *generalization,* he repeats it several times but always in somewhat different words, as in these expressions: "The feeling is that the adult Establishment is phony or self-interested, composed of people you can't trust." . . . "*Hyprocrisy* is a big word with us, and it's a mortal sin in our moral code." . . . "Why would you teach us unreality if you didn't accept it?" . . . "Most of us think that such things insult our intelligence."

His choice of *point of view* was also appropriate. He is addressing the *Saturday Evening Post* range of readers, and he talks straight from the shoulder as a spokesman for "The Kids," with whom he identifies himself through the consistent use of the first-person-plural pronoun, "we." He is blunt with this personal point of view: "When we take a look for ourselves," "It's said that we're know-it-alls," "It all starts in first grade. There we are treated to a candy-cane world," "One kid told me that he feared becoming a writer because of what high-school English teachers would do to his books," "For we know that in this world nothing is so simple." Another reason for his successful communication with his readers is that his illustrations, supporting his main complaints, come out of his own experiences, which he describes in graphic detail.

In adopting the *deductive order* of leading down from the generalization stated in his *introduction,* Kelman found an order of development natural to his subject. He felt strongly about what he wanted to say and so used the opening portion of his essay to prepare the reader for the bitter generalization soon to come. Then in a *sequence* of increasing importance he took up the specific points indicated in the outline in order to build up the *body* of the essay. In the *conclusion,* he once more reminded his audience: "Adults often like to pretend the real world doesn't exist. Kids can't." And his final sentence is also frank and direct: "And that's what really worries us."

In your own writing assignments, strive to give your generalizations this kind of unity and order. You have probably discovered that the hardest part of writing often lies in finding a problem that you can phrase into a generalization, as Kelman did. Here are some suggestions. First, from the topic suggestions in the following "What Do You Think?" items, choose one that you, like Kelman, have strong feelings about, and then give it some thought and brooding time. Second, keeping Kelman's essay in mind, write a first draft of a generalization supported by facts and ideas drawn from your own experiences. Then still trying if possible to outdo Kelman, begin the rewriting and revising necessary to almost all good compositions.

Write what you sincerely believe, and enjoy discovering things about yourself and your world that you have never before realized existed.

WHAT DOES IT SAY?

1. What is the difference between a *rebel* and a *skeptic?*

2. Why would novels like *1984* and *The Grapes of Wrath* be barred from the reading lists of some high schools?

3. In what sense is the school "society's agent"?

4. How do you interpret the expression "You must be putting me on"? Would you use it in a written composition? Why or why not?

5. Who or what are "nervous Nellies"?

6. Have you observed any signs of "our fetish with objectivity"?

7. What is Kelman trying to say when he says "Love is not objective"?

8. What is *hyprocrisy* and why does Kelman label it "a mortal sin in our moral code"?

WHAT DO YOU THINK?

Here are other views of this same "rebellion." Choose one or more of them as a basis for an essay having a distinct introduction and conclusion in support of your agreement or disagreement with Kelman.

1. The young TV generation has a completely different sensory life than the adult generation which grew up on hot radio and hot print. Hence, young people today reject jobs and goals—that's linear thinking. They reject the consumer life—that's fragmented and specialist. They want roles, that is, involvement.—Marshall McLuhan quoted in *Newsweek*, March 6, 1967, p. 54.

2. a) Stay clear, don't get involved.
   b) Society nowadays makes you a hypocrite.
   c) Find out what the prof wants, give it to him, and get the grade. That's what counts.
   d) The "Generation Gap" starts at 30. People older than that can't understand us.
   e) It's not what you learn in college but whom you meet.
   f) What's wrong with having a good time if it doesn't hurt anybody?

3. "My parents," said a senior, "expect more of me than I can possibly put out. I have even cheated on exams to get B's and A's because I didn't want to let them down." It is a sad and bitter thing when the "helpful" efforts of parents end this way.—Dr. Wilbur F. Pillsbury, "Learn to Leave Your Student Alone!" *Better Homes and Gardens*, October 1966, p. 20.

4. Running away from home is something kids have been doing for hundreds of years. Most merely have an argument, pack a bag, get 150 yards from the door and go back. But more and more young people from respectable homes are really running away—disappearing for days or weeks. Last year, there were 100,000 and one third of them were girls.—Jhan and June Robbins, "The Nice Girls Who Ran Away," *McCall's*, November 1966, p. 115.

5. It isn't a question of moderate versus militant but of responsibility versus irresponsibility, sanity versus insanity, effectiveness versus ineffectiveness.—Whitney M. Young, Jr., National Urban League director, *Time*, August 11, 1967, p. 13.

A VOTE
FOR STUDENT
PROTEST

MARY N. GONZALES

IN THE present era university students and their professors, who are, it must
be immediately established, only older students paying their debt to scholarship by inducting a new generation, have been passionately involved in debating and protesting the political and social events of their time.

The students who demonstrated on campuses across the country last year
against the U.S. position in Vietnam were acting within their rights as citizens.
Where they infringed the constitutional rights of others—by breaking up
assemblies of fellow students or inhibiting the free speech of others—they
deserved to be, and were, punished. But the fact that some of the students
who demonstrated were rowdy (or dirty or bearded or *wrong*) is no more
logical as an argument against demonstrations than the fact that Americans
have often elected incompetent men to office can be considered a reason for
abandoning democratic elections.

The human fact is that a student of any age cannot read analytically the
works of Locke, Jefferson, Ortega, Shaw, Ibsen (much less Sartre, Osborne,
or Baldwin) without recognizing much that is stupid and evil in our society.
In the way of people who are young, free, and relatively innocent of the
adult world's experience, he believes that there's no point arguing because no

one listens to him anyway, so he makes his anger known in other ways. His righteous wrath and insistence that society take steps to improve itself immediately are not the products of inflammatory texts or teachers; they are the inevitable concomitants of the intelligent student's attempt to relate what he hears in class to himself and his world.

No pat on the head for youthful idealism is intended here. Youthful idealism is widely known to curdle into middle-aged cynicism, and both are diffuse, unproductive ways of meeting social problems. The past year's crop of demonstrators made it clear that they were not claiming to have answers to problems that have required years of persistent effort and will require many more to produce results. They wanted to express their attitude on issues of the greatest importance—war and peace, and foreign intervention, the rights of small nations and defenseless citizens—and to communicate these attitudes as widely as possible.

Any student who can sit through four years of college without once getting excited enough about the war in Vietnam or Communism in Cuba, voting discrimination in the South or the plight of the Jews in Russia to investigate the problem (study) and find others who agree with him and make some public protest—any student so dense or just plain selfish that he has not perceived the relation between his university education and the pressing questions of his society has undoubtedly been wasting his time.

COMMENTARY

This brief essay was chosen by the *Atlantic Monthly* staff as the best comment received from campus activists on the issues and temperament of student radicalism as they knew it. Note that Mary Gonzales has a passionate *point of view,* clearly expressed. Although the *generalization* of this essay appears in the opening sentence, the movement and *order* are mainly inductive, leading to the rousing final paragraph which makes up the *conclusion.* Observe how this one-sentence paragraph ends with an outspoken declaration that echoes the "passionately involved" state of the students and professors described in the *introduction.*

WHAT DOES IT SAY?

1. *Activists* is a term applied to those persons who are willing to *act* upon the basis of their principles. Does Mrs. Gonzales in her opening paragraph maintain that all professors *have been passionately involved* in these controversial events?

2. What are the connotations of her expression "inducting a *new genera-tion*"?

3. In the second paragraph, are her adjectives describing the demonstra-tors—(*rowdy or dirty or bearded or "wrong"*)—of equal weight? In her opinion, is there any difference among these words when applied to the demonstrators?

4. What in the context of paragraph 3 does she mean by "read analyt-ically"? How does this kind of reading differ from other kinds of reading?

5. Also in paragraph 3, after consulting library sources, explain why the two sets of authors' names are grouped as they are (the second group is enclosed in parentheses).

6. *Righteous wrath* has biblical overtones of what kind?

7. What examples of beliefs and public acts do you associate with *youth-ful idealism? With middle-aged cynicism?*

8. What is the "plight of the Jews in Russia"?

WHAT DO YOU THINK?

1. Mrs. Gonzales implies that professors owe it to their students, as a way of paying their "debt to scholarship," to take part in debates and protests on political and social events. Do you agree? Or do you think that a professor's "debt to scholarship" can be equally well paid in other ways, such as by good teaching and further study in his field? Write a 500-word letter-essay of reply suitable for *Atlantic*-level readers.

2. In a brief essay discuss the different situations of social protest wherein city officials would probably move to curb "freedom of expression" as explained in the following statement:

The most stringent protection of free speech, said Holmes, would not protect a man from the penal consequences of falsely shouting "fire" in a crowded theater. The question in every case is whether words are used in such cir-cumstances and are of such a nature as to create a clear and present danger.— Leo Pfeffer, "Freedom of Expression," *Nation,* October 3, 1966.

3. What is your literate reaction to this judgment voiced by a prominent university professor?

We need a rigorous definition not merely of student rights but of student responsibilities. We need clearer apprehension of the truth that though the university should not close its doors to public discussion, it cannot be flooded by public passions. We need universities. We are not going to get them by following the Berkeley pattern.—Howard Mumford Jones, *The Atlantic Monthly*, September 1966, p. 87.

4. Analyze the position of the faculty and their role as "citizens" as outlined in the following postinaugural statement by the president of a large urban college. After carefully summing up its views, write your reactions to them as if you were one of the faculty or a student body officer.

Lest there be any doubts about the position of the College, faculty should be assured that their right of free speech is one that the College takes for granted. Each member has the right to speak his thoughts and opinions, to communicate his general and specialized knowledge as freely as he wishes outside the College, as long as he does not put himself in the position of appearing to speak officially *for* the College. Within the classroom, traditionally he speaks with a degree of objectivity, in an attempt to illuminate matters of partisan interest with knowledge and viewpoints providing broader perspective and an increase of understanding. Outside the College, these obligations and restraints do not apply, and he may speak more freely; he acts as a private citizen and has no obligation to the College for his opinions and actions. As a private citizen he may make important contributions to the life of the community by virtue of his knowledge and experience, and may exemplify to the community the vital force of the intellect—of learning and rationally considered values—upon practical affairs. In doing so, he will reflect credit upon the College, and the College places a value upon such activities.

For such reasons, and because the individual has the right no matter what the College's views, the College takes for granted that members of the Faculty will continue to speak freely as private citizens, and that the College defends this right and has in mind no tests of conformity or popular approval. The College's administration will also continue to reject any criticisms from outside the College which attempt to interfere with this right or to discipline the individual. The College's simple requirement upon its members is the devotion of fitting attention to their academic tasks and obligations.—Branford P. Millar, President, Portland State College (Oregon). [Dr. Millar resigned the presidency of P.S.C. in June 1968.]

FREE SPEECH IS NOT FOR SPEAKERS

ART BUCHWALD

THE FREE speech movements on various campuses have become more militant in recent months and I naturally was interested to know what they were up to. So I went over to the Sitdown Institute of Technology to confer with an organization called the Students for Utterly Free Speech and the Preservation of Democratic Institutions Through the Exchange of Ideas Movement.

The young man in charge of the organization was very happy to speak to me.

"Sir," I said, "what is the purpose of the Students for Utterly Free Speech?"

"Our main purpose is to keep speakers who come to college campuses from speaking."

"That's a very idealistic goal," I said. "How do you do this?"

"It's quite simple. When the speaker starts talking we begin to heckle and shout at him so he can't be heard. The more he persists, the noisier we get and pretty soon everyone is shouting and if we're lucky it turns into a brawl."

"This probably sounds like a stupid question but if your organization is presumably for free speech, why don't you let the speaker say what he has on his mind?"

"But we're not for free speech for the speaker. We're for free speech for ourselves. We demand the right to interrupt anybody any time he opens his mouth. This is still a democratic country and we have a right to prevent anyone we want from speaking."

"But if you don't hear what the speaker has to say, how do you know you disagree with him?"

"We know we disagree with him before he comes. Anything he says might just confuse us. We're not fools, you know."

"I didn't say you were," I said. "But let's say, for argument's sake, that a speaker may have something new to add to the debate. Don't you think he should be able to put forth his position at the university?"

"None of the speakers has anything new to say. Besides, if we let one speaker put forth his arguments, then we'd have to let other speakers put forth their arguments, and pretty soon you'd have all sorts of ideas floating around and it would hurt the free speech movement."

"How could it hurt the free speech movement?"

"Well, our members don't want to sit around listening to people making a lot of speeches all day. They like action. That's why they joined the free speech movement. We prefer to boo and shout a lot. It gets rid of our hostilities."

"I can see that. But on the other hand, look at it from the speaker's point of view. He's probably worked on his speech for several days; taken time off to come to the university. Shouldn't he be allowed to talk?"

"It's not our fault he went to all that trouble. If he were smart he would have just written the opening lines of his speech, and we would have seen to it that no one knew that was all he had to say. We'll co-operate with a speaker if he co-operates with us."

"Is there any situation where you would allow a speaker to finish his speech?"

"We don't like to make exceptions but I guess if he used four-letter words we might let him finish. You see, our free speech movement believes we should be allowed to use four-letter words."

"How do four-letter words contribute to the cause of free speech?"

"It helps us understand the exchange of ideas."

COMMENTARY

This kind of question-and-answer technique originated with the ancient Athenian philosopher Socrates, but Art Buchwald often adopts it, as he has here, to ridicule those policies and practices in the news which he considers objectionable. This dialogue form differs from a regular newspaper reporter interview in that Buchwald arranges the *sequence* of inquiries and replies in such a manner that they support two different *generalizations*. One of these is clearly stated, but the other is only implied and never spelled out. In the *introduction,* the "strawman" being interviewed is made to overstate his stand so that he will appear preposterous—"But we're not for free speech for the speaker. We're for free speech for ourselves." As the interviewer, Buchwald's own views have to be drawn from the kind of questions he asks and from the way he makes the "strawman's" final replies in the *conclusion* reach the limits of nonsense:

"How do four-letter words contribute to the cause of free speech?"
"It helps us understand the exchange of ideas."

This dialogue method appears easy to imitate, and its humorous treatment of serious topics tempts one to adopt it in order to strike out at one's own favorite targets. Also its 800-word brevity and its wit seem within reach. Its irony in saying one thing and meaning another also is beguiling.

If you should decide to emulate Buchwald, make up your mind that you will have to keep a consistent *point of view* throughout your essay and never lose sight of your implied *generalization.* Also you will want to exercise some restraint in toying with the delights of irony.

WHAT DOES IT SAY?

1. What is Socratic irony? Is there Socratic irony in the name Buchwald gives to the "movement" he visited?

2. What incongruity lies in his addressing the young man with the term *sir?*

3. Did you find the reply to the first question ironical? Why?

4. What does Buchwald intend when he calls the purpose of the group "very idealistic"?

5. What ironies do the questions and answers give to the term "free speech"?

6. Does the student's derogatory expression "pretty soon you'd have all sorts of ideas floating around" roughly state Buchwald's own idea of free speech?

7. How do the final absurdities of the interviewee's replies exemplify Buchwald's broad use of Socratic irony?

8. Buchwald's use of the term "four-letter word" obviously does not mean all four-letter words (*hurt,* for instance). How do you know what he

means? This is another figure of speech called a *euphemism*. Look up *euphemism* in a dictionary to discover its meaning. When do you think the use of euphemisms is desirable?

WHAT DO YOU THINK?

1. Solely on the basis of this dialogue, what very definite views on college education and college life do you think the interviewer himself has? Write a dialogue-essay in which you interview the interviewer.

2. Point out in an essay any absurdities or contradictions you may have detected in the speech of some visiting lecturer to your own campus.

3. Write an imaginary interview with an influential leader on your campus such as the newspaper editor, a dean, a fraternity spokesman, an athlete, or a librarian.

4. The Associated Press (April 6, 1967) carried the following news story. In what respects do you agree or disagree with the kind of decisions announced in the report?

The Seattle School Board reaffirmed Tuesday its decision to deny the use of Garfield High School here for a speech by "black power" advocate Stokeley Carmichael April 19.

Board chairman Robert A. Tidwell said the local branch of the Student Non-Violent Coordinating Committee, of which Carmichael is national chairman, rejected a suggestion that "a panel of reactors" appear on the same program.

5. Formulate a generalization based on some problem suggested by the following topics, and develop it into a 500-word essay.
   a) Freedom does not mean license.
   b) Rights have corresponding duties.
   c) What "being trusted" means to me.
   d) How important are rules and regulations?
   e) Freedoms now lacking on this campus.
   f) Changing student attitudes.

DEAR MISS O'NEILL

LEO ROSTEN

ON THE HELLISH HOT DAYS (and the only city more hellish than Chicago, where this happened, is Bombay), Miss O'Neill would lift her wig and gently scratch her pate. She did it absently, without interrupting whatever she was saying or doing.

We always watched this with fascination. Miss O'Neill was our 7th-grade teacher, and it was the consensus of my more sophisticated peers that Miss O'Neill had, until very recently, been a nun. That was the only way they could explain the phenomenal fact of her baldness. Miss O'Neill, they whispered, had left her holy order for heartrending reasons, and the punishment her superiors had decreed was that she become a slave in the George Howland Elementary School on 16th Street.

We never knew Miss O'Neill's first name (teachers never had a first name), and when my mother once asked me how old she was, I answered, "Oh, she's *old*." All teachers are *old*. And "old" meant at least 30, even 40—which, to an 11-year-old, is as decrepit and remote and meaningless as, say, 60 or 70, though not 100.

Miss O'Neill was dumpy, moonfaced, sallow-skinned, colorless, and we loathed her as only a pack of West Side barbarians could loathe a teacher of arithmetic. She did not teach arithmetic—but that is how much all of us hated her.

She was our English teacher, a 33rd-degree perfectionist who drilled us, endlessly, mercilessly, in spelling and grammar and diction and syntax. She had a hawk's eye for a dangling participle or an upright non sequitur, a "not *quite* right" word or a fruity solecism. (Did you know that "solecism" comes

Reprinted from *Look* Magazine, September 20, 1966, by permission of the editors of *Look* Magazine, copyright © 1966, Cowles Communications, Inc.

from the contempt of Greek patricians for the dialect that thrived in Soloi?) Whenever any of us made an error in composition *or* recitation, Miss O'Neill would send the culprit to the blackboard to "diagram" the sentence! That was the torture we most resented.

We had to designate the function of every word and phrase and clause; we had to describe how each part of every sentence worked; we had to explain how the parts fit together, and how they mesh and move to wheel out meaning. Before our whole runny-nosed congregation, an innocent child had himself or herself to locate an error, identify a malfunction, explain the *reason* for the correction Miss O'Neill impassively awaited. She waited as if she could sit there until Gabriel blew his kazoo, as our devastating humor had it. And if the offered correction was itself wrong, Miss O'Neill compounded her discipline by making the errant urchin diagram *that* on the board, instructing him to persevere.

Some kids would break into a sweat as they floundered around, failing to hit the bull's-eye, praying that Miss O'Neill would end their agony by the generous gift of the one good and true answer. But that Miss O'Neill rarely proffered. Instead, she would turn her inquisition from the pupil at the blackboard to the helots in the chairs. "Well, class? . . . Jacob, do *you* know the answer? . . . No? . . . Shirley? . . . Harold? . . . Joseph?" So heartless and unyielding was her method.

Each day, as we poured out of George Howland like Cheyennes en route to a scalping, we would pause briefly to pool our misery and voice our rage over the fate that had condemned us to such an abecedarian. Had we known Shakespeare, we would have added one word to Hamlet's brutal advice to Ophelia, making it, with feeling, "Get thee back to a nunnery."

Miss O'Neill never raised her voice, never lost her patience, never got angry. What was even more surprising, she never had to punish or even threaten our most ingenious troublemakers. For some reason we never discovered, the small impertinences and sly infractions and simulated incomprehensions with which we shrewdly persecuted our other teachers never seemed to get anywhere in the tight, shipshape world of Miss O'Neill's classroom.

I say that my comrades and I hated Miss O'Neill—but that is not entirely true. I only pretended to hate her. In our sidewalk conclaves, when we chortled over the latest tour de force of Douglas Fairbanks, or mourned the defeat of the noble Cubs by the disgusting White Sox, or matched extravagances about what we would do if we found *ten million dollars,* or imagined the possible surrender of one or another maiden to our lascivious fumblings, I, too, would howl about Miss O'Neill's tyranny, cursing her adamantine ways as fervently as any of my companions. So strong is the desire of a boy to "belong," to be no different from even the grubbiest of his fellows.

But secretly, my respect for Miss O'Neill—nay, my affection—increased week by week. For I was exhilarated by what I can only call the incorruptibility of her instruction. I found stirring within myself a sense of excitement, of discovery, a curious quickening of the spirit that attends initiation into a new world. Though I could not explain it in these words, and would have scorned the Goody-Two-Shoes overtone, I felt that Miss O'Neill was leading me not through the irksome labyrinth of English but into a sunlit realm of order and meaning. Her iron rules, her crisp strictures, her constant corrections were not, to me, the irritating nit picking they were to my buddies. They were sudden flashes of light, glimpses of the magic hidden within prose, intoxicating visions of that universe that awaits understanding. It was as if a cloak of wonder had been wrapped around the barren bones of grammar. For it was not grammar or diction or syntax that Miss O'Neill, whether she knew it or not, was introducing me to. She was revealing language as the beautiful beat and life of logic. She was teaching what earlier generations so beautifully called "right reason."

The most astonishing thing about Miss O'Neill was that she proceeded on the sanguine assumption that she could actually teach a pack of potential roller-skate-derby fans how to write clear, clean, correct sentences, organized in clear, clean, correct paragraphs—in their native tongue.

I do not think Miss O'Neill had the slightest awareness of her hold and influence on me. Nor was she especially interested in me. She never betrayed an inkling of preference or favoritism for any of her captive flock. Nor was she interested in the high, immortal reaches of the language whose terrain she so briskly charted. She was a technician, pure and simple—efficient, conscientious, immune to the malarkey some pupils resorted to. Nothing derailed Miss O'Neill from professionalism.

And that is the point. Miss O'Neill did not try to please us. She did not even try to like us. She certainly made no effort to make us like her. She valued results more than affection, and respect more than popularity. Not endowed with loving or lovable qualities, she did not bother regretting it, or denying it, or trying to compensate for it. She went about her task with no concessions to the we're-all-friends or think-of-me-as-your-pal gambits. She used the forthright "I want" or "You go" instead of the repulsive "Shall we?" Alien to humor or affection, she concentrated on nothing more than the transmission of her knowledge and her skill.

I think Miss O'Neill knew what the evangelists of "progressive" education are bound to rediscover: that the young prefer competence to "personality" in a teacher, and certainly to camaraderie; that a teacher need be neither an ogre nor a confidant; that what is hard to master gives children special rewards (pride, self-respect, the gratifications of succeeding) precisely because difficulties have been conquered; that there may indeed be no easy road to learning some things, and no "fascinating" or "fun" way of learning some things really well.

I do not know whether Miss O'Neill infected anyone else in my 7th grade with a passion for, or even an abiding interest in, English. To me, she was a force of enlightenment.

She has long since shucked her travail among the West Side aborigines. Perhaps she has departed this baffling world to don wings—and, I hope, golden locks, to replace that wig under whose gauzy base she scratched relief from itching. If she is still alive, she must be in her dotage. And if she is among us still, I hope she somehow gets word of these long-belated thanks for a job supremely well done. I have never forgotten what she taught.

To this day, whether I am wrestling an intransigent sentence, or stand glazed before a buck-passing phrase whose improvement eludes me, or flagellate myself for some inspiration that might light up the drab texture of tired prose, whether I am winded by a rodomontade clause in Shaw or knocked cold by a tortured sentence in Talcott Parsons, I find myself thinking of Miss (What-oh-what?) O'Neill—and sighing, take a sheet of paper and diagram the English until I know—and know *why*—it is right or wrong, or how it can be swept clean of that muddle-headedness that plagues us all.

COMMENTARY

It should be increasingly clear that any explanation of the meaning of facts or experiences calls for some definite order in the presentation of the details supporting a generalization. We have seen how Steve Kelman found the *deductive* order helpful to his purposes in telling his readers "why the kids rebel." Now in "Dear Miss O'Neill" Leo Rosten offers us a fine example of *inductive* order, the one wherein the *generalization,* which underlies the essay, does not appear until near the very end.

At the outset it appears that Rosten is concerned merely with poking fun at Miss O'Neill for having been just another "old" teacher. Not until near the middle of the essay do we learn that he "only pretended to hate her." Then, little by little, he goes on to pay tribute to her teaching and influence upon him. The climax of his appreciation and the clear statement of his generalization come near the end of the essay when he states: "To me, she was a force of enlightenment."

Rosten's essay, therefore, contrasts with Kelman's in the order of its development. Each writer apparently chose the order he did because of his feelings regarding his subject matter, yet both employed a plan of procedure, a *sequence* of details appropriate to their respective purposes. Perhaps to beguile us, Rosten chose not to start out with telling us that Miss O'Neill was "a force of enlightenment." He preferred, instead, to lead us to that statement as he continued recalling details for us in the form of appreciative memories.

In considering the organization of possible essay topics, you also may now wish to experiment with the *inductive* order. It need not be applied only to topics of reminiscence, such as this one by Rosten. It lends itself to any topic on which you have come to a conclusion in the light of certain evidence. Before you decide about anything, you examine the facts and circumstances. Thus the *generalization,* or judgment, reached is a reasoned conclusion, not a mere prejudice. In presenting that conclusion to the reader, then, you can follow your own thought processes, leaving the conclusion, or generalization, to come at the very end. The inductive order also lends itself well to a sequence of increasing importance, as we noted in Buchwald's implied generalization in the previous essay.

WHAT DOES IT SAY?

1. Why does Rosten start his essay talking about Miss O'Neill's wig, and how she would "lift her wig and gently scratch her pate"?

2. What does *old* mean in this generalization: "All teachers are old"? Did you share that belief when you were in grade school? Why?

3. Do *you* think of all teachers whom you once disliked as "arithmetic teachers"? Why would Rosten have *loathed* them?

4. What does he mean by calling Miss O'Neill a "33rd-degree perfectionist"?

5. What does *syntax* mean? What does it have to do with a *dangling participle*?

6. Wherein lies the "devastating humor" of until *Gabriel blew his kazoo*?

7. What typical examples of the following do you recall having been offered to former grade school teachers you knew: *small impertinences, sly infractions,* and *simulated incomprehensions*?

8. Why can Miss O'Neill be considered "a force of enlightenment"?

WHAT DO YOU THINK?

1. This essay includes also a detailed definition of "the ideal teacher." Write a summary of "Dear Miss O'Neill," listing in detail the excellences that Rosten assigns her, and then apply that definition as a measure of your own description of "the ideal teacher" you remember.

2. In the light of your own experiences with them, which of the following activities of a teacher are the most typical? "She's mother, father,

warden, clergyman, traffic controller, philosopher, friend, psychologist, hygienist everyday, maybe zoo-keeper some days."—Harper & Row advertisement.

3. Goodman Ace, a sharp critic of American mores, recently poked fun at eighty New York City teachers who demanded "that the Board of Education protect them from unruly pupils." Mr. Ace fondly remembers his sixth grade teacher: "The school was her kingdom and she was its ruler. And when she couldn't rule she had a ruler 12 inches long that she rapped across knuckles."—*Saturday Review*, April 15, 1967, p. 8. Have times changed, do you believe, since Mr. Ace was in the sixth grade to the extent that teachers in some city schools today do need protection from their pupils? Have students become more unruly, less receptive to discipline? What are your views on how classroom discipline should be maintained?

4. All things considered, do you believe that school officials should have the right to regulate the clothing and hair styles of students? Support your opinion with detailed reasons and well-chosen examples. Try the inductive order if you wish.

5. Rosten remarks that conformity to the ideas held by the group is a powerful influence on youth. His statement reads: "So strong is the desire of a boy to 'belong,' to be no different from even the grubbiest of his fellows." Do you find this compulsion true in your own experience? Discuss. Is it as true of girls as of boys?

WHAT'S THE USE
OF EDUCATING
WOMEN?

EDWARD D. EDDY, JR.

IN HIS vigorous defense of Scotland and Protestantism, John Knox addressed several communications to his enemy, Mary, Queen of Scots. One such discourse was labeled "The Second Blast of the Trumpet Against the Monstrous Regiment of Women." In recent years there have been blasts from many quarters concerning the future of women's education and particularly of women's colleges.

Much of the published commentary on women's education either shows a sickening condescension toward womanhood, *or* tries bravely to rise above the fact that many women like to get married. Many writers seem embarrassed by the fact that a majority of educated women choose marriage and that a number of people question the wisdom of giving a college education to the woman who is *just* a wife and mother. As little Sally in *Peanuts* observed: "I never said I wanted to be somebody important. All I want to do when I grow up is to get married and be a good wife and mother. Why should I have to go to kindergarten?"

Other commentators on women's education appear baffled by the eager-

Reprinted from *Saturday Review*, May 18, 1963, by permission of the author and publisher. Dr. Eddy, Jr., is President of Chatham College.

ness of women undergraduates to jump at the opportunity of marriage rather than complete their education. David Riesman says that this is due to a pattern of thought among college women which he calls "very much a bird in hand—or, rather, bird in nest" philosophy. He remarks wistfully, "If only I could convince the young people I know that 'life' *will* catch up with them even if they try to escape it."

Historically, women's colleges emerged from America's reaction against the classical and European models of higher education that the new nation had originally adopted. Privately endowed Chatham College, for example, was founded in the same decade of educational rebellion that gave birth to the great majority of state universities and land-grant colleges. While Congress was struggling over the lack of practicality in education—a struggle that led to the passage of the Morrill Act in 1862—the founding fathers of the Pennsylvania Female College were worrying about ignorance among the Pittsburgh ladies.

This special concern for education of women did not, however, lead to a special education for women. Indeed, from the outset it was considered proper to provide women with an education designed primarily for men. Diana Trilling has observed that as long as women feel inferior to men, they ought to get an education at least as bad, in order to feel that they are not being discriminated against. Thus, to this day, women's colleges have achieved little educational distinction. Essentially they offer male education to the female, who prefers to keep men at a suitable distance for the greater part of the week.

This absence of distinction in the female college raises serious questions of justification. Without such distinction, women's colleges might as well fold their elaborate tents and creep into the coeducational camp.

Why does the education of women so often lack distinction? Partly, I suspect, because American women aren't sure they really want to be women. There is a frustrating ambivalence in their concepts of themselves. On the one hand, women luxuriate in the male's over-idealization of the female creature; Pearl Buck calls it "angels on pedestals." The proper education of "angels" is of course that offered by the best finishing schools. Round them out, and send them out—like angelic ornaments for a Christmas tree—fragile and glittering. The male, too, relishes this over-idealization of the female. It makes him feel more masculine to be surrounded by brainless beautiful women.

Thus, the American female of the past century has been caught between the desire to enjoy the view from the pedestal and the desire to kick over the pedestal and achieve equality with men. Generally speaking, however, the modern woman who is content with equality makes the tragic mistake of confusing it with conformity. And, if we are to perpetuate the human species, *this* is an impossibility.

What's the use, then, of educating women? First we must determine how their education will be used.

The current discussion of women's education appears to center on several supposedly distinct approaches. We can, for instance, educate the career woman, or educate all women with the idea that some (but who knows which ones?) will stake out justifiable claims in man's world of science, business, or the professions. And this is a strategic function of higher education. Without it, colleges would be robbing society of the immense contributions of many highly qualified women. Since comparatively few actually do have professional careers, however, we cannot stop here. The colleges can't be just multi-million dollar siphons.

This leads us to a second possibility: the postponed career. This alternative assumes that many women will go into hibernation long enough to bear and raise children and will then return to their career in their "middle years." Some educators are so concerned with middle-year productivity that they would have women's education concentrate on this point. Lois Irish, for instance, concludes that "what is needed . . . is an extension of the student's sights beyond the early romantic stages of her life to the years when her principal occupation ceases to be a full-time job in the home."

The third possibility, the one most frequently ignored or ridiculed, is that of educating women who simply want to be intelligent and perceptive wives, mothers, and citizens.

The college graduate who becomes a housewife is said to suffer from confusion and frustration. According to Carolyn Heilbrun, she is "dropped from the heights of Olympus to the depths of the washing machine." This is nonsense. What man in any profession remains continually, if at all, on the heights of Olympus? College presidents, for example, spend a good part of their time pulling socks out of the stuck guts of academic washing machines. Life just requires these unromantic details.

Miss Heilbrun goes on to say that:

> . . . The modern woman, graduating from college at an age entirely suitable to the life pattern of a man seeking his place in the world, finds herself launched, not into the world, but into domesticity. She progresses through diapers to the companionship of other three-year-olds, without privacy, without time to recollect herself, without time *to be*. Ahead lie unplanned years for which she weaves nebulous schemes. She thinks that when her children are old enough she, like MacArthur, will "return." Too late she will discover that she is out of touch, out of training, and out of demand, and to be out of demand is to be excluded from that public realm where excellence is honored.

Miss Heilbrun seems to be suffering from that dreadful self-pity that afflicts a good many women who confuse equality with conformity.

This condescension toward the female-in-the-household is reflected in both the passionate feminist urge for conformity and the male attempt to keep the upper hand. In an unusual editorial confession, *The Saturday Evening Post* conceded that "masculine bravado" has permitted the male to picture the female as "the poor bedraggled little housewife, bogged down in her scullery, lulled by her soap operas while she ironed our shirts, and tended our runny-nosed offspring."

We do a great disservice to American women by dismissing their role as wives and mothers as unfortunate dissipations of time and talent. The educated woman who becomes a wife and mother has an enormously important job to do. If done well, it cannot help but engage every aspect of her education. If we regard the housewife and mother as simple fools, we only penalize and even jeopardize our own future. It is the mother, almost single-handedly, who will raise a generation of potential peace-makers.

Beyond these alternatives, what special responsibilities devolve upon educated women *because* they are women, regardless of how they use their talents?

The *Post* editorial again observes: "We have, in the American woman, one of the nation's great neglected resources. We have always admired her, pursued her, whistled at her—even enshrined her. Now we need to use her. Not just for the jobs men don't want to do. Not begrudgingly because we want to shut her up. Not slyly because we think she's cute. But thankfully—because she has brains, time, knowledge, courage, sensitivity, and dedication that are needed in our struggle for survival."

The educated woman, viewing life in perspective, is free to seek an answer to the old question: What, after all, is *man*? The educated woman can keep the male eye from trivia, and the male mind from preoccupation with immediate effects. The educated woman can encourage a man to rise above self, can make community service something more than a hollow status race, can insist on an intelligent approach to foreign aid, desegregation, taxes, and federal aid to the schools and colleges that educate her children. As James Reston observed recently in the *New York Times*: "Somebody has to find a new way to get around old men and old problems, and since women have been doing precisely that for several thousand years, why not pass the problem to them?"

To achieve these larger goals, the educated woman will have to fight the contagion of self-pity that periodically overcomes anyone not sufficiently recognized. And, above all, she must keep a perspective that allows her on occasion to have a good, hearty laugh at herself, the kind of laugh that the proud, self-righteous male usually denies himself.

Considering the nature of a woman, then, the prevailing structure of male education is not sufficient. The male version of higher learning is tied down by the short strings of utility. Vocational education is basically informational. It lacks the sensitive nuance. It is preoccupied with the immediate job.

The last true stronghold of the liberal arts may be the college that is free to concentrate on the education of women, and free from the utilitarian emphasis that distorts the liberal arts. Women are, of course, important in the labor market but they are not just one more unit of trained manpower, and their education should not be directed as if they were.

In decrying the utilitarian approach, Joseph Wood Krutch has observed that "what philosophers used to call 'the good life' is difficult to define and impossible to measure. In the United States today . . . we substitute for it 'the standard of living', which is easy to measure if defined only in terms of wealth, health, comfort, and conveniences."

Krutch thus points out that our concept of "the good life" has become strongly materialistic, and vocational education tends, by its very nature, to emphasize this materialism. Put the man or woman in the right job slot, and, inevitably, "the good life" will be his or hers.

The education of women, less constricted by utility, is more likely to awaken the student to a larger sense of value, to an idea of man and what makes him what he is. The result of liberal education can be a better person, a better life. The liberal arts—the reflection of man's heritage and hope— can thus be studied without the problem of post-college placement, which restricts the imagination and interest of both students and professors.

Unfortunately, too, coeducation today requires a sublimation of female leadership. The male is dominant on the majority of coeducational campuses. Diana Trilling declares that "No woman—no reasonably normal woman— wants to assert superiority over men, let alone dominate them. On the contrary, women want to be cherished and protected by men and dependent on men's superior strength. It is by this that they are made to feel most feminine."

Again, the pedestal. And again, the women's college is about the only place left where a woman can be knocked flat off that pedestal and not want to crawl back. The women's college allows women to be women—unashamed, uncluttered, humble, confident, and, above all, excellent in all respects. Such an education must also be thoroughly academic and completely demanding lest it be condescending.

The danger exists, of course, in Mervin Freedman's words, that the women's college will be left with "passive appreciation of what others, chiefly men, have done—with insufficient emphasis upon what the student herself may be able to do." The women's college, therefore, must put over-riding stress on the necessity for *action*, not pleasant, safe, harmless contemplation. The educated woman must develop for herself and transmit to her family a social conscience, and indeed, most major social reforms were originally championed by women. If we are wise, we will sustain this pattern.

We conclude that women's colleges have no reason whatever to be on the run or on the defensive—so long as they perform with distinction the basic task of preparing women as women for rich, useful lives. If women are to be educated as men, there is no cogent reason why they should not attend coeducational institutions. But if women are not only to learn about the sun but also to enjoy the radiance of the sunset, as one essayist has put it, then separate education in the liberal arts makes sense. As a rule, women want to be better, and men *better off*.

COMMENTARY

After discussing five commentators on womanhood and the education of women, with some reference to the college for women he himself heads, Dr. Eddy at the end of the *introduction* raises the question serving as the title of the essay. Instead of answering it then, he holds back, telling the reader, "First we must determine how their education will be used." It would appear he has also chosen the *inductive* order as the organizing form of his composition.

In the *sequence of their increasing importance* to him, Dr. Eddy next lists three possible uses women may make of their college education. He deals at some length with the third of these possible approaches, and goes on to quote the opinions of others. Then in a separate paragraph he reframes his original question but again refrains from answering it directly. So we still have not been given the *generalization* underlying his essay.

Not until he has defended the liberal arts against utilitarian curriculum, and has protested that "coeducation today requires a sublimation of female leadership," does he begin detailing his long awaited answer. But by now it seems he has somewhat changed the question, for he is explaining the importance of the college for women only and stressing the need of liberal arts education for them.

Perhaps no one sentence serves as an adequate statement of his basic generalization. And none is absolutely required as long as it is evident that the author had one basic purpose guiding him and giving his essay *unity* and *order*. In the final paragraph of the *conclusion*, the second last sentence, although somewhat figurative in language, does state the kind of education that Dr. Eddy wants for women: ". . . then separate education in the liberal arts makes sense."

By means of *inductive* order, the author has moved gradually towards a larger view of his topic than perhaps his opening remarks promised. The method gave him opportunity to explore possibilities and in doing so keeps the reader in some suspense, thereby encouraging him to read on—a desirable quality in any form of composition!

WHAT DOES IT SAY?

1. The opening reference to John Knox and his "Blast Against the Monstrous Regiment of Women" refers to what earlier religious views of the woman's place in the world?

2. What typical expressions regarding women's education could be classified as "sickening condescension"?

3. How does the observation of "little Sally" compare with David Riesman's "bird in the nest" expression?

4. What does Dr. Eddy mean in saying, "Life will catch up with them [women] even if they try to escape it"?

5. What is ironical in the Diana Trilling remark: "As long as women feel inferior to men, they ought to get an education at least as bad"?

6. When can women's colleges be thought of as "just multimillion dollars siphons"?

7. What kind of wives are *perceptive* wives?

8. Rephrase in your own language, the concluding sentence: "As a rule, women want to be *better,* and men want to be *better off.*"

WHAT DO YOU THINK?

1. If you find it suitable to your chosen topic, try adopting the *sequence of increasing importance* or one of the other forms of *inductive* order in developing a generalization based on some aspect of one of the following wide topics:

Working wives	Women and the medical profession
Teen-age marriage	Women as concert musicians
Women athletes	Teaching as a career
Women in the armed services	Mother vs. wife
Angel on a pedestal	

2. Do you agree with the author's sweeping statement: "It is the mother, almost singlehandedly, who will raise a generation of potential peace-makers"? If so, describe who raises all of the potential and actual *hell-raisers.*

3. Urging more education for women, a government consumer affairs adviser to President Johnson maintains that a "woman must be scientist, researcher, and economist," because she has to make difficult choices in shopping for the family. Develop an essay regarding her generalization.

WHY

ROOMMATES

MAKE

THE BEST WIVES

JOAN PAULSON

I WONDER whether American men realize what a debt they owe to the custom of unmarried young ladies sharing living quarters with roommates or apartment-mates from the time they venture away from the family bosom until the triumphal march into matrimony.

An Oriental girl devotes her whole life to learning how to please her future spouse—how many men have told me that? And once upon a time in this country, finishing schools and anxious mothers instructed young ladies in the art of disciplining servants, embroidering linens and other domestic chores. But nowadays, most girl high-school graduates (and college graduates, for that matter) can rarely do anything more mechanical than dialing a telephone, and are hard put to heat a TV dinner.

The only remaining bulwark between this state of domestic ignorance and the collapse of marriage in America (it's not doing too well anyway) is the custom of having roommates. When I, for example, graduated from high school I couldn't even light a gas stove. ("Where are the buttons?") After having lived with 15 roommates, from one to five at a time, during five years of college

Reprinted from *Ladies Home Journal*, March 1967, by permission of the author.

and two of a "career," I can now, if necessary, bake a loaf of bread, change a fuse, bait a mouse trap (and dispose of it when it's served its purpose), cook 43 different dishes starring hamburger, and look on almost all quirks of behavior with equanimity. I'm also a whiz at providing three meals a day for $5 a week per person, and if, after marriage, I discover that my husband has no more trying habits than snoring, strewing his clothes on the floor and eating crackers in bed, I'll consider him a miracle.

Take cooking. Unlike new husbands roommates have no qualms about judging a dish to be a disaster. However, as long as you don't have to cook it yourself, you're not going to demand just what Mama used to make, so they're tremendously good sports if you want to take a try at flaming shish kebab or *ratatouille*. And if your *Sachetorte* emerges with a drunken lean, it's less embarrassing among roommates. After all, who burned the biscuits last week?

Roommates are also a fruitful scource of culinary tips that you don't find in cookbooks. Lael, one of my first apartment-mates, taught me how to test if spaghetti is done. You throw a piece at the wall. If it sticks, it is; if it doesn't, it'll probably fall behind the stove where nobody will ever see it. Even my mother didn't know this technique. When I casually demonstrated it at home one day she was speechless.

As in a marriage, money is probably the most common bone of contention among roommates. Luckily, community living teaches you the basic tenets of economy. Like how to prove that you weren't the one who used the extra message units listed on the phone bill. (*"He* always calls *me!"*) Once a group of us completely furnished a five-room apartment with wooden milk crates, which we removed under cover of night from the neighborhood supermarket.

I had one roommate, Pam, who, in the interests of economy, tried to convert us to a permanent diet of brains, kidneys and the other less expensive but more nutritious parts of various animals' anatomies. Her meals invariably featured something on toast covered with a thick cream sauce. It wasn't bad . . . if you like cream sauce.

I've discovered that roommates are divisible into two types. First, those who are messier than I am. They're generous and lovable and kind to animals—though somewhat difficult to room with because you can't get in the closet and strange smells emanate from forgotten foods left under the bed. Then there are those who are organized, efficient, neat and even harder to live with on civil terms, though they're more educational in the long run—or, as my mother would say, a challenge.

Like Madeleine, whose first salary was $75 a week. On that, she managed to support herself completely and save $100 a month. She allowed herself $8 spending money a week (including clothes, which she made herself), and at the end of the week she remarked pointedly that she had money left over because she couldn't find anything worth spending it on. Madeleine now dates her stockbroker, makes plenty more than $75 a week, and will certainly be a millionaire.

Since Madeleine is as economical with words as she is with money, her statements come out sounding like axioms or epigrams. I always imagined them neatly capitalized. I have a collection of several hundred of Madeleine's Laws, such as: "The Only Reason a Sandwich Has Two Slices of Bread Is to Keep the Filling From Falling Out When You Take It to Work; At Home, You Only Need One Slice of Bread Per Sandwich." Or, "If You Empty Ashtrays Into Wastebaskets, You Will Have Dirty Wastebaskets. People Who Smoke Deserve Dirty Wastebaskets."

Madeleine was also opposed to, among other things, eating or drinking foods that have no nutritive value, such as coffee and diet drinks—wasted energy, she said—which drove the rest of us off into dark corners when we indulged. She also believed that dry milk is not only cheaper than whole milk but also tastes better. Since Madeleine has never been known to be wrong, we drank lumpy dry milk for three years.

Perhaps the greatest value of having roommates is that it provides what a professor of mine used to call a Cross-Cultural Experience. I remember every one of the 15 with varying degrees of affection. There was Kathleen, whose grandmother had founded a religious sect that included yoga. Every now and then Grandmother would appear on our doorstep wearing brown sateen bloomers, accompanied by a 7-foot-tall Boris Karloff type who was her guru (or she was his, I forget which). Even though Grandmother and Boris might startle a date, they always brought a huge floral offering from some ritual, and Grandmother could really whip up a mean curry.

Then there was little Pru, who was younger than the rest of us and quite naïve. Except for her lingerie. She favored red-fringed, black lace or leopard skin on the theory that they don't get gray like white does. Every Saturday, Pru would go to the corner laundromat to wash all her underthings. Lovingly, she would pull each piece separately out of the dryer and fold it. By the time she was through, she was surrounded by an admiring throng of male onlookers. They would follow her home, and litter our front stoop until we dispersed them.

Then there was Macy, who played harpsicord music at top volume on her stereo during every waking minute; Jill, whose boyfriend came with a boa constrictor, which he carried with him wherever he went; and Bobbi, who created metal sculpture with a blowtorch in her room.

Personal idiosyncrasies manifest themselves most drastically in sleeping habits, however. In self-defense, you therefore learn to train yourself to sleep through practically anything. Everyone runs into teeth grinders and snorers, but I've roomed with chucklers and even singers (Bobbi sang nursery rhymes in her sleep). And Candy would get up in her sleep and curl up on the floor of the closet, where she would be found sleeping happily, come morning, among the galoshes. I shouldn't really complain. At the time, I was going through a phase of sleeping with my shoes on and, on really bad days, my coat as well, and I can't remember anybody suggesting that my sleeping attire was somewhat unorthodox.

But roommates are so understanding. Who else would call up your current love and pose as a television survey just to find out what he's doing? Or lend you her new blouse for a special date before she'd even worn it and then iron it for you? Or feed live goldfish to your baby alligator because you couldn't bear it? Or tell you that you look just like Audrey Hepburn, only fatter? Or look at your baby pictures when your mother comes to visit? Or bring you fig bars that she made from *real* figs, and *Lady Chatterley's Lover* when you're sick in bed with a terminal cold?

But that's what roommates are for. Among other things.

COMMENTARY

Any essay that lacks sufficient *detail* will disappoint its readers. Details are the items of fact, the minute particulars of an idea, or the parts of a design that give full meaning and substance to a generalization. The earlier selections by Kelman, Rosten, and Eddy are particularly rich in details supporting the generalizations made in them. In the essays comprising Part 2, you will find the various kinds of details specifically defined and exemplified. It is sufficient now just to point out the general character of these supporting materials.

Joan Paulson's essay provides us with an especially colorful example of how details expand a generalization and hold reader attention. Here, as the title promises, the author explains *why* "roommates make the best wives." She gives specific reasons why, by having shared living quarters with other single girls, she has been prepared for some of the trials of marriage. She has learned to be economical and resourceful in housekeeping and to be able to get along with people having unusual tastes and living habits. Her anecdotes describing the behavior of some of these roommates contribute minute and interesting particulars as details.

Just as some people never seem to know when to stop talking when they try to tell us something, so the danger in writing is to bring in unnecessary details—facts and particulars having little or no bearing on the immediate topic. Needless repetition is as much the bane of writers as it is of gossips.

In the essay suggestions appearing below, you may find one that can be developed in much the same manner as Joan Paulson handled the details of her essay. Whatever your choice, avoid irrelevance and needless repetition. Stay in sequence and watch for unity. Your readers will thank you for it with their gift of attention.

WHAT DOES IT SAY?

1. In the opening, how do expressions like "the family bosom" and "the triumphal march into matrimony" set the tone for the rest of the essay?

2. Why does Joan Paulson resort to exaggeration by claiming that having roommates provides "the only remaining bulwark" between "domestic ignorance" and "the collapse of marriage"? What is the literary term for this kind of exaggeration?

3. What delicacies are these: *shish kebab, ratatouille,* and *Sachetorte?*

4. What is the literary term applied to the substitution of an expression like "*removed* under cover of night" for *stolen?*

5. Why can the statement "or, as my mother would say, a challenge" be termed an *understatement?*

6. How does an *axiom* differ from an *epigram?*

7. Are *orthodox* or *unorthodox* appropriate terms to be applied to "sleeping attire"? Why, or why not?

8. And is *Lady Chatterly's Lover* appropriate reading fare for someone "in bed with a terminal cold"?

WHAT DO YOU THINK?

1. Describe in detail the behavior patterns of roommates you have observed, and project what kind of marital mates you think they will make.

2. In the order of their obnoxiousness to you, list and explain in detail the types of roommates you would *not* like to have.

3. How does the following quotation by a famous psychiatrist about husbands and wives also apply to roommates or friends?

Talking to each other is loving each other. Expressing our anger and resentment is, in large part, conquering it. Aggression expressed in words is no longer the same aggression. There is the silence of understanding—communication. And the silence of denial—excommunication from verbal intercourse.

Talking unburdens the mind and heart and relieves tension. . . . Most people feel the vacuum of silence to be a sinister threat . . . more disconcerting than outright contradiction, more hateful than open aggression.—William Cole, "Toward Better Husband-Wife Communication," *Family Circle,* October 1966, p. 55.

4. If you have traveled with a group of people your own age, explain in detail what personal values you now can find in that experience.

5. Point out what you have learned from your experiences with various neighbors that you hope will, or will not, ever be your experiences when you have a family of your own.

THE COLLEGE GRAD
HAS BEEN
SHORT-CHANGED

ANDREW HACKER

STUDENTS at schools as widely contrasted as Berkeley, St. John's and Yale have rallied, marched, signed and sat in displays of vehemence and in numbers not equaled in this generation.

A major reason for these stirrings is that not a few American undergraduates have become convinced that they are being short-changed. Feeling cheated on the educational end, especially at the larger institutions, they are ripe for any demonstration against authority in general and campus officialdom in particular. Nevertheless, it must be recorded that the protests over the quality of higher education are foredoomed to failure. They are outcries against conditions which will become even further entrenched in the years to come.

What is distressing is that so many students, faculty members and observers of the educational scene still think that serious reforms are possible. For this reason the facts of modern university life deserve to be catalogued, if only because so many of us will have to live with them.

In the first place, colleges and universities will become larger, and consequently more bureaucratic and impersonal. Within a generation, only a minor fraction of the student population will be attending small, independent colleges. Already 6 out of every 10 students are in institutions having enroll-ments of over 5,000, whereas a dozen years ago, less than half were in schools of that size.

The reason for this is not that small colleges are going out of business—hardly any do—but that most of them are becoming larger. This is especially the case with publicly supported institutions. Whereas every state used to have its network of normal and A.&M. schools, these are now being trans-formed into universities with no ceilings foreseen for their enrollments. What was once a teachers' college in Carbondale is now Southern Illinois Uni-versity, with over 17,000 students. Plans are being made to expand New York's old normal schools—like Brockport, Fredonia, Geneseo, New Paltz, Oneonta, Potsdam—so they can absorb the tens of thousands of students in search of a college education. And except for a handful of Amhersts and Swarthmores, virtually all of the small private colleges are anxious to raise their enrollments, sometimes for financial reasons but also for purposes of prestige.

It is easy to give publicity to projects and experiments intended to counter this trend. About 10 years ago, for example, California declared that it would make its Riverside campus the "Amherst" of the system, with an enrollment limited to about 1,000 liberal arts majors. As of now, Riverside has grown to some 3,000 and its plans are to have as many as 14,000 students on the campus by 1980, many of them working for advanced degrees. So much for the "Amherst" idea.

Now we are hearing about the new Santa Cruz campus, this time to be the "Oxford" of the Coast, having a series of small colleges, each with its own professors giving tutorials, on a prominence above the Pacific. It is impossible to see how such an educational luxury can survive, especially in a state with so many teenagers knocking on college doors. The Santa Cruz plan, like Riverside's before it, is expensive in fact and undemocratic in theory. These are two powerful strikes against intimate education, public or private.

Larger enrollments mean larger classes. In a small school, only 15 students would elect medieval history and a professor would be assigned to teach them. In a large place, 150 sign up for such a course—and the professor lectures to them en masse. (Why not have 10 professors, each teaching a class of 15? The answer, apart from the fact that no department has 10 medievalists, is that such an arrangement is outrageously expensive. That is why colleges are ex-panding their enrollments to begin with.) One result is that students will come to know fewer and fewer professors on a personal basis. But if they will have less to do with the faculty, they are destined for many more encounters with the administration.

On every campus, students find they must spend more and more time deal-ing with an expanding bureaucracy. Regular visits must be paid to administrative purlieus to fill in forms in triplicate, to be photographed in duplicate (face and lungs), to appeal, to petition, to ask permission. They must not fold, mutilate, staple or spindle the I.B.M. cards representing their student-hood; they must secure prior approval for all manner of social, political and domestic arrangements if they are to ensure that their existence does not violate the rules contained in the thick handbooks of codes and regulations. (One might ask if this is not the case in every sphere of modern organized life. The answer is that a university is supposed to be a realm of scholars, a community of ideas and hence to be spared such encumbrances.)

The ranks of the administrators have been expanding much faster than those of the teaching faculty and this trend will doubtless continue. I have yet to learn of a single college or university where the growth rate of its administrative corps is less than that of the professoriat. Educational administrators, like their counterparts elsewhere, are adept at discovering new services they can perform, new committees they can create, new reports they can write.

They have an advantage over the professors in this respect, for they possess both the will and the skill for arrogating new powers and functions to themselves. And they have, after all, a sweet reasonableness on their side. Would anyone care to suggest that a college could operate without registrars, controllers, deans of men, house-mothers, public-relations emissaries, guidance counselors, activities advisers, residence managers, proctors, pastors, research coordinators, placement officers, clinic technicians and development directors?

Every day these officials find new ways to intrude their presence into student life. It may well be that undergraduates are looked after better than ever before: they are ministered with food and housing, counseling and recreation, medicine and religion, career guidance and financial assistance. Yet if undergraduates are driven into the arms of the burgeoning bureaucracies this is partly because the professors are so seldom at home.

Much has been written and said about the retreat from the classroom, about the increasing unwillingness of professors to teach or otherwise to meet with students. No elaboration is needed here, except to say that the charges are true. This is the age of the foundation grant, of prolonged academic travel, of frequent leaves. It is also the era of conferences, workshops and symposia that draw professors (all expenses paid) away from the campus, frequently in the middle of classes. The mere murmuring of the sacred incantation "research" is sufficient excuse to bow out of introductory courses, to confine one's offerings to graduate seminars, to depart for another institution where more grandiose projects will be more generously underwritten.

But the focus here is on the future of higher education, and it is relevant to consider the rising generation of professors. These young men are being suitably indoctrinated even while in graduate school. For one thing, they learn the dominant fashions in their disciplines and commit themselves intellectually (if that is the word) to the going trends. This is especially necessary for the less talented (in other words the majority) for the rising tide of fashion offers the safest haven for mediocre minds.

Just a few months ago I was lecturing at a liberal arts college, a small up-state institution, with a strong teaching tradition. I was told by several department chairmen of their great difficulties in attracting new faculty members. The men they interviewed, most of them in their middle 20's, all wanted to be assured about research funds, abbreviated teaching schedules, grants, leaves and the other prerequisites they are coming to expect. Even undergraduate colleges are being forced to match these demands if they are to recruit for their faculty—and what amounts to a part-time faculty at that.

Most of the new professors like to think of themselves primarily as scholars, and this attitude is held even by those incapable of making more than a quite minimal contribution to human knowledge. This being the case, who is going to do the teaching? This question would be a pressing one even if the every-man-a-researcher fetish did not exist.

The result will be larger classes, more machine-graded examinations and more televised instruction. (The "solution" of less classroom work and more "independent" study is another delusion; it takes a professor far more time to supervise and evaluate the independent work of students than it does to teach them in groups.) It is fruitless to discuss the wisdom of developments such as electronic education. They are going to come, like it or not, and whatever is inevitable ceases to be a worthwhile issue for discussion. If three million new places are going to be created for students over the coming decade, the 300,000 new professors who will be needed to teach them are nowhere in sight. And those who are recruited will spend less time in actual teaching than ever before.

Colleges and universities as constituted at present have too many contented constituents for them to change their ways. Most of the students, at least half of the professors and all of the educational administrators are faring better than ever before and are experiencing opportunities that only a favored few knew in earlier days. The dissenting members of the academic community are setting themselves against the combined forces of democracy in education and technology in learning. Like many rebels they are nostalgic for a society they never knew and a world they can never know.

COMMENTARY

How much space, how many details, should be allotted to any one part of an essay is a question of *emphasis*. If you have found yourself wondering just what portion of the total length of your own essay you should give to its introduction, conclusion, and to the various subtopics developed in the body, you will find the following analysis of "The College Grad Has Been Short-Changed" helpful. This essay, as well as the others so far discussed, can serve as a model showing the amount of space that might well be allotted to the various sections of an essay under 2000 words.

Emphasis in composition, as we indicated in the introduction to this part of the text, is in part a matter of *proportion*—the amount of space given to the respective parts. The more space, the more details you give, the more attention you are calling to that part.

Hacker's *generalization* appears in the last two sentences of his opening paragraph: "Nevertheless, it must be recorded that the protests over the quality of higher education are foredoomed to failure. They are outcries against conditions which will become even further entrenched in the years to come." The following paragraph concludes his introduction by announcing that the "facts of modern university life" are to be catalogued. This introduction takes up approximately 170 words.

The facts of modern university life, as Hacker outlines them, turn out to be three: (1) Colleges and universities will become ever larger. (2) They will become increasingly bureaucratic. (3) They will become even more impersonal. A discussion of these "facts" furnishes the body of his essay. A look at the space devoted to a consideration of each of these facts suggests the importance that Hacker assigns to each:

"Fact" 1: 570 words
"Fact" 2: 470 words
"Fact" 3: 620 words

This proportion suggests that Hacker considered the increasing impersonality more important than the other "facts," and the increasing bureaucracy the least important.

This relative importance of ideas is enforced by another consideration—*position*. Hacker knows that the items placed first and last usually attract the most attention from a reader, and consequently become more emphatic than items placed in between.

The conclusion takes up approximately 120 words. Introduction and conclusion together take up considerably less space than any one of the items discussed in the body of the essay—a warning against a long-winded introduction and a long-drawn-out conclusion, which are always to be avoided, in case the reader should comment: "Come to the point!" and "You've said what you intended, so why don't you stop?"

WHAT DOES IT SAY?

1. Give the literal meaning of *short-changed*. How does it fit in tone with the rest of the language of the introduction?

2. What are the connotations of *foredoomed* in the sentence "the protests over the quality of higher education are foredoomed to failure"?

3. What *prestige* can a large enrollment give a small private college?

4. In calling the Riverside campus the "Amherst" of the system, what is Hacker trying to suggest?

5. And if the Santa Cruz campus were to become the "Oxford" of the Coast, what unique qualities would it have?

6. Knowing your professors "on a personal basis" suggests what special advantages?

7. What do you associate with "an expanding bureaucracy"?

8. Hacker writes of administrators having "after all, a sweet reasonableness on their side." What does he mean?

WHAT DO YOU THINK?

1. Although you expected to find differences between your high-school teachers and those in college, what have been the main kinds of discoveries you have made regarding the college faculty? Remember to give the respective differences the proper *emphasis* each one proportionately deserves.

2. Formulate a generalization and write an essay showing the allotting of due emphasis to the major details on a topic suggested by one of the following:

Bureaucratic impersonality	Campus planning
Library overcrowding	Preregistration procedures
Campus organizations	Large classes
Parking problems	Residence rules
Campus dining	Campus distractions
Use of gymnasium	Big time athletics

3. Do you feel as this Ohio student does? "The whole bit on this campus now is about 'the needs of society,' 'the needs of the international

situation,' 'the needs of the IBM system.' What about *my* needs?" *The Reader's Digest,* January 1967, p. 96.

4. How just do you consider the following observation made by a New York City school principal?

It may be that college students are miserable. At the same time they are one of the most favored groups in our society. They are fairly wealthy; and they are the largest leisure class in America—our mass consumers of culture, the advance guard of the great owning and managerial orders into which they will move at graduation. Far from being exploited, they ride on the backs of all of us—and sometimes they use spurs.—Spencer Brown, "What's the Matter with the Younger Generation?" *The New York Times Magazine,* November 27, 1966.

1. *What is the mood of the group?* 2. *What possible problems could this group be discussing?* 3. *What is the man on the left, obviously the leader, proposing?* 4. *Put yourself in the place of the girl in the center, facing the camera. What does she seem to be thinking?* 5. *What seems to be the reaction of the girl who is biting her lip?* 6. *What social background would it appear that this group is from? Would they be conservative in their thinking? Liberal? Radical?*

Photo by Paul Conklin from Pix

Part 2

MORES
AND MORALS

Development
by
Details

How do the authors of articles like "You Force Kids to Rebel" and "Dear Miss O'Neill" find so many interesting and significant things to say about their topics? The first answer is obvious: they know a great deal about their subjects, and they have strong feelings about them. But this answer is not complete. To explore and clarify their topics both for themselves and for their readers, these authors have employed certain effective devices of exposition, or "explanation."

To "explain" means to make clear or plain. It requires giving all the *details* necessary to make your ideas clearly comprehensible. Of course, before we can explain something to someone else, we must first understand it in our own mind. Perhaps in a friendly conversation we could get by with smiling apologetically and saying, "Oh, you know what I mean!" But this is not possible in written composition. Here, adequate details are expected as much as a definite point of view, a carefully maintained unity, and a logical ordering of our subject within an introduction, body, and conclusion, as we noted in Part 1.

Let us assume that we have chosen a topic with which we are familiar, a topic that interests us deeply. What are the devices, the various kinds of details, that every knowledgeable writer has at hand to help him clarify and develop his ideas so that they support his basic generalizations?

One of the devices that Steven Kelman used in explaining the revolt of today's youth was a detailed discussion of the *causes* of that revolt. Every effect presumably has certain causes. Therefore, if you give a clear explanation of the causes, you make the effect understandable. That is basically what Kelman did in showing that the revolt of youth today was due to the gap between what the student discovers the world to be in reality and what he has been taught about it in his years of schooling.

Another type of detail used by Kelman was *illustration*—giving specific instances or examples. When he was talking about the inadequate textbooks used in schools and colleges, he gave examples from a junior high-school civics book and a specific instance of J. Edgar Hoover's high-school guide *A Study of Communism*. Note the occasions Kelman has for saying "for example," "for instance," or "these are only random examples." A well-chosen illustration can be very effective in making an idea clear.

Closely allied to illustration is *comparison* or *contrast*, a type of detail that helps to explain what something is by showing its similarity to or difference from something else that may be more familiar. Andrew Hacker, in "The College Grad Has Been Short-Changed," used comparison and contrast very effectively in pointing out the way in which the college of tomorrow will differ from the college of today. A type of comparison which points out parallels between things that are, in one sense, categorically different, is called an *analogy*. In her article "Why Roommates Make the Best Wives" Joan Paulson constantly draws upon situations that are like those one meets in married life to show why rooming with another girl makes one a better wife in future years. Girls living together are not an *example* of marriage, but the problems that arise are similar, or analogous, to those one confronts in marriage.

Again, almost every writer has to make use of *definition* to explain some of the terms he uses which might be unfamiliar to the readers, or which he wants to be construed in a certain way. Note how Leo Rosten, for example, includes definitions of *non sequitur* and *solecism* for his readers.

Two devices that help a writer look clearly at his topic and sort out appropriate details to develop it are the devices of *analysis* and *classification*. *Analysis* consists of breaking something down into the parts of which it is composed. The advantage of explanation by means of analysis is that by looking carefully at the parts one can better understand the whole. Note that Kelman subjected the causes that underlie student revolt to detailed analysis. He divided into numerous areas the unrealities that he saw being taught to young people: social conditions, love and sex, literature, racial problems, and so forth, and he discussed each one in turn.

Classification consists of arranging things into categories. (For example, oranges, lemons, and grapefruit all belong to the category of citrus fruits.) In discussing the education of women, Dr. Edward D. Eddy, Jr., classified women into those seeking an immediate career, those seeking a postponed career, and those who "simply want to be intelligent and perceptive wives, mothers, and citizens." Explanation by analysis and classification, then, consists of breaking-down the subject to be explained into its separate parts, and then grouping those parts under various categories (or headings) so that they can be discussed in a logical, coherent fashion.

These practicable means of finding and adding significant details will be our special study here in Part 2, especially as they contribute to the development of paragraphs.

DEVELOPING PARAGRAPHS

For all practical purposes a good *paragraph* is one that explains in adequate detail just what an author means when he makes a general statement. The sentence in the paragraph which expressly makes this statement is called the *topic sentence*. It serves as a base from which the writer deliberately sets out, and to which he can constantly refer as he works his way through the supporting detail. For the reader it is a signboard telling him definitely what lies ahead, or, should the topic sentence appear at the end rather than at the beginning of the paragraph, just what ground he has covered. Even if there is no topic sentence, the reader should be able to deduce from the details given, the one that the writer had in mind.

To explain and expand the idea of the topic sentence, one can use the devices of illustration, comparison or contrast, analogy, definition, causes underlying the effect—either alone or in any combination. If, for example, you wished to write about some phase of the riots in Negro slums, you might well want to give what you felt were the causes leading to the outbreak of such violence. You would surely want to give ample details to illustrate the action, with typical instances of the kinds of violence and terror occasioned by such riots. You might want to define terms, which emerged during the riots, such as "Black Power," and you might want to indicate by comparison and contrast the similarities and differences in viewpoints between rioters and nonrioters, participants and law-enforcement officials.

LINKING PARAGRAPHS

Since each paragraph consists of a central generalization or topic sentence, developed by one or more of the supporting details that we have discussed, an essay may be regarded, really, as an organic chain of paragraphs, each expressing and developing an idea of its own, but with a central generalization or purpose governing the whole. Study the development of the paragraphs in the articles that follow with a view to using them as models for your own writing.

Be careful, as well, to guide your reader from one paragraph to the next by skillful *transitions,* for it is only by linking paragraphs smoothly in that "chain" that the writer makes it easy for the reader to follow the progress of his ideas. By means of *transitional words* (such as *nevertheless, for example, but, yet*), by the repetition of *key words,* and by the use of sentences that lead directly to the next paragraph-idea, the careful writer encourages the reader to read on.

GENERATION
OF ZEROS

PHILIP WYLIE

NEWSPAPERS recently reported that a leading educator was advocating the total abandonment of marks and grades in school and high school. His cause was an extension to its absolute of what has been, for more than a generation, the basic philosophy of our educators— education must avoid traumatizing the pupil, must spare tot and teen-ager alike; any experience that might tend to hurt feelings gives a sense of inferiority.

INTRODUCTION

Opening statement (dramatic, belligerent): Education is coddling students

Innumerable schools already move students on, without reference to effort or capability. Such automatic promotion is presumed to prevent the trauma that used to occur when a poor or lazy student was kept back a grade. Yet, these educators still maintain that they are preparing youth for adult life.

A lively attack: Yet educators pretend they are preparing youth for adult life

Grown-up life is, still, a life of ruthless competition where promotion depends on the equivalent of marks. And these are accorded by business, industry and the professions—publicly and without the slightest consideration of potential trauma. The man who makes it to a corporation presidency is *never* one who was sheltered from competition and spared the spiritual

Coddling is no preparation for ruthless competition

Reprinted from *This Week* Magazine, February 5, 1961, by permission of Harold Ober Associates, Inc. Copyright © 1967 by Philip Wylie.

blow of constant comparative rating with his associates. Nor was he the man who went up the ladder with what would have been a D-minus grade at every rung. In sum, education by the philosophy now inbred into teaching is utterly unsuitable as preparation for real life in a real world because it is, basically, *nothing education.*

Thesis statement (a grave criticism): We are becoming a "nothing" people

Another and even darker thought is likely to follow—a growing realization that much of all we consume, do, think and believe is, in one way or another, *also* a "nothing." Wherever one looks for the evidence, the evidence can be found without too much difficulty.

BODY
Adult "nothing readers"

The generation, now adult, that by and large wasn't taught how to read is an example. Perforce, it has recourse to that illiterate form of so-called communication, TV. *Nothing readers* are, in consequence, know-nothings, or near to it.

Campus "nothing thinkers"

Again, in the current campus uproar, the anti-Vietnam demonstrations, the undergraduate opposition to the draft and so on, one perceives how nothing-teaching has created nothing thinkers. For, in all this passionate protest, there is virtually no intimation, even in the loud negatives, of what these young people are *for*. The simple truth of the intent of Communism is either unknown to them or beyond their understanding.

Campus "nothing citizens"

They claim to want freedom—yet they libel the very men who are now dying to save their own. They want equality and even go into the South to face possible martyrdom in the effort to win Negro enfranchisement. Yet they reserve the right to judge who's equal *to them*. All persons who oppose their "right" to ordain what their professors shall teach, or their "right" to take drugs if they wish, or to parade, strike, riot, burn draft cards and stop troop trains, are held to be far from equal. They are squares. To be anti-square, without considering the problems, ideas, efforts and attainments of squares is, I think, to be a *nothing citizen* and near to a *nothing person*.

"Nothing" art

Art generally runs ahead of human conditions. Art shares one property: creativity. And creativity implies what genuine art achieves—some new value, perception, insight or direction that, then, becomes the general possession. So art is prophetic; art that arises from denial cannot be called creative. But, even before the First World War, many painters had become enamoured of what will certainly be termed, if mankind lasts long enough to regain some sanity, *nothing art.*

Today, of course, many major art forms plainly produce nihility. Yet leading critics, art judges, museum directors and gallery owners have created entire languages to accord the stuff their loftiest praise —nothing languages, of course, explaining why a blow-up of a tin-can label (Pop) is terrific, why mere optical illusion (Op) is worth a fortune per doodle and, lately, why a half-burned mattress, a dirty and paint-bloodied quilt or some heap of plastic chips glued together at random is also Art, as much as anything the Florentines ever did.

"Nothing" languages

In music, the solemn farce has become a similar religion. I remember when George Antheil's "Ballet Mécanique" had its Manhattan premiere. I was there. Besides an orchestra, the composition required synchronized pianos—13, as I recall—some airplane engines with attached propellers, going full blast at one point, and doorbells, too. Many in the audience laughed at the concert. Some booed. But certain highbrow critics undertook, even then, to find a way of talking that would dignify that cacophonous travesty. Nowadays, of course, music that isn't—*nothing music* —has become a cult.

"Nothing" music

Let's examine *people themselves* in the light of this lust for nothingness. The reduction of man's sense of his own worth is often set forth as an effect of our civilization. Crowded living-space diminished his sense of private dignity. Repetitive chores at assembly lines, desks or machine-controls reduce him to a seemingly petty object. Instead of resisting these pressures, man seems to be growing ever more willing, in America at least, to abet his own shrinkage. Made to feel less, he wants to become less still.

Man shrinking into "nonperson"

His version of the "new morality" shows how he goes about that sickly deed. The "new" morality relates to sex and followed the sexual revolution undertaken with the century's turn. It assumes that once truth and decency replace the venerable doctrine of "evil," sex

The "new morality"— perverted attitude toward sex

and its consummation would heighten the value men placed on themselves. The assumption was logical since the old dogma demeaned and besmirched man's sense of self.

"Pleasure morality"

But people are not using this new enlightenment as the "new moralists" intended. On the contrary, many tend to employ the newly revealed "truth" as a means to achieving private pleasure, without reference to any human value. Wives are swapped. Clubs for such trading and for other mass sex "games" abound. The only rule is that the players must not become concerned with any partner as a person. They must purge themselves of *humanity*.

Reflexion of "nothing sex" in modern dancing

This is reflected, too, in contemporary dances, where each one of any pair stands apart from the other and performs his exercises, however erotic, with no physical touch—depersonalized and wholly self-immersed. Such behavior cannot be called "nothing sex"—but it is sex by persons who make themselves into nothing much—nonpersons shorn of their very identity!

Noninvolved "nothing people"

Another evidence of the self-reduction of mankind is noninvolvement. The first instance to receive national attention concerned a horror in Kew Gardens, New York. There, a woman was twice attacked by stabbing and spent an hour crawling in the lighted streets begging for help. No one came to help. No one even called the police—not even anonymously. Afterward, investigators found 38 people who had watched the event—not one had made any effort to aid the woman who was being slowly murdered.

"Subhuman, nothing people"

From many American cities, innumerable examples of exactly that sort of behavior have since been cited. And, always, those who could have aided but merely watched, explained that they "didn't want to become involved." Since, to remain human, humanity must be and remain *involved* with itself, such persons are subhuman, nothing people.

"Nothing" theologians

There is an even more astonishing example of this national trend—a growing group of theologians are developing a theology (sic!) on the premise that "God is dead." Being professional religious men they hold, or some do, anyhow, a second premise of the cunning sort typical of dogmatists: that "God" could be "resurrected"—presumably by following *them*.

The fact that even a few "theologians" can take up such a monstrously incongruous idea shows how hard-put and how diminished *they* are in their search for a gimmick that might explain and suit the nothingness of the times. Now, *I* believe man's potential is nearly or truly infinite, supposing he gives himself time to approach that state—or infinite time to achieve it. But if man's potential is even near infinite, it includes the potential to destroy his species. Lately, we have acquired the means for that—and found ourselves in a scary new situation. Are we, perhaps, dedicating our lives and love and energy to nothingness, to diminishing ourselves as an unconscious means of easing the blow, should something slip and man's extirpation follow? The less we value ourselves, as individuals and as a species, the less would be the loss.

Eventual end of this nothingness

That *may* be the motivation of the nothing-seekers.

In any event, many Americans in high places are very disturbed about the poor "condition" of the citizens. Of them, one group attributes the phenomenon to materialism—a passion for acquiring things and gauging importance by relative piles of possessions, tends to diminish everybody, as human beings. But materialism has always been man's main folly and other civilizations have been more dedicated to things, and more ruthless in their collection, than we.

Main cause of nothingness: not materialism

It is odd, furthermore, that another group of American "analysts" and "thinkers" ascribe their worry about manifestly poor public attitudes to the *lack* of things— to the failure of our society to spread enough of everything among everybody.

Not inequal distribution of wealth

None of them seems to see, however, what I have tried to make evident, here. Prior societies of a materialist caste have, after all, valued real things. People have not, till now, accepted ersatz products and substitute acts save when the corresponding reality was unavailable. We seem, rather, to be trying to de-materialize—to be non-involved—when there *is* no alternative for involvement short of the abandonment of any claim to being human.

The real cause: noninvolvement and lack of values

Consequences for a nation
of "nothing people"

And if that's right, or if any similar evasion of reality *as a defense* is our motive, where will it leave us if the bombs never fall—if whatever situation we are trying to prepare for and cope with, by a massive shrinking toward zero, doesn't occur?

A nation, I suggest, so tremendously engaged in becoming nothing people—a nation motivated by unconscious fear—can hardly hope to create a Great Society, the precondition of which is a great citizenry.

Such a nation can hardly hope at all, in fact: Hope —like faith—is founded on something, however frail, and not on nothing.

CONCLUSION

Urgency to seek answers

Anybody who would study his fellow Americans to discern how much of nothing enters into their being and doing will find my sketchy samples sound, if merely a scratch on the surface. So, I think this hitherto unnoticed orientation-toward-nothing needs watching, needs further documentation and also deep contemplation. It may not be too late, though the reason for so much self-swindle may be more complex and obscure than I've suggested. Whatever it be, it needs seeking.

Too late?

Perhaps, however, it *is* too late. Too late to restore something to ourselves in order that we as a people may reverse the trend and become something, eventually. A dubious prospect.

Key terms for this search

For the scrutiny needs what we are running short of—*Entity. Identity. Presence.* And perhaps we already have become terrified of our own selves—and don't know it.

Dramatic close with
stinging challenge

Correct?

Or wouldn't you know?

COMMENTARY

Some years ago, Philip Wylie criticized a generation of Americans for their "Momism," or excessive devotion to motherhood. Just as he subjected "Momism" to a thorough *analysis,* so he now has treated what he considers our "nothing" society with similar severity. Once more, as the marginal comments and the accompanying outline show, he has applied the processes of *analysis* to his topic in order to develop its details. He lays bare the various dangers he deplores, and he gives them such labels as "nothing readers," "nothing thinkers," and "nothing citizens." As the outline also suggests, he has, moreover, with obvious care *classified* these various elements of danger under the general headings of faulty education, morality, personality, and social goals.

Wylie has analyzed the American plight as he sees it; he has pointed out specifically what practices and attitudes he finds alarming for the future. One after the other, in sequence of increasing importance, he ticks off the types of "nothing" young people and adults whom he holds responsible for the disintegrating social structure. He has detailed what rightly or wrongly he believes he has detected at work today under the surface of our national life.

This method of developing an essay topic cannot be applied to every subject, nor will every student find it a congenial process. It requires something of an analytical mind, one interested in the "why" of things and given to at least some reflection on what has been observed. It is the method of the scientist and the engineer, who have eyes trained to observe the nature and functioning of things. The social scientist, too, sets himself tasks of analyzing and classifying social behavior of all kinds. And both the artist and the critic, of course, also depend upon *analysis,* one to create imaginative works growing out of his examination of man and nature, and the other to appraise and interpret those works.

Look below the surface of your chosen topic. Try to see what underlies any troublesome situation, and then you will find *analysis* and its companion process, *classification,* helping you discover significant detail.

OUTLINE

Generalization: "Another and even darker thought is likely to follow—a growing realization that *much of all we consume, do, think, and believe is, in one way or another ALSO a 'nothing'.*"

    I. Faulty modern education has had dire consequences.
        A. It has seriously harmed the students.
            1. Adults are now "nothing readers."
            2. College students are too often "nothing thinkers."
            3. Many people are "nothing citizens."
        B. It has corrupted the arts.
            1. Painting has become a "nothing art."
            2. Music has become "nothing music."
   II. Man, as a result, has lost the sense of his own worth.
        A. He has deteriorated into a "nonperson."
        B. He has taken up a perverted "new morality" of sex.
        C. He has taken on a policy of noninvolvement.
        D. His religious leaders have encouraged "nothing seekers."
  III. The causes for this devaluation of the person can be found.

    A. The main cause is not a growing materialism, a passion for acquiring things.

    B. Neither is it the poor distribution of material goods.

    C. Rather, it is the lack of value for things that are real.

IV. A "Nothing people" cannot create a Great Society.

    A. Orientation toward "nothing" needs to be watched.

    B. Something must be done—or is it already too late?

WHAT DOES IT SAY?

1. What evidence could lead Wylie to brand television as "that illiterate form of so-called communication"?

2. What is "Pop Art" and how does it differ from "Op Art"?

3. Wylie insists people are motivated these days by a "lust for nothingness." What is the meaning of *lust* here?

4. What reactions from his readers is Wylie striving for in using language like "wives are swapped"?

5. Explain why the word *theology* is followed by "(sic!)" in this sentence: "There is an even more astonishing example of this national trend—a growing group of theologians are developing a theology (sic!) on the premise that 'God is dead.' "

6. What possibilities does Wylie refer to when he says, "Man's potential is nearly or truly infinite. . . ." ?

7. What do you think Wylie means by "a Great Society" in this context: ". . . a nation motivated by unconscious fear—can hardly hope to create a Great Society, the precondition of which is a great citizenry"?

8. What significance do the concluding words in italics each bear: "*Entity. Identity. Presence.*"?

WHAT DO YOU THINK?

1. Exercise your own powers of analysis and classification by concentrating your attention upon some area of collegiate or non-collegiate activity, and after you have isolated the various features distinguishing it, write an essay approving or disapproving Wylie's attack on types of "nothing citizens," "nothing music," or "nothing morality."

The Pro Deo study, however, will not be confined to problems of precise translation. The major emphasis has to do with something even more fundamental: the dangerous misconceptions and prejudices that take root in language and that undermine human values. The color of a man's skin, for example, is tied to plus-or-minus words that inevitably condition human attitudes. The words "black" and "white," as defined in Western culture, are heavily loaded. "Black" has all sorts of unfavorable connotations; "white" is almost all favorable. One of the more interesting papers being studied by the Pro Deo scholars is by Ossie Davis, the author and actor. Mr. Davis, a Negro, concluded on the basis of a detailed study of dictionaries and *Roget's Thesaurus* that the English language was his enemy. In *Roget's,* he counted 120 synonyms for "blackness," most of them with unpleasant connotations: blot, blotch, blight, smut, smudge, sully, begrime, soot, becloud, obscure, dingy, murky, threatening, frowning, foreboding, forbidden, sinister, baneful, dismal, evil, wicked, malignant, deadly, secretive, unclean, unwashed, foul, blacklist, black book, black-hearted, etc. Incorporated in the same listing were words such as Negro, nigger, and darky.

In the same *Roget's,* Mr. Davis found 134 synonyms for the word "white," almost all of them with favorable connotations: purity, cleanness, bright, shining, fair, blonde, stainless, chaste, unblemished, unsullied, innocent, honorable, upright, just, straightforward, genuine, trustworthy, honest, etc. "White" as a racial designation was, of course, included in this tally of desirable terms.

No less invidious than black are some of the words associated with the color yellow: coward, conniver, baseness, fear, effeminacy, funk, soft, spiritless, poltroonery, pusillanimity, timidity, milk-sop, recreant, sneak, lilylivered, etc. Oriental peoples are included in the listing.

As a matter of factual accuracy, white, black, and yellow as colors are not descriptive of races. The coloration range of so-called white people may run from pale olive to mottled pink. So-called colored people run from light beige to mahogany. Absolute color designations—white, black, red, yellow—are not merely inaccurate; they have become symbolic rather than descriptive. It will be argued, of course, that definitions of color and the connotations that go with them are independent of sociological implications. There is no getting around the fact, it will be said, that whiteness means cleanliness and blackness means dirtiness. Are we to doctor the dictionary in order to achieve a social good? What this line of argument misses is that people in Western cultures do not realize the extent to which their racial attitudes have been conditioned since early childhood by the power of words to ennoble or condemn, augment or detract, glorify or demean. Negative language infects the subconscious of most Western people from the time they first learn to speak. Prejudice is not merely imparted or superimposed. It is metabolized in the bloodstream of society. What is needed is not so much a change in language as an awareness of the power of words to condition attitudes. If we can at least recognize the underpinnings of prejudice, we may be in a position to deal with the effects.

To be sure, Western languages have no monopoly on words with connotations that affect judgment. In Chinese, whiteness means cleanliness, but it can also mean bloodlessness, coldness, frigidity, absence of feeling, weakness, insensitivity. Also in Chinese, yellowness is associated with sunshine openness, beauty, flowering, etc. Similarly, the word black in many African tongues has connotations of strength, certainty, recognizability, integrity, while white is associated with paleness, anemia, unnaturalness, deviousness, untrustworthiness.

The purpose of Pro Deo University in undertaking this study is not just to demonstrate that most cultures tend to be self-serving in their language. The purpose is to give educational substance to the belief that it will take all the adroitness and sensitivity of which the human species is capable if it is to be sustained. Earth-dwellers now have the choice of making their world into a neighborhood or a crematorium. Language is one of the factors in that option. The right words may not automatically produce the right actions but they are an essential part of the process.

COMMENTARY

How do the languages that men daily speak shape their thinking and help or hinder mankind in attempts to attain peace and understanding? In this essay Norman Cousins answers that question by an *analysis* of the nature of language showing that language is the most powerful force in determining any man's cultural environment. Every paragraph *analyzes* one important phase of this capacity of language to determine one's way of looking at things and other people.

The paragraphs show also how the device of *analysis* can combine with that of *illustration* to supply the details needed to support the *topic sentence*. In the second paragraph, for example, the topic sentence is the opening one. Cousins cites examples of how words in diplomatic messages can undergo dangerous shifts in meaning while being translated. The third paragraph, which deals with "the dangerous misconceptions and prejudices that take root in language and that undermine human values," also relies upon illustration, or example, to provide details. The lists of synonyms for "black" reveal surprising facts in support of the topic sentence. Paragraphs 4 and 5 really belong to that same one topic sentence. They are given separate indentation probably to break up a too massive appearing column of print. They illustrate how "white" and "yellow" affect our thinking from childhood on, regarding people who happen to have skins differing in color from our own.

Each of the paragraphs is a unified "miniature essay" progressing in a suitable sequence. Note also with what care Cousins has provided paragraph *transitions*. Paragraph 2 begins with a "key word" transition: the work of the Pro Deo University is stressed in the final sentence of the preceding paragraph, and then the next paragraph is made to begin with repetition of that key word "One aspect of the Pro Deo study." In the opening sentence of paragraph 3, the word "however" is a *transitional word,* warning the reader to watch for a shift in attention. Key words—"In the same *Roget's*" and "No less invidious than black"—also serve as links in paragraphs 4 and 5 respectively. Throughout, Cousins has linked and ordered his paragraphs of analysis and example.

If you want to improve the clarity and interest of your own written work, try adopting these devices of analysis and illustration and also using these transitional devices of coherence.

WHAT DOES IT SAY?

1. What is meant by the statement: "Language is an instrument; it is even more an environment"?

2. Point out the critical distinctions between *I assume, I deduce,* and *I consider.*

3. What is *Roget's Thesaurus?* Why would Mr. Davis regard its listed synonyms so important that he would say that "the English language was his enemy"?

4. Why does Mr. Cousins imply that definitions and synonyms for color words, such as *black, white,* and *yellow* have "sociological implications"?

5. What does he mean by the following question: "Are we to doctor the dictionary in order to achieve a social good"?

6. What is "negative language"? What is the meaning of this statement: "Negative language infects the subconscious of most Western people from the time they first learn to speak"?

7. Does Mr. Cousins say that Western languages are the only offenders in the matter of synonyms for color words that carry a loaded connotation? What conclusion do you draw from his remarks?

8. What is the meaning of "loaded words"?

WHAT DO YOU THINK?

1. On the basis of your own firsthand knowledge and experience, analyze the circumstances of the occasion when you first discovered what particular meaning one of the following kinds of words had for others and

now for you. Discuss as part of that analysis the effect that word has had in shaping your own personal "environment" socially, morally, and intellectually and why it is also a "loaded" word for others.

a) Any derogatory term for a person of another race or color
b) Any disparaging term for a person of a different religion
c) Any hostile term for a person of another nationality
d) Any cruel expression for one physically or mentally handicapped
e) Any taunting expression for a weaker or less advantaged person

2. Follow the same instructions given in the above assignment.

Red	Loudmouth	Nut	Punk
Cop	Gang	Fatty	Do-gooder
Chicken	Scout	Squealer	Christer
Runt	Bully	Goof-off	Junky

3. Write an essay analyzing the kind of "environment" the special vocabulary of your planned college major can be expected to create for you in the future. (Analyze the shaping influence intellectually, socially, and morally that the typical terms and expressions common to your profession will have on you.)

THE TOSSPOET

RICHARD WHITTINGTON-EGAN

DYLAN AND DRINK. The easy conjunction slips across the tongue smooth and savoury as finest malt beer. It has the salt and tang of saloon-bar truth—but is it no more really than a public legend?

Was Dylan Thomas, singer of womb and tomb, creation and crucifixion, a *poète ruiné*?

Did he end up written-out, prodding a stumbling talent with alcoholic shots in the arm? Or was he, dying, the living witness to the truth of that cardinal tenet in the drinker's shaky ordinal—that life develops significant new facets, seen through a glass brightly?

What, in short, was the part that drink played in Dylan's work? Was he a better poet with it? Would he have been no poet at all without it? Was drunkenness the tax that talent paid to turn itself to genius? Or did genius prematurely drown in a sparkling foam of alcohol?

All sound case histories must begin with familial considerations affecting the subject's heredity. Here at least we are on positive ground, for David John Thomas, the poet's father, was a reformed drunkard. Thomas senior, respected and respectable schoolmaster, himself confessed to his son that, when young and smarting from the discovery that the poetry which rang in his skull proved intractable to melodious transcription, he had solaced himself over-liberally with whisky, and had come within a short measure of ruining his life.

That the tilting Welsh elbow manifested itself among other of Dylan's relations too, is implicit in Dylan's own stories.

Still traversing medical territory, physiological factors have to be taken into

Reprinted from *Books and Bookmen,* November 1966, by permission of the author and publisher.

the reckoning. Dylan was of a somatic type (pyknic) frequently associated with diabetes and, although there is no evidence of his having been diabetic, we know of his remarkable addiction to sweet things. Indeed, at one stage this taste took the repellent form of plunging an ice-cream into his tankard of fizzy light ale. And alcohol itself is generated by the fermentation of sugar.

There is, too, abundant evidence that Dylan found a partial solution to the problem of his continual insomnia in alcohol.

Any, or all, of these somatic reasons may have contributed to Dylan's drinking habits, and the circumstance that he was so frequently and indubitably intoxicated may have been a purely mechanistic concomitant of the further physiological fact that the horizon of his alcoholic tolerance appears to have been low. *Vulgatim:* he had a poor head for drink.

But by far the greatest weight of evidence would seem to indicate that the basic motivation of Dylan's massive ingestion of alcohol was psychological —a matter of emotional need.

The drinking began, in the early days, as bravado; as part and parcel of a deliberately cultivated persona. At 17 Dylan was working as a cub reporter on the *South Wales Daily Post*. He was ever a lad of parts, and the role of tough, hard-drinking newshound would inevitably involve him in ritual bouts of bar-counter bonhomie. At 17, too, a youth of Dylan's rebellious, self-willed temperament would be eagerly reaching out for the status of manhood. How better to grasp it than grasp the handle of a tankard, a sophisticate's fistful, standing your corner like a man? *Here* was manliness. *Here* was FREEDOM.

And all the while, behind the journalist's façade, the poet was inching up. The young Dylan's conception of the poet was old-fashioned. The Poet was Marlowe carousing at the Mermaid, Dowson reeling eastwards down the Strand, a roistering Rimbaud, tipsy, tatterdemalion Verlaine. The Poet was a practitioner of vice as well as verse—and what more wicked in the white-washed Wales of 30 years ago than public-houses and DRINK? How better to kick against the Chapel pricks and prigs than to have hot and rebellious liquors in his blood? At 17 defiance for its own sake can be a divinely satisfying thing.

So it was that Dylan, always a great actor, oozed and boozed his way from the bit part of gulping journalist to the lifelong role of wild, romantic tosspot poet. And with practice came pleasure. One cannot discount the strong down-to-earth possibility that, once set upon his initially imitative course, Dylan discovered that he liked the taste of beer, enjoyed the ethos and rites of beer-drinking—. . . *its live, white lather, its brass-bright depths, the sudden world through the wet-brown walls of the glass, the tilted rush to the lips and the slow swallowing down to the lapping belly, the salt on the tongue, the foam at the corners.*

In November 1934, when he was 21, Dylan moved to London. Here, in the Soho pubs, the romantic emphasis shifted. In bohemian London everybody drank. Drink was no longer the wickedly interesting thing that it had been back home in Swansea. So now Dylan became the doomed consumptive poet.

Cyril Connolly remembers:

When I first knew him, soon after he had come to London, he was determined to drink as much as possible and to imagine that he had T.B. He was already obsessed with the idea that a poet should die young and live in such a way as to risk his own destruction. At an age when many an undergraduate is doing the same thing, it did not seem pernicious that he should aim at the intoxication of a Marlowe, a Baudelaire, a Rimbaud, or a Dowson, because he seemed able to do without drink for his creative country-periods, and because he was still a young poet, not the heavy-drinking Fleet Street character which he afterwards became.

Indeed, such drinking as he did in the 1930s seems to have been no more than a social drinking. The pub was his club, the place to which at day's work's end he went to see his friends, to exchange the lonely isolation of his working hours for the convivial relaxation which he felt that he had earned. He was a sociable man. He loved company. He loved to talk. Yet withal he was a surprisingly timid man. Within those "wet-brown walls" he found great draughts of Dutch courage. Drink oiled the stiff wheels and gears of intimidating intercourse.

By the 1940s Dylan was undoubtedly drinking heavily—and becoming a roaring success. Asked point-blank by John Arlott why he got drunk so often, Dylan replied, "Because it's different every time." A typically Dylanesque ambiguity. It *could* have meant that on each occasion the reason that he got drunk was different, that the constellation of circumstances which precipitated the unintended drunkeness was different. Or it *could* have meant that he became intentionally drunk because in that way he discovered exciting new experiences and visions of the world.

On another occasion, replying to the same question, Dylan said, with all-embracing (and highly suspect) simplicity, "Because they expect it of me."

In other words, Dylan-the-actor was playing the role which he had created for Dylan-the-poet.

Was it really, then, all make-believe? Or was he a fringe alcoholic, stalwartly refusing to admit the fact even to himself?

Dylan could, indeed did, go for weeks on end taking no more than a few glasses of weak beer, and seldom, in the privacy of his own home, did he drink to excess. He was, in what one may call his pre-American Period—that is prior to 1950—able to keep his social drinking life and his creative working life more or less satisfactorily separate.

The late Julian Maclaren-Ross has written illuminatingly of Dylan's habits in this context.

The scene: A rooftop, attic office at Number 1 Golden Square, Soho. It is the office of Strand Films, where Dylan and Maclaren-Ross are working on scenarios for documentary films.

The time: August 1943.

The speaker is Dylan.

"Now where's this bloody script got to? Ah, here we are. 'Home Guard.' I expect you'll want to start work right away?"

Maclaren-Ross: "We could discuss it over drinks. They'll be open time we get there."

(Dylan seemed delighted with this suggestion, which he'd plainly not wanted to be the first to make.)

Dylan. "We mustn't get tight though."

The pair adjourn to the nearby Café Royal, where Dylan rations himself to a single pint of bitter and watches anxiously over Maclaren-Ross and his intake of Irish whisky. Thanks to his vigilance they regain the office—both sober—at 2 P.M.

Scene Two: The same as above.

The time: Twenty-four hours later. In the meantime Dylan and Maclaren-Ross have survived a wild, besotted night.

Maclaren-Ross. "Look here, Dylan, I don't feel too good myself. Why don't we have a bottle up here, guard against these hangovers in future?"

Dylan. "A bottle?"

Maclaren-Ross. "Whisky. We could go halves. I know a fellow can get it on the black market. I'll ring him now if you like."

Dylan. "Whisky. *In the office?*" (Absolutely appalled.)

Maclaren-Ross. "Don't be silly, why not?"

Dylan. (Firmly shaking his head) "Not for me. You please yourself, of course, but I won't, if you don't mind."

And so the bottle was never imported.

Similarly, it was, I think, the sober, bottle-spurning, temptation-resisting Dylan, sitting perched and parched in his cliff-top hut at Laugharne, who did the best work.

I say "I think," because, short of directly questioning Dylan himself, I do not think that one can really resolve the problem of how much or how little the inspirational quality of his work was affected by his drinking.

The mythology of alcohol is copious. Literary legend overflows with bibulous whisperings of the beneficent djinn (or should it perhaps be gin?) in the bottle, who has brought the gift of inspiration to his uncorking slave-master. But this semi-mystical, wine-borne increase in perception and sensitivity is, if I may be permitted a Smilesian, militant, Victorian teetotalitarianism, a snare and a delusion. To the scientist, alcohol is a poison . . . and there is precious little mystery as to the effect that it produces.

The action of ethyl alcohol on the human system is lamentably predictable. Its acute effects are sensations of warmth and relaxation, euphoria, camaraderie and the release of inhibition. Pharmacologically, this corresponds to the gradual administration of general anaesthesia.

Alcohol is not a stimulant. The drinker may feel stimulated, may believe that his abilities are enhanced, but actually his intellectual functions are undergoing progressive impairment.

The inflexible prognosis for the chronic alcoholic is one of irreversible deterioration.

Abnormal drinkers are of two kinds—those who can stop if they want to, and those addicts who cannot.

Dylan Thomas's drinking was, I suspect, non-addictive. It was, more likely, hedonistic, a method of combating symptoms—to allay anxiety, to point-up pleasure. Throughout the greater part of his life its *direct* effect on his work was probably negligible. On the credit side, it may even have contributed a felicitous phrase here, a lingering image there. But its long-term consequence was *bound* to be destructive. And indeed it was—utterly destructive.

It killed him.

The pieces of the pattern of annihilation are fragmented over the 46 months of Dylan's post-American Period—that is, from the time of his first visit to America in February 1950, to the moment of his death, three years and four visits later, in November 1953. Something happened during that time which fatally tipped the chemical balance, turning Dylan from a heavy drinker into an alcoholic, rushing him through the hell of delirium tremens into the mercy of coma, and the final absolution of death.

What that something was, it is difficult, in defect of more precise data, to speculate. To suggest that it was purely and simply the result of the accessibility of free alcohol, in a new land flowing with the milk and honey of excessive hospitality, is naive. To conclude that it was a compensatory ploy to alleviate the distress caused by the realization of a waning poetic talent is to put the cart before the hearse.

My own belief is that it was not the poet who destroyed the man, but the man who destroyed the poet. There is evidence, discreetly swathed but visible through its swaddlings, that in America Dylan, for the first time since his marriage, fell in love with a woman other than Caitlin. I suspect that the dilemma produced by this situation affected him so profoundly that it became unbearable. Not only was he incapable of facing the decision which he knew the future must thrust upon him, but the very contemplation of that impending choice made the present so hideous that he sought to escape it in continual alcoholic anaesthesia. He deliberately opted out of the emotional conflict, even though he must have dimly realized that, in so doing, he was opting for death instead of life.

And, shortly before the end, he even verbalized the old self-destructive urge, hardened now into an invincible death wish, to Liz Reitell, "I want to go to the Garden of Eden . . . to die . . . to be for ever unconscious . . . I truly want to die."

He had his wish.

"Insult to the brain" was the medically ambiguous diagnosis on his death certificate. It might, I think, have been no less scientific, and certainly nearer to the truth, if the doctors had written, "Overdose of guilt."

Alcohol was, as it were, the gun, but the gun is not the killer. The killer is the idea that lies behind the finger that pulls the trigger.

In the case of Dylan Marlais Thomas, the miracle is that alcohol had so *little* effect on his work. The *man* played a kind of desperate Russian roulette . . . and the *poet* it was who died.

COMMENTARY

One standard, and excellent, method of explanation is the use of cause and effect. Every *effect*, presumably, is the result of some *cause* (or variety of causes), so in examining in detail the cause of any situation, action, or accomplishment one can consequently understand and explain the effect. This method can also operate in reverse—that is, an examination of the effect can illuminate the cause.

In this essay the author attempts to explain Dylan Thomas the poet, by looking closely into one of the causes (heavy drinking—note the title of the essay) that has been suggested as being responsible for his death. The author's concern is clearly with two items: the poet's achievement and his early death; both, *presumably*, due to the same cause. What conclusion does the author reach in his analysis? And where, in the essay, does he state that conclusion? How carefully does he examine the supposed cause?

One must be careful in dealing with cause and effect to watch out for several pitfalls. (1) Because *A* comes before *B*, can we conclude that *A* is the cause of *B*? For example, was a football game won because just before the opening whistle an announcement reached the locker room that the coach had been fired? (Presumption: the players went out on the field to prove how valuable the coach was to the institution.) (2) Does any end-result, like the too-early death of Dylan Thomas, have only one cause, or does it have several? If several, which is the main cause? Again, for example, did the football team lose the big game of the year merely because one of the players was forced out of the line-up with an injury in the first quarter? Note how the author of this article avoids such pitfalls in his essay.

WHAT DOES IT SAY?

1. What words and phrases suggest that the author himself likes beer?

2. The expression *the salt and tang of saloon-bar truth* is very appropriate in the opening paragraph. Do you know any other such "truths" that have become almost "gospel truths"?

3. In what way can a finished poem be called a *melodious transcription?*

4. Is there any difference between "playing a role" and "cultivating a persona"?

5. To read intelligently one must recognize people and places, as well as various allusions, literary or otherwise. Who, for instance, was Marlowe? What and where is Soho? What was the Mermaid? Information of this kind is readily available in any good dictionary or encyclopedia or in a variety of reference books such as the *Oxford Companion to English* (or *American* or *Classical*) *literature.* Consulting one or more of these sources, you will learn that Christopher Marlowe was an English dramatist and poet who was born the same year as Shakespeare, 1564; that Soho is a district in central London; and that the Mermaid was a tavern in London, a favorite gathering place for Elizabethan poets and dramatists. Look up the following: Dowson, Baudelaire, Rimbaud, Verlaine, Swansea, the Strand.

6. Why should *Chapel pricks and prigs* encourage rebellion?

7. Give equivalents for *ritual bouts, bar-counter bonhomie, oozed and boozed, ethos of beer-drinking, convivial relaxation, bibulous whisperings,* and *tosspoet.*

8. Why is the medical diagnosis explaining his death—*insult to the brain* —ambiguous?

WHAT DO YOU THINK?

1. David Holbrook, the critic, sharply attacks Dylan Thomas as a poet and applies Karl Menninger's famous psychoanalytical analysis of alcoholism to Thomas. Examine the analysis and Holbrook's use of it. Then show in what respects "The Tosspoet" cause-and-effect explanation supports or differs from the Holbrook-Menninger account.

   It is true that alcohol has the quality of giving some degree of relief from the pain of facing reality and also from other psychic pain resulting from emotional conflicts. . . . The use of alcohol can be regarded as an attempt at self-cure. . . . Such individuals, as children, have endured bitter disappointment—*unforgettable* disappointment, *unforgiveable* disappointment. They feel, with justification, that they have been betrayed, and their entire subsequent life is a prolonged, disguised reaction to this feeling. . . . He remains all his life what we call an "oral" character . . . one characterized by conspicuous residual of the stage of psychological development in which the child's attitude toward the world was determined by his wish to take it in through the mouth and to destroy with his mouth anything which resisted his demands. In drinking [then concludes Holbrook] the alcoholic performs with his mouth, takes in a magical substance and may become aggressive. The same elements are found in the oral imagery and babble-quality of Dylan Thomas's poetry, its magical attitude (as of incantation) to reality, and what John Bayley calls "the sense of being assaulted by something other than words." David Holbrook, *Dylan Thomas and Poetic Dissociation,* Carbondale, Illinois: Univ. of Illinois Press, 1964, pp. 14–15.

2. Take some situation (one that is an effect), such as the increasing number of drop-outs in the schools, or the increasing crime-rate, or the steadily mounting number of accidents on the highways, and discuss it by looking into the possible causes. Be careful to avoid the two pitfalls mentioned earlier.

3. In addition to reporting your own feelings on the matter, question some of your fellow students on one of the following subjects and then write your own analysis of that situation:
   a) Why do some young people like to violate laws prohibiting the sale of alcoholic beverages to minors?
   b) Why do young people start smoking cigarettes now that there appears to be a definite causal relationship between smoking cigarettes and lung cancer?
   c) Why do you (or don't you) attend church services regularly?
   d) Why do so many students postpone doing class assignments?

THE NEW
PORNOGRAPHY

from *Time*

JOHN CLELAND was a luckless little hack who in 1748, destitute and desperate, scribbled *Fanny Hill* or *Memoirs of a Woman of Pleasure* for a flat fee of 20 guineas. He went on to become an inept philologist, ducked creditors much of his life, and died aged and unsung. If the poor fellow were only alive today, he could be a Big Writer, for critics on both sides of the Atlantic have acclaimed his ability to describe repetitive fornication with elegance and grace. He could wear hand-sewn Italian loafers, sell his still unwritten books to the paperbacks and the movies for a cool million, and lecture at progressive colleges on "Erotic Realism in the Novel."

But he would have to work hard, very hard, to keep up with the competition. For just about anything is printable in the U.S. today. All the famed and once hard-to-get old volumes are on the paperback racks, from the *Kama Sutra* to the Marquis de Sade's *Justine*. Henry Miller's *Tropic of Cancer,* once the last word in unprintable scatology, can often be picked up in remainder bins for 25¢. Miller has almost acquired a kind of dignity as the Grand Old Dirty Man of the trade, compared with some of the more current writers. Krafft-Ebing's *Psychopathia Sexualis* is out in two new editions, which for the first time render all those horrendous Latin passages in English—and, surrounded by the author's quaint 19th century moralizing, they seem tame alongside *Candy* or Norman Mailer's *An American Dream.*

Maurice Girodias, the shy little Parisian who was the world's foremost publisher of English-language pornography until tightening French censorship

Reprinted from *Time,* April 16, 1965. Courtesy *Time;* copyright Time Inc. 1965.

put his Olympia Press out of business, often talks about setting up shop in the U.S., but it is difficult to see what he could peddle. Barney Rosset, publisher of Grove Press and in a sense the American Girodias, is way ahead of him. Says Rosset hopefully: "Who knows if the limits have been reached? Just because the scientists split the atom, did they sit back and say, 'Well, that's it'?" The pioneering publisher could always push the limits a little farther by trying the notorious *Story of O.* or *The Debauched Hospodar*. But one of these days even Rosset may run out of material.

The avowed professional pornographers face a related dilemma. The fact is that all kinds of respectable hard-cover books now contain subject matter and language that would have brought police raids only a few years ago "is really killing us," says a West coast practitioner. Far from giving up, the cheap paperback pornographers are diversifying by expanding their old pre-occupation with lesbianism and sado-masochism, while searching for ever more bizarre combinations and settings. Still, it is tough trying to stay ahead of the avant-garde.

With everyone so afraid of appearing square, the avant-garde is obviously trying to determine just how far things can be pushed before anyone will actually admit to being shocked. New York now exports to various other centers of culture a mimeographed magazine whose title is somewhat stronger than *Love You, A Magazine of the Arts*; its pages are filled by some certified avant-garde writers, many homosexual, who mostly write *pissoir* poetry.

While cheap "nudie" movies are branching out into torture and lesbianism in a desperate attempt to keep a few steps below Hollywood, the far-out new wave in New York and San Francisco is also creating a cinema of sorts; such "underground" films as Jack Smith's *Flaming Creatures* and Andy Warhol's *Couch* feature transvestite orgies with masturbation and other frills—although they seem even more concerned with an almost narcotic attack on the concept of time, since most of them are interminable.

After a visit to the U.S., Malcolm Muggeridge, onetime editor of *Punch*, complained: "I'd have joined a Trappist order rather than take more. All those ghastly novels—sex is an obsession with the Americans." Besides, adds Muggeridge, "if the purpose of pornography is to excite sexual desire, it is unnecessary for the young, inconvenient for the middle-aged, and unseemly for the old."

Unnecessary or unseemly, or just unpleasant, what young and old may now read or see is part of the anti-Puritan revolution in American morals.

The Greek term *pornographos,* meaning literally "the writing of harlots," has always been relative and subjective. As D. H. Lawrence put it, "What is pornography to one man is the laughter of genius to another." Until the 1930s, U.S. courts generally followed a celebrated 1868 ruling of Britain's Lord Chief Justice Sir Alexander Cockburn, whose test for obscenity—used more or less interchangeably with pornography—was the effect any material might have on a hypothetical schoolgirl, or its tendency to "deprave and corrupt those whose minds are open to such immoral influences." This ruling, which bedeviled and outraged the literary world for some 65 years, ignored the over-all literary or educational merit of a book for the adult reader.

The schoolgirl test began to crumble in 1933 with the famed ruling by the U.S. Circuit Court of Appeals in New York, which held that James Joyce's *Ulysses* was not obscene—despite its impudent pudendicity and ovablastic genitories—since the "proper test" is a book's "dominant effect." In 1957, in decisions that upheld the conviction of two mail-order pornography dealers, the U.S. Supreme Court finally defined its own views on the matter. First, it flatly denied the smut peddlers' contention that the 1st and 14th Amend-ments guaranteeing freedom of speech and press gave them a right to sell obscene material. Second, the court held that the Constitution does guarantee freedom for ideas "having even the slightest redeeming social importance—un-orthodox ideas, controversial ideas, even ideas hateful to the prevailing climate of opinion." The court defined obscenity as material "utterly without redeem-ing social importance," and set up as its test "whether to the average person, applying contemporary community standards, the dominant theme of the material taken as a whole appeals to prurient interest."

This does not establish a uniform permissiveness across the U.S. Each city, county and state can bring actions that publishers or distributors must defend individually, at sometimes prohibitive costs. But in general, what constitutes "redeeming social importance" is endlessly arguable, and even plainly unre-deemed "hard-core" pornography is easier than ever to buy, particularly since the Supreme Court ruled that allegedly obscene books or movies cannot be seized by police until they have been so adjudged in the courts.

Lately, a distinct reaction against permissiveness has begun. Pressure is increasing from citizens' organizations such as the Roman Catholic National Organization for Decent Literature, the Protestant Churchmen's Committee for Decent Publications, and Citizens for Decent Literature, a nonsectarian organization that now has 300 chapters around the country. These groups are shrill, sincere, and sometimes self-defeating. When a Chicago court ruled three years ago that Henry Miller's *Tropic of Cancer* could be sold locally, the C.D.L. flooded Chicago with excerpts of outrageous passages in the book, undoubtedly giving them wider circulation than they had ever before enjoyed in the city.

Miller, for one, considers such alarms trivial in the light of the Bomb. "We are now passing through a period of what might be called 'cosmic in-sensitivity,'" he says, "a period when God seems more than ever absent from the world and man is doomed to come face to face with the fate he has created for himself. At such a moment, the question of whether a man be guilty of using obscene language in printed books seems to me incon-sequential. It is almost as if, while taking a walk through a green field, I espied a blade of grass with manure on it, and bending down to that obscure little blade of grass I said to it scoldingly, 'Naughty! Naughty!' "

Not everybody can be as cosmically insensitive as that, particularly when, as it sometimes appears, there is so much manure and so little grass. Actually, there is relatively less indignation from the pulpits of any denomination than one might expect. Says Harold Bosley, pastor of Manhattan's Christ Church Methodist: "The new license in the arts is one of the major problems in the church today. But none of us are interested in rigorous public censorship. We must help create an attitude of self-censorship and responsibility, otherwise we're dead ducks." And Baptist Minister Howard Moody of the Judson Memorial Church in New York's Greenwich Village feels that a new Christian definition of obscenity should not concentrate on sex or vulgar language alone, but on anything, particularly violence, whose purpose is "the debasement and depreciation of human beings."

As for psychiatrists, they are great believers in the Jimmy Walker dictum that no girl was ever ruined by a book, asserting, in effect, that no one is harmed by pornography who is not sick to begin with. The young, it is widely conceded, are more vulnerable, but no one has yet devised a practical way of keeping books from the young by law without also keeping them from adults —which would mean a return to the Cockburn rule.

Perhaps beyond questions of law, even beyond concern for morals, the problem is one of taste.

An open mind toward the new, the shocking, even the intolerable in art is an intellectual duty, if only because so many great and shocking artists from Swift to Joyce were so vehemently condemned at first. It hardly follows that any writer who manages to shock is therefore automatically entitled to respect as a worthy rebel. Yet this is how their followers regard the heroes of today's avant-garde, notably Jean Genet (*Our Lady of the Flowers*) and William Burroughs (*Naked Lunch*). "The new immoralists" is what they are labeled by *Partisan Review* Editor William Phillips, who is anything but a literary reactionary. He adds: "To embrace what is assumed to be beyond the pale is taken as a sign of true sophistication. And this is not simply a change in sensibility; it amounts to a sensibility of chaos."

Genet, Burroughs and other chroniclers of fagotry and fellatio are different from the realists of sex like Zola, the sentimentalists of sex like D. H. Lawrence, the poetic demons of sex like Baudelaire. They are different from the good old-fashioned pornographers like *Fanny Hill's* Cleland or the masters of bawdry from Ovid to Aretino, Rabelais, Boccaccio and (in an off moment) Mark Twain. However unconventional, these writers found delight in sex; however critical of human folly, they were partisans of mankind. The new immoralists attack not only society but man and sex itself. Their writings add up to homosexual nihilism, and what Fanny Hill would have thought of them is made clear by her "rage and indignation" when she observed a pair of "male-misses, scare less execrable than ridiculous."

Writing in *Commentary*, William Phillips nails the whole genre by devastatingly describing Burroughs' *Nova Express* as "the feeding almost literally of human flesh and organs on each other in an orgy of annihilation. The whole world is reduced to the fluidity of excrement as everything dissolves into everything else." And Critic John Wain adds: "A pornographic novel is, in however backhanded a way, on the side of something describable as life. *Naked Lunch,* by contrast, is unreservedly on the side of death."

In their defense it is often said that the new immoralists merely seek to show the world as they see it, in all its horror and lovelessness; but that is simply the old error of confusing art with event, a propagation of the notion that a novel trying to convey dullness must be dull. Sheer nightmare does not redeem a book any more than sheer pollyannaism. The Genet-Burroughs crowd, including such lesser sensationalists as John Rechy (*City of Night*) and Hubert Selby (*Last Exit to Brooklyn*), are not pornographers, if pornography is defined as arousing sexual excitement. These writers have created a pornography of nausea, which if anything has the opposite effect. They are thus the enemies of the hedonist almost more than the enemies of the moralist.

Apart from making sex hideous and inhuman, the new pornographers also make it hopelessly dull. They should have learned from Sade, who used sex to assert the impossible—the totally unlimited freedom of man—and pushed the concept into insanity. Along the way Sade desperately tried to force his imagination beyond human limits by inventing inhuman horrors, but he only managed to make his compilation shatteringly dreary. Toward the end of his *120 Days of Sodom* he was no longer really writing, but simply setting down long lists of neatly numbered and tersely outlined enormities— the effect being ludicrous and totally unreal. Much of the current writing on sex approaches this quality of mechanical repetition and unreality.

For one thing, the constant use of the limited four-letter vocabulary tends to rob the words of what legitimate shock effect they used to have. "Powerful words should be reserved for powerful occasions," says Novelist Philip Toynbee. "Words like money can be devalued by inflation." Stuart B. Flexner, coauthor of the authoritative *Dictionary of American Slang,* believes that this is already happening. "The next step is to find a new crop," he says, "but I don't know yet what these will be."

Secondly, it is becoming ever clearer that, as Novelist Saul Bellow said not long ago, "polymorphous sexuality and vehement declarations of alienation are not going to produce great works of art." The vast majority of writers, publishers and critics rejoice over the decline of censorship. While it permits the emergence of much trash, they feel that this is the necessary price for the occasional great work that might otherwise be taboo—for example, Nabokov's *Lolita,* a brilliant *tour de force.* But they concede that the new permissiveness paradoxically imposes a more difficult task on the writer; in a way it is harder to work without than within limits. Says Critic-Author Leslie Fiedler: "We've got our freedom. Now the question is what do we do with it."

Joseph Heller, author of the far from prudish *Catch-22,* adds: "Now that we have established more dirty talk and more promiscuity in literature, we've established the obvious. What is accomplished by being specific? A reader's imagination is a more potent descriptive power than any author has. When everything is told, what you're left with is pretty crude and commonplace. The love scenes in *Anna Karenina* are infinitely more intimate than any explicit sex scene I can recall."

Besides, Tolstoy did not suffer from the pathetic phallacy according to which all existence revolves around sex. Many authors today treat sex the way Marxists treat economics; they see it at the root of everything, and day-dream about sexual triumph the way revolutionary writers daydream about power. Thus in the tirelessly explicit writing of Norman Mailer, sex is a personal boast, a mystique and an ideology—and, in all three capacities, solemn and unconvincing.

Sex has, of course, infinite variants and imposes many compulsions. There will always be cheap pornography, and in a permissive age it will flourish openly and, perhaps, eventually fade; in a restrictive age, it will live clan-destinely and, probably, remain a hardy growth. The purpose of sex in serious literature is to help convey the feeling and meaning of life as it is. Thus litera-ture neither denies the existence of the wildest aberrations nor the use of the most clinical or bawdy language—but does not celebrate them as norms.

In the long run a sense of humor may be far more effective against the new pornography than censorship ever could be. "A return to ribaldry would be a very good thing," says Methodist Minister Tom Driver. "People ought to laugh in bed, and at some of the current writing about bed." There are signs that some are indeed laughing—and laughing at the authors of por-nography. For sex is far too important a matter to be left merely to writers.

COMMENTARY

This *Time* essay on a highly controversial topic shows how *illustration,* or *example,* provides the kind of dramatic detail that only this expository device can give the reader. By definition, an *example* is something selected to show the typical character of others like it: a sample to illustrate a principle or generalization. Naturally the examples in this essay illustrate the range and quality of the contemporary pornography that is analyzed. The candor and objectivity of the writer's point of view make the inclusion of the names of authors, publishers, and movie-makers, with representative titles of their works, reasonable if somewhat startling. Yet such specific examples center the dis-cussion upon definite cases and works and leads to a frank consideration of the principles underlying them, whereas an evasive article dealing only with vague generalities and issues would avoid all direct and analytical airing of the topic.

Drama lies in the specific, individual instance or example. And as we shall see in Part 3, we tend to jump to conclusions on the basis of individual experiences. In fact, the whole process of inductive logic is based upon this manner of arriving at a generalization through repeated observations. In the following assignment suggestions, you will find opportunity to bring in examples supporting your opinion of some generalization quoted from the essay.

One word of warning about examples, however: be sure that the instances you cite are really relevant as samples of the principle they are intended to support.

WHAT DOES IT SAY?

1. How in the terms of the definitions found in this essay do *pornography*, *hardcore pornography*, and *obscenity* differ as legal terminology?

2. What was "the schoolgirl test" for decency in literature?

3. How can the present vogue of pornography be termed "the anti-Puritan revolution"?

4. Who are *avant-garde* authors? Are they all primarily purveyors of pornography?

5. Can you explain the distinctions between "the realists of sex like Zola, the sentimentalists of sex like D. H. Lawrence, the poetic demons of sex like Baudelaire"?

6. "Words like money can be devalued by inflation," Philip Toynbee is quoted as saying. How is this statement applicable to the "shock" value of the usually objectionable "four-letter" words?

7. Is the phrase "the new immoralists" appropriate for those grouped here under "new pornography"? Why?

8. The opening sentence of the fourth paragraph states: "The avowed professional pornographers face a related dilemma." What is this "dilemma"?

WHAT DO YOU THINK?

1. Select one of the following generalizations found in "The New Pornography" and develop it by means of analysis supported by illustrative examples. Make sure that the examples are representative samples.
   a) "Sex is an obsession with the Americans."

b) "We are now passing through a period of what might be called 'cosmic insensitivity.'"

c) "An open mind toward the new, the shocking, even the intolerable in art is an intellectual duty."

d) "No girl was ever ruined by a book."

e) "Many authors today treat sex the way Marxists treat economics: they see it at the root of everything, and daydream about sexual triumph the way revolutionary writers daydream about power."

f) "The purpose of sex in serious literature is to help convey the feeling and meaning of life as it is."

g) "Perhaps beyond questions of law, even beyond concern for morals, the problem is one of taste."

h) "In the long run a sense of humor may be far more effective against the new pornography than censorship could ever be."

2. Support with examples your analysis of the possible harmful effects that "dirty books and pictures" may have on children.

3. During a recent nationwide television report on "The Pill," one of three mothers who were interviewed explained that when the time came to send her daughter to college, she probably would be given a prescription for the Pill as a safeguard. If you were the mother, would you make a similar decision "in order to be safe rather than sorry"?

WHAT IS "BRAINWASHING"?

ROBERT JAY LIFTON, M.D.

WHEN CONFRONTED with the endless discussion on the general subject of "brainwashing," I am sometimes reminded of the Zen Buddhist maxim: "The more we talk about it, the less we understand it." The confusion begins with the word itself, so new and yet already so much a part of our everyday language. It was first used by an American journalist, Edward Hunter, as a translation of the colloquialism *hsi nao* (literally, "wash brain") which he quoted from Chinese informants who described its use following the Communist takeover.

"Brainwashing" soon developed a life of its own. Originally used to describe Chinese indoctrination techniques, it was quickly applied to Russian and Eastern European approaches, and then to just about anything which the Communists did anywhere (as illustrated by the statement of a prominent American lady who, upon returning from a trip to Moscow, claimed that the Russians were "brainwashing" prospective mothers in order to prepare them for natural childbirth). Inevitably, the word made its appearance closer to home, sometimes with the saving grace of humor (*New Yorker* cartoons of children "brainwashing" parents, and wives "brainwashing" husbands), but on other occasions with a more vindictive tone—as when Southern segregationists accused all who favor racial equality (including the United States Supreme Court) of having been influenced by "left-wing brainwashing"; or equally irresponsible usages by anti-fluoridation, anti-mental health legislation, or anti-almost anything groups leveled against their real or fancied opponents.

Then there is the lurid mythology which has grown up about it: the "mysterious oriental device," or the deliberate application of Pavlov's findings on dogs. There is also another kind of myth, the claim that there is no such thing, that it is all just the fantasy of American correspondents.

Finally, there is the more responsible—even tortured—self-examination which leads professional people to ask whether they in their own activities might not be guilty of "brainwashing": educators about their teaching, psychiatrists about their training and their psychotherapy, theologians about their own reform methods. Opponents of these activities, without any such agonizing scrutiny, can more glibly claim that they are "*nothing but* brainwashing." Others have seen "brainwashing" in American advertising, in large corporation training programs, in private preparatory schools, and in congressional investigations. These misgivings are not always without basis, and suggest that there is a continuity between our subject and many less extreme activities; but the matter is not clarified by promiscuous use of the term.

Behind this web of semantic (and more than semantic) confusion lies an image of "brainwashing" as an all-powerful, irresistible, unfathomable, and magical method of achieving total control over the human mind. It is of course none of these things, and this loose usage makes the word a rallying point for fear, resentment, urges toward submission, justification for failure, irresponsible accusation, and for a wide gamut of emotional extremism. One may justly conclude that the term has a far from precise and a questionable usefulness; one may even be tempted to forget about the whole subject and return to more constructive pursuits.

Yet to do so would be to overlook one of the major problems of our era— that of the psychology and the ethics of directed attempts at changing human beings. For despite the vicissitudes of brainwashing, the process which gave rise to the name is very much a reality: the official Chinese Communist program of *szu-hsiang kai-tsao* (variously translated as "ideological remolding," "ideological reform," or as we shall refer to it here, "thought reform") has in fact emerged as one of the most powerful efforts at human manipulation ever undertaken. To be sure, such a program is by no means completely new: imposed dogmas, inquisitions, and mass conversion movements have existed in every country and during every historical epoch. But the Chinese Communists have brought to theirs a more organized, comprehensive, and deliberate —a more *total*—character, as well as a unique blend of energetic and ingenious psychological techniques.

The Western world has heard mostly about "thought reform" as applied in a military setting: the synthetic bacteriological warfare confessions and the collaboration obtained from United Nations personnel during the Korean War. However, these were merely export versions of a thought reform pro-

gram aimed, not primarily at Westerners, but at the Chinese people themselves, and vigorously applied in universities, schools, special "revolutionary
colleges," prisons, business and government offices, labor and peasant organizations. Thought reform combines this impressively widespread distribution with
a focused emotional power. Not only does it reach one-fourth of the people of
the world, but it seeks to bring about in everyone it touches a significant
personal upheaval.

Whatever its setting, thought reform consists of two basic elements: *confession*, the exposure and renunciation of past and present "evil"; and *re-
education*, the remaking of a man in the Communist image. These elements
are closely related and overlapping, since they both bring into play a series
of pressures and appeals—intellectual, emotional, and physical—aimed at
social control and individual change.

The American press and public have been greatly concerned about this
general subject, and rightly so. But too often the information made available
about it has been sensationalist in tone, distorted because of inadequate
knowledge, or obscured by the strong emotions which the concept of brainwashing seems to arouse in everyone. Its aura of fear and mystery has been
more conducive to polemic than to understanding.

Still the vital questions continue to be asked: Can a man be made to
change his beliefs? If a change does occur, how long will it last? How do the
Chinese Communists obtain these strange confessions? Do people believe their
own confessions, even when false? How successful is thought reform? Do
Westerners and Chinese react differently to it? Is there any defense against it?
Is it related to psychotherapy? to religious conversion? Have the Chinese discovered new and obscure techniques? What has all this to do with Soviet
Russia and international Communism? with Chinese culture? How is it
related to other mass movements or inquisitions, religious or political? What
are the implications for education? For psychiatric and psychoanalytic training and practice? For religion? How can we recognize parallels to thought reform within our own culture, and what can we do about them?

It was with these questions on my mind that I arrived in Hong Kong in
late January, 1954. Just a few months before, I had taken part in the
psychiatric evaluation of repatriated American prisoners of war during the
exchange operations in Korea known as *Big Switch;* I had then accompanied
a group of these men on the troopship back to the United States. From the
repatriates' descriptions of what they had experienced, I pieced together a
great deal of information about Chinese Communist confession and re-education techniques, and was convinced that this process raised some basic human
issues; but the expediencies of the military situation made it difficult to study
them with the necessary depth and thoroughness. I thought then that the
most important questions might best be approached through work with people
who had been "reformed" within China itself.

Yet I had not come to Hong Kong with any clear intention of carrying out this detailed research. I had planned only a brief stopover on my way from Tokyo back to the United States after having lived in the Far East for almost two years, serving as an Air Force psychiatrist in Japan and Korea. But plans can be changed; and such change is sometimes an expression of an inner plan not yet consciously understood by the planner himself. Thus as long as I was in Hong Kong, I decided to make a few inquiries into a subject that seemed so important.

As soon as I did, I discovered that a number of Western scholars and diplomats there had also been asking themselves these questions. They had been shocked by the effects of indoctrination programs applied on the Chinese mainland. They told me of Western missionaries who, after having made lurid "espionage" confessions in prison, arrived in Hong Kong deeply confused about what they believed; of young Chinese students violating the most sacred precepts of their culture by publicly denouncing their parents; of distinguished mainland professors renouncing their "evil" past, even rewriting their academic books from a Marxist standpoint. My Western acquaintances had been both troubled and fascinated by these events, and welcomed my interest in the problem. At my request, they arranged for me to meet a few people like the ones they had described.

The impact of these first encounters was not something one readily forgets: an elderly European Bishop leaning forward in his hospital bed, so deeply impressed with the power of the prison thought reform program he had just experienced that he could only denounce it as "an alliance with the demons"; a young Chinese girl, still shaken from the group hatred that had been turned upon her at a university in Peking, yet wondering if she had been "selfish" in leaving.

I realized that these two people had both been through China's most elemental thought reform programs; and that these programs were much more powerful and comprehensive than the modifications which had been applied to United Nations' troops in Korea. I also realized that Hong Kong offered a unique opportunity for the study of thought reform, although, surprisingly enough, no one was taking advantage of it. I sought a means of remaining there to undertake prolonged and systematic research into the process; and with the help of two research grants, my stay was extended into seventeen months of stimulating psychiatric investigation.

COMMENTARY

As the title of this essay denotes, Dr. Lifton has relied largely upon the expository device of *definition* to explain "brainwashing" as he scientifically knows it. Many of his paragraphs also afford good examples of how definition can provide the details needed to develop a topic sentence. Four of the first five paragraphs are definition paragraphs in that they describe the various notions popularly associated with "brainwashing."

Definition is the identification of something by setting bounds to its meaning through explaining what general class it belongs to (*genus*) and just how it differs from all others of its kind (*differentia*). For instance, according to the dictionaries, "football" is any of several games played with an inflated leather ball by two teams of eleven players each on a field having goals at each end. But Rugby (English football), soccer, and American football are three different forms of the general game. In defining each we should have to show exactly how each differs from the others in all basic essentials of rules and even in the kind of ball itself.

Dr. Lifton begins the second paragraph by limiting the meaning of "brainwashing" as a term that was "originally used to describe Chinese indoctrination techniques." He then gives details of the many popular misconceptions that have developed around the term as mistaken definitions. This listing arouses interest in the reader as well as indirectly stressing the need for the kind of exact definition yet to come.

His method of first showing what "brainwashing" is *not* before presenting the correct definition is an excellent one which you may want to try yourself, although it requires considerable familiarity with the term you are defining. Still, since definitions and their processes are fundamental to all the sciences and the arts, we should take particular care to define accurately. Your reputation as clear thinkers, or at least as earnest students, may depend upon it.

WHAT DOES IT SAY?

1. Can you give any other examples of things to which the Zen Buddhist maxim in the opening paragraph can be applied?

2. Why is *brainwashing* a term used incorrectly in ordinary, everyday usage?

3. What is the difference between *myth, mythology,* and *lurid mythology*?

4. If *semantics,* in brief, is the science dealing with the relation between symbols (words, signs, and so forth) and our behavior reactions to them, why does Dr. Lifton prefer the term "thought reform" as a means of eliminating "semantic confusion"?

5. Why does he link the terms *dogma* and *inquisition*?

6. In context, what is the meaning of *revolutionary colleges*?

7. How does *education* differ from *re-education?*

8. Does Dr. Lifton define *confession* and *re-education?* What would be the *genus?* What the *differentia?*

WHAT DO YOU THINK?

1. Write a 500-word essay defining one of the following terms, on which you consider yourself something of an authority. If you know of current and misleading definitions or concepts of the term, be sure to include them as a means of establishing your familiarity with the subject.

Fink	SNIC
Hippy	Curfew
Square	All American
TV documentary	Electronic music
Peace Corps	Sonic boom

2. Define "military training" if it is to include training against such Chinese-refined *thought-reform* methods as those complained of in the following report:

Life, in its April 7, 1967 issue, published photographs taken in Hanoi of Lt. Cmdr. Richard A. Stratton, navy pilot captured in January, which showed him acting like an automaton. Ambassador-at-Large Averill Harriman is quoted as saying: "From the photographs, video tapes and descriptions by eyewitnesses that I have seen of the so-called 'news' conference at which Commander Stratton was exhibited, it would appear that the North Vietnamese authorities are using mental or physical pressure on American prisoners of war. We all remember the ugly record of 'brainwashing' during the Korean war. It would be a matter of gravest concern if North Vietnam were using similar means against the prisoners."

SHOULD

GOD

DIE?

GRAHAM B. BLAINE, JR.

TO ME the greatest paradox of modern times is the attempted murder of God by some of those who were formerly His strongest supporters. We have always been faced with militant atheists and rationalist unbelievers, but never before have we seen ordained ministers rise against their God—and all He stands for—in the defiant fashion we now witness.

The image of God as an old man with flashing eyes and flowing beard is still held by very few, but God as a presence, whose guiding influence is communicated and explained to us by the ministers of His Church, is a powerful force in the lives of many. For the average young adult in today's world it can serve as an essential reinforcement for earlier moral standards learned at home, and as a continuing source of direction and inner strength. But religion can only have real meaning if it is the medium through which the word of God is transmitted. Without God, religion is merely a man-made philosophical framework. If God is destroyed, then with Him is destroyed the entire basis for traditional and absolute morality.

Parental example and control begin to become less effective with the start of adolescence, and as the adolescent moves on to college he looks almost entirely for example and advice to those whom he respects in his school and church community. He may need to challenge these individuals fairly brashly, but essentially he respects them for their consistency and firmness. Though he may openly disagree, inwardly he usually believes in them and with them.

Many of today's proponents of the New Morality, such as the Right Reverend John A. T. Robinson, the Bishop of Wollwich, and Joseph Fletcher, Professor of Social Ethics at the Episcopal Theological Seminary in Cambridge, Massachusetts, hold high positions in their churches and are not out of favor with the hierarchy, even though they have blatantly contradicted the most basic tenets of Church doctrine. Perhaps these men cannot be defined as the original death-of-God theologians but, in denying the existence of an absolute system of ethics, they are essentially denying the existence of God.

The Reverend Fletcher, in his book, *Situation Ethics,* argues in favor of judging the right and wrong of every decision in the light of the total context in which this decision must be made. He is against prejudging a situation or entering any moral crisis with a previously determined set of values, no matter how much experience one may have had or what precepts one might have acquired from wise individuals. According to him, so long as one feels sure that no one will be hurt, anything goes. He states: "People are learning that we can have sex without love and love without sex; but if people do not believe it is wrong to have sex relations outside marriage, it isn't—unless they hurt themselves, their partners, or others." This would seem to give religious sanction to adultery as well as to premarital intercourse—so long as those who might be hurt by it do not find out about it. How easy it would be to convince oneself that such an act, in a particular situation, would be entirely harmless!

John A. T. Robinson is more subtle, but equally permissive, when he says:

> I recognize to the full that all of us, especially young people, have to have working rules. But my point is that when these are questioned as they are being questioned, the Christian is driven back to base them not on law ("Fornication is always wrong") but on love, on what deep concern for persons as whole persons, in their entire social context, really requires.

This seems to state that if some people object to some laws, then we should eliminate them and rely instead on one of our emotions (love), even though this emotion is usually characterized as blind, and leads often to biased or distorted judgment.

There are situations in which a law cannot be sensibly applied as written, but this does not seem a logical reason for eliminating it entirely. Joseph Fletcher describes four cases involving, respectively, prostitution, adultery, suicide, and mass homicide, which clearly demonstrate the impossibility of formulating a law that is right for every situation; but if his premise is correct, then because an ambulance or a fire engine must exceed the speed limit in order to save lives in special situations, we should have *no* speed laws. Perhaps love and, as Robinson says, "deep concern for people as whole persons in their entire social context" *would* keep everyone driving at a safe speed, but I doubt that any of us would be willing to count on it.

Theologians may readily argue among themselves about the logic or even the existence of absolute morality, but when they talk from the pulpit or write popular books, they may well do great harm if they promote new—and unproved—theories of ethics. A young adult, faced with many conflicting internal emotions and, at the same time, vast numbers of external temptations and enticements, needs to know where he stands on important issues before he finds himself in a decision-making situation. At such a moment, there is usually no time to step back and view the entire context with coldly calculating calm. More often, reason has been submerged by passion, and decisions are made from the dictates of a conscience developed over the years as a result of training from Church and home, rather than a cool appraisal of the possibility of someone's being hurt by the action (or inaction) of the moment.

Why does a psychiatrist like myself get involved in matters of ethics, since his main job should be to treat the emotionally ill and, in the process, remain neutral and nonjudgmental? Professionally, a psychiatrist should try to understand and explain, rather than to criticize or punish. But in his job he needs to have limits not only clearly set but also firmly maintained by society. This is society's business. When a medical or psychiatric approach is adopted by others, it may do more harm than good to those in trouble. For example, a theological student who had been caught stealing—in fact, had a long history of it—was not reprimanded by his dean but was, instead, referred to a psychiatrist for help. When asked why he seemed so desultory about his treatment, he explained that he did not understand in what way he was ill. He still had the money he stole, he continued to be a student in good standing at the seminary, and he was able to chat with a psychiatrist when he wished to, at the school's expense. The rules were there, but they had no real meaning for him. In ignoring its obligation to make these rules clear by enforcing them, the theological school was contributing to the perpetuation of this student's illness rather than its resolution.

Some campus ministers, today, claim that students are no longer interested in traditional religion and that the concept of God has no meaning for them. They blame the emphasis on science, the popularity of existentialism, and the current college student's reliance on logic and rationalism, for what they see as the recent movement away from the Church. Their concern does not seem to be entirely warranted. Surveys have shown that college students profess more faith than seminarians, and it is also true that enthusiasm is still high on most campuses when religious leaders who follow traditional and orthodox patterns of belief appear.

I do not think that the situationists will succeed in murdering God. My fear, instead, is that, in their attempts to kill Him, His attackers will so maim and mutilate His image that they will seriously contribute to moral softness and irresolution in our young people, and that this, in turn, will have lasting ill effects upon them and their own children (both wanted and unwanted) in the years to come. Personally, I believe that God will prove to be indestructible.

COMMENTARY

In explaining something we generally sort out facts and ideas and check them for their relevance—at least, we do so if we do not want to be thought of as being empty headed. But usually we choose those that show immediate promise and shun those that threaten to involve us in contradictions. Dr. Blaine has evidently confronted the contradictions he describes in his opening sentence paradox (a statement expressing an apparent contradiction). He devotes the rest of the essay to contrasting some new theological doctrines with the traditional one which he thinks all theologians should still be teaching.

This expository device of *contrast* and *comparison* derives from our natural way of making judgments by comparing and contrasting things that please or displease us. How we use them to argue the relative merits of athletic teams, entertainers, artists, and even colleges! And what would producers of TV commercials and politicians do without these methods?

Whether the whole essay or only some of the paragraphs deal with comparison and contrast, the process is the same. In the second paragraph, for example, Dr. Blaine contrasts the religion having "real meaning" with the kind lacking "God." This contrast provides the main supporting detail for the topic sentence, with which the paragraph ends. Then in paragraphs 4, 5, and 6 he gives explicit details comparing the doctrines of Bishop Robinson with those of the Reverend Fletcher. When he has clearly presented those doctrines he attacks them by contrasting them with the values he sees in traditional ethics.

Dr. Blaine makes only those comparisons and contrasts which specify the essential and highly relevant points of similarity and difference in the doctrines that he places in juxtaposition. Note that he has avoided making pointless referrals.

WHAT DOES IT SAY?

1. How do militant atheists differ from *rationalist unbelievers?*

2. What is the difference between an *absolute morality* and a *relative morality?*

3. How would you very briefly state the principle behind *Situation Ethics* as that ethical system is explained herein?

4. Also in this context what is the meaning of *love*? Does *love* mean "Just don't hurt anybody"?

5. How is God conceived of in an *existential* philosophy?

6. What is the literal meaning of *orthodox* and what is its relevance in the article?

7. An analogy is a form of comparison. Note the author's analogy between laws governing prostitution and speeding. Is this a sound comparison?

8. What is meant by *rationalization*? Is there any indication that the author is suggesting that certain attitudes toward sex are a rationalization of desire?

WHAT DO YOU THINK?

1. Compare or contrast the views and concepts you had of "God" when you were a child with those you now hold. Explain any changes and how you feel about them.

2. Compare and contrast the following views with those of Dr. Blaine and the theologians he quotes.

When asked for his views on the "God is dead" statement, Dr. Harry Emerson Fosdick, an 88-year-old-minister-author, said there are many concepts of God that should die. Here are some of these concepts he considered outmoded: the God who either bores or scares you to death, God who will take care of everything, God the venerable bookkeeper, God the king of glory on a golden throne, the man-size anthropomorphic God, the God who is on our side, the God of battles, the God who makes everything come out right.— "Whose God Is Dead?" *The Reader's Digest*, October 1966.

3. Compare your experience with the average college student that Dr. Blaine says "looks almost entirely for example and advice to those whom he respects in his school and church community." How accurate do you find that statement? Looking to your own experience, has there been some one person outside your home for whom this is true? If so, what qualities in this individual attracted you?

4. Write an essay discussing the religious atmosphere on your campus as you see it, and contrast it with (1) what you expected or (2) what you have heard is true of other campuses.

THE HIPPIES:
MUSIC AND
TRIBAL CEREMONY

JACK BERRY

TITLES OF the art works are things like "At the Zoo," "Strawberry Fields Forever," "Ruby Tuesday," "Love Minus Zero-No Limit," "The Black Angel's Death Song," "Tiny Bubbles," "The Dis-Advantages of You," "Voodoo in My Basement," "Help I'm a Rock," "Sensory Overload," "Plastic Fantastic Lover," "The Return of the Son of Monster Magnet," "Hung Up in Your Eyes," "Queen Jane Approximately," and "Sit Down, I Think I Love You."

They call themselves "The Electric Prunes," "Harper's Bizarre," "Country Joe and the Fish," "Mogen David & The Grapes of Wrath," "The Mothers of Invention," "The Congress of Wonders & Morning Glory," "? (Question Mark) & the Mysterians," "The Nitty Gritty Dirt Band," "Simon and Garfunkel," and "Big Brother and the Holding Co.," "The Mamas and the Papas."

Their instrumentation is standard rock—lead guitar, rhythm guitar, electric bass, and drums—and any other instrument which catches their eye, from jews harp to the chitarrino diuerfo.

A by no means inclusive list of their subjects would include love, sex, fun, beauty, despair, disgust, contempt, admiration, grass, marijuana, cars, betrayal, loyalty, abandonment, indifference, seduction, violent death, pacific life, war,

Reprinted with permission from *The Sunday Oregonian Northwest Magazine*, Portland, Oregon.

nonsense, magic, LSD, youth, speed, fame, trouble, cruelty, stupidity, innocence and bitterness with an emphasis on fun and games. With rhythm
deriving from the hardest of blues drivers, men like Bo Diddly and Chuck
Berry, they have evolved a sound which can rasp, tear, howl, and blast but
is erected on a fundamental tone, the electric base line, which has a muffled,
internal resonance, very close to the sound of an amplified heart beat. It is
the aural symbol of the times.

It was in the mid-'50s when Chuck Berry told Beethoven to "roll over" and
things have been rolling ever since. Youth has always demanded, with little
success, that adults pay attention to their reality. Now there are more of them,
and the petition is more insistent. . . .

In a recent series of articles on psychedelic or "head" community, one in-
habitant, a musician, objected to respectable society's constantly iterated charge
that the heads are parasites.

While the group's most central tenet, withdrawal from society's power and
competition games, would appear to make the "parasite" label inevitable and
correct, the musician pointed out that respectable society's merchandisers have
been drawing heavily on discoveries made by the psychedelic movement.
"They call us parasites and keep sucking us dry." Perhaps the field in which
the best argument can be made for this notion is that of popular music. And
the head rock music, along with psychedelic drugs, astrology and charity, is an
article of faith in the hippie community. Music and dance is the central
tribal ceremony and the head musician has about the same status in the
psychedelic community as the astronaut has in ours.

American popular music, although a realm largely unexplored by sociologists, is a direct and useful reflection of the disposition and priorities of the
times. It is also amusing and, frequently, musically satisfying.

It's true the head musicians are making some unique contributions to this
music but, before examining them, a look at the musical resources which were
available to them seems in order. For this, one is required only to inspect the
juke box in the nearest tavern or burger bar, a display of the most incredibly
varied and vital body of musical styles and sources ever assembled by a single
nation on earth. One area in which the results of America's great melting pot
experiment has been an unqualified success is in the absorption, extension and
transformation of scores of musical traditions.

Talking about his musical background and interests, John Browne, a Portland head musician, said, "I went through the stages of listening to a lot of
jazz, then the country blues and folk thing before I got into this." The number
of musical options contained in that journey are barely suggested by the statement. Included in just "the folk thing," for instance, would have been
generous exposure to the English, Irish and Scottish ballad, martial song,
boozing tunes, street song and music hall turns, the great variety of Jewish
music, flamenco from the Spanish gypsy, polka from Scandinavia, fado from

Portugal, the ancient and sophisticated music of India and Africa and the endless permutations of all these in the New World. With African music alone, you have the Latin American rhythms, calypso from the Caribbean, Louisiana Cajun and, more influential than any other element of current popular music in America, the blues.

The strangest aspect of this remarkable phenomenon is that until the "folk" boom of the late 50s and early 60s, much of the variety of American music was restricted to regions, ethnic pockets or small groups of enthusiasts. The musical appetite of mass America was fed an unvarying diet of saccharine written by hacks on Tin Pan Alley, delivered by sweeties, male and female, whom somebody old would like on their knee.

Now if the music business is not the nation's most venal, neither is it the least. The radical alteration in its complexion was simply another manifestation of the dollar impulse, but this time it led into realms dotted with islands of imagination, energy and sincerity. And if imagination, energy and sincerity are where some dollars are, they can still get a hearing. From this point, two startling events extended the possibilities of expression in popular music immeasurably, Bob Dylan and his impact on the Beatles.

As an erratic child of the "folk" craze, Dylan sold a fairly interesting number of records. Then, however, his erraticism ran wild. Disassociating himself from doctrinaire social consciousness, a strength and weakness of the folk movement, Dylan began a career of free association. And while prominent authorities have snubbed claims of poetic greatness by Dylan's devotees, few language watchers could deny that he has a gift for arresting utterance. That he decided to deliver his verbal collage with the assistance of a hammering rock band has had a very extraordinary effect on American pop culture. The Beatles, noting the amount of whimsey and weirdness Dylan was getting away with, were deeply stimulated and influenced. And Dylan, in the zenith of his popular success (the "Like a Rolling Stone" period), never approached the sway which the Beatles possess over the marketplace. Even now, in semi-retirement, they can turn the business upside down at will. (It is true but almost beside the point to note that the Beatles are English, not American. Except for the Liverpool accents and most music hall touches, their musical sources have been almost entirely from the U.S.)

Into this unprecedented situation the head musicians have jumped and clearly intend to push the new freedom as far as possible. Their primary contribution to popular culture at this point is their function as custodians and synthesizers of available musical diversity. The synthesis they are in the process of forging may go in any of a number of different directions and undoubtedly will.

The central obstacle of "folk" performers was the felt need to test themselves against a notion of "authenticity." If you hadn't "plowed that row" the use of blues tonality was suspect. Little concern is evinced by the head players about "authenticity." If a form, style, inflection or attack seems appropriate to their song making idea, they use it. Often, they use it in a novel and effective way. The forms may not stay pure but they are staying alive.

Of the hugely successful pop groups operating now, about the only people who could be considered hard core hippies are "The Mamas and the Papas," "Donovan," and "The Rolling Stones." Much of the music's innovations, however, are now coming from the head center of San Francisco and groups that get plenty of work in the Bay Area. An appearance by one of these in Portland recently, the C.I.A., indicates that the tendency is toward more and more electronic frenzy (it is presupposed that the listener is high on psychedelic drugs or acquainted with what music sounds like when one is high) with dynamics ranging from throb to the pain threshhold and collective improvisation. Drumming is becoming more sophisticated and a jazz style walking bass line is commonly used. Some observers have even predicted a merger between the advanced head music bands and the free playing jazz avant garde.

Whether the old school of jazz critics or older generations generally ever decide to extend serious consideration to this musical development is not a matter of overwhelming concern to its exponents. They have their exotic equipment and their market.

COMMENTARY

Once more we can observe how the relating of specific details closely related to one another with logical ties catches the reader's attention. But besides having interesting subject matter this article is also an example of development of the topic by a *combination* of all the expository devices so far examined: analysis, classification, example, definition, cause–effect, and comparison and contrast.

Let us take a closer look at some of the paragraphs exemplifying one or the other of these devices. Certainly the opening paragraph begins with a host of typical samples as details of the "titles of the art works," just as paragraph 2 does for the names of the groups, and paragraphs 3 and 4 do for their instrumentation and the classifications of the themes of their songs. This four-paragraph section pretty much serves to define Hippy music; it offers an analysis of five essential aspects of what makes this kind of music what it is—the titles, the special groups, their instrumentation, the subject matter of the songs, and the unique "sound." Among the many other details in this fact-crammed article are those of comparison of the Beatles with Bob Dylan.

In brief, this article, like the one to follow it, shows that complex subjects lend themselves to this manner of *combination* development. A brief introduction, a few paragraphs of one method or the other, a conclusion—and there you have a complete and probably interesting essay!

WHAT DOES IT SAY?

1. Can you trace the derivation of any of the names given to the groups? Or add interesting names of new groups?

2. What are "blues drivers" and "the electric base line"? Why does Jack Berry call it "the aural symbol of the times"?

3. To a Hippy "head" what are the connotations of "the folk thing"?

4. Name some samples of the "diet of saccharine written by hacks on Tin Pan Alley" and the "sweeties" who deliver it.

5. What is the typical subject matter of the Bob Dylan songs that Berry describes as "doctrinaire social consciousness"?

6. In what sense can "heads" be considered "custodians and synthesizers of available musical diversity"?

7. "Authenticity" has what special meaning for a "head" musician?

8. What are your responses to Berry's statement: "It was in the mid-'50s when Chuck Berry told Beethoven to 'roll over' and things have been rolling ever since"?

WHAT DO YOU THINK?

1. Through a combination of expository devices develop your own personal views and reactions to the following facts.

   Thousands of rock 'n' roll fans have rioted in Zurich, Switzerland, and in Warsaw, Poland—to mention only two cities—in trying to hear such music performed by groups like the Beatles, the Rolling Stones, Chuck Berry, and Muddy Waters. As many as 40 million recordings by The Stones have been sold.

2. Here are several opinions on the present state of jazz. By means of definition, classification, example, and comparison or contrast, discuss your feelings on the subject.

America goes on kicking jazz music, using its life-blood for political purposes, and then leaves it limp and battered in the alley.—Michael Zwering, *Commonweal*, Feb. 3, 1967, p. 491.

Jazz doesn't make it any more with the young crowd.—Garry Paul Gates, *Holiday*, March 1967, p. 122.

Now everybody is writing jazz masses. Hip clergymen are sponsoring them apparently in the belief that jazz will reinstate the dialogue between the church and the common man. Hip networks are broadcasting them, apparently in the hope that jazzy religion might offset the death of god dirges.—Tupper Saussy, *Motive*, March 1966, p. 35.

3. Through a combination of methods, develop a topic chosen from among the following subjects:
   a) Pleasures and discipline of being a musician
   b) My favorite music
   c) "Canned" music
   d) Records I buy
   e) A new dance

1 IN 7:

DRUGS

ON CAMPUS

RICHARD GOLDSTEIN

MARIJUANA has become this generation's illicit pleasure. In the '20's, illegal booze parties took place on ivy-covered campuses on which golden Scott Fitzgerald characters frolicked. In the '50's, when the Kinsey Report stunned a "Puritan" America, college students were experimenting with sex—and bragging about it. Now it is drugs. On campus after campus, scandal and denials follow the revelation that students are "turning on." Administrators deny it, and alumni doubt it. But the police know about it. Health officials and school psychiatrists are aware of it. The students themselves are not only sure it exists but they can usually tell you where to find the action.

In Harvard Square you can obtain marijuana within 30 minutes. Near Columbia University, on Upper Broadway, it takes 20 minutes. From Princeton's Nassau Street to Minnesota's Dinkytown to Seattle's University Way, students are experimenting with nonaddictive drugs.

Marijuana is, after alcohol, the most popular intoxicant in the world. Scientists call the plant *Cannabis savita*. Indians call it *bhang*, Turks *hashish*, Chinese *ma*, Moroccans *kef*, Mexicans *marijuana*. Most Americans who have used the drug call it pot, though other names—boo, grass, mary-jane, stuff— appear as rapidly as the cult tires of the old words.

The long-haired element on campus (those who are variously called "ethnic," "beatnik," "folkie" or "fringie") is often a major source of marijuana, but it is a grave mistake to assume that the students are the only ones who use

Reprinted from *Saturday Evening Post*, May 21, 1966 by permission of Walker and Company. Reprinted here in part.

drugs. Drugs have begun to invade "respectable" areas of campus life, like Fraternity Row. Special names are given to locally grown marijuana— Brooklyn green, Berkeley boo, Wisconsin weed, Kentucky blue-grass, Kansas standard. When so many are certain that the law is wrong, illegal activities become a huge game like the activities many Americans indulged in during prohibition. When you considered liquor harmless and fashionable, the fact that it was illegal seemed laughable. College students today feel that way about marijuana. Pot smokers, to a man, find their vice "enjoyable" and "harmless." They deny that student users graduate to heroin.

To many college students, marijuana is illegal but safe, and heroin is dangerous, and therefore uncool. The few students who use heroin are referred to as "sickies" by even the most Bohemian of students. Most important, they suddenly become "square." They have allowed the body to dominate, and they have exhibited vulnerability and dependence; cool people do not depend. Most important, with their glazed faces and drug obsession they scare even the habitual marijuana users, or "potheads."

Police estimate that 30 percent of all heroin addicts begin with marijuana —but these statistics simply do not apply to the college scene. A former narcotics commissioner at the New York City Health Department has reported that 90 percent of the city's heroin addicts are school dropouts, and concludes that few college students are likely to use addictive drugs. The slum drug addict, caught in a hopeless, dismal existence, turns to drugs as an escape from slum life, but our student population is the most pampered and worried-about in history.

The question of the danger or safety of marijuana, however, is by no means settled. By general medical agreement, marijuana is nonaddictive. It almost never leaves a hangover. It is less damaging, physically, than alcohol. Some psychiatrists and doctors believe that the drug should be legalized, and eventually will be. They predict that marijuana will someday rival liquor as the prime social intoxicant.

Other experts, however, point out that marijuana may be "psychologically" habit-forming, although it is probably less so than either tobacco or alcohol. Some doctors believe that, taken in excessive quantities, marijuana can produce brain and lung damage. Most experts say that, for people who are already emotionally disturbed, marijuana sometimes uncovers psychological problems. And some doctors see dangers in the very fact that marijuana users can still function while "high." One doctor asserts: "The user will be able to perform feats on marijuana, while he would probably just pass out on liquor. For instance, he can drive a car under the influence of marijuana, even though his judgment is impaired. And he can commit acts of violence under marijuana, since it sometimes creates a sense of ultimate power that can be dangerous to the abnormal personality. Liquor does this also, but it also makes it hard for the individual to do physically what he may feel like doing emotionally."

The reasons students use marijuana vary from group to group, but the great majority claim they take the drug simply because it gives them pleasure. Some experimenters give up after one or two times, because "It made me nauseated," or "It didn't do anything for me," or "It's like parachute jumping. Once is enough." But marijuana users claim that a pleasurable experience always comes with practice. Medics are not so sure. One doctor says, "It's a very mild psychedelic [psychedelics are drugs which change perception and disorient the mind]. It just gives you a head start on yourself. For many, it does nothing at all, and they have to fake it." Boston police report one "pot party" in which authorities found a group of teen-agers who seemed to be very high on "marijuana." But little could be done, once the police realized they had confiscated ordinary cigarette tobacco, bought at marijuana prices from a clever pusher.

The marijuana user, on almost any given campus, may be placed in one of three categories: a dabbler, a user, a head.

The dabbler has experimented with marijuana, but does not use the drug frequently. For the dabbler, marijuana is something daring—something to tell them about at home. The dabbler refrains from extensive drug usage out of fear, out of moral qualms, or out of immunity to the drug. The large majority of students who try marijuana belong in this category. It is in this group that the "respectable" pot smoker is usually found.

The user indulges on weekends, much the way the rest of the campus uses beer. It is here that the "cult of marijuana" begins. The user enjoys smoking pot, but he also enjoys the mystique surrounding the drug. He is likely to exaggerate the impact of his experience, since he smokes for social as well as psychological reasons. Emotional disturbance is present in such a group, but it does not predominate. What is outstanding is the importance of the group itself. It survives police raids, and even graduation. Often its members dress alike and hold similar political opinions. Drug obsession is rare, and the occasional graduation to stronger psychedelics and amphetamines, or pep pills, is a matter of personal choice rather than group pressures.

The heads, the smallest segment of the drug-taking population, probably make up no more than five percent of all students experimenting with marijuana, but they are often the center of the marijuana cult. The head is high on marijuana most of the time. He often turns on by himself, or with a small group. No matter what the reasons behind his initial experiments with drugs, he now finds an entire personality in this solipsistic world. His most dangerous enemy, as one head says, is any authority, from police to deans and parents; he must learn to live like somebody who is hunted, with the whole respectable world as an enemy. To enhance his stability, the head may often be a supplier. The head may drop out of school, but he continues to make his home on or near the campus. He may eventually become a victim of hard narcotics.

The college student who uses marijuana does not conform to any stereotype, but it is possible to make some rough generalizations about him. He is likely to be either apolitical or liberal; drug experimentation fits into a general pattern of rebellion against society's values. Marijuana was used in Berkeley's Free Speech Movement, as it is within many activist groups.

Sexually the marijuana user claims to be experienced. Most students were contemptuous of promiscuous sex, but many reported favorable experiences under marijuana. Doctors are uncertain of the sexual effect of the drug. Though no one has been seduced merely because he or she is under the influence of marijuana, many have found that the drug reduces their fears about sex.

Academically, the marijuana user spans the entire spectrum of grades. The pot smoker may be a dropout or an honor student.

Drug usage also cuts across social classes, but a distinction can be drawn between urban and rural campuses. The use of marijuana is prevalent in the cities. On many Midwestern campuses it is the cliques from New York and Chicago that first experiment with the drug. On rural campuses, where the student body is composed mainly of local residents, the symbol of rebellion and cool seems to be alcohol, often beer. On Friday afternoon many Southern campuses undergo what is referred to as T.G.I.F.—Thank God It's Friday. The drinking, to hear students tell it, begins Friday afternoon and ends Sunday evening, around curfew time. In urban colleges marijuana plays a similar role for students. Marijuana users call beer-guzzling students "hicks" or "foamies." The beer drinkers call the potheads "junkies" or "fringies." One Southern student summed up the reaction to marijuana in rural areas: "Man, you could tie me down. You could do anything, but you'd never get me to go near the stuff." Police officials point to the Northeast megalopolis and the West Coast urban sprawl as the chief areas of marijuana consumption. Except for such areas as New Orleans and parts of Southern Texas, pot is less of a problem in the South. In the Midwest, it is a problem mainly in urban areas, or where urban students gather.

Why do the students use marijuana? The pressures at Harvard are mentioned. "Pot takes the pressure off in a very real way," says one honor student. "There's a sense of total, timeless ease."

The impersonality in a large university is blamed. "When you smoke," says one student, "it's like a big conspiracy. It's personal; there's a common enemy for the whole group."

A long-time administrator asserts: "Kids are rebelling against adult norms. They think they are more rational and realistic than their parents and smoking marijuana is a way to prove it."

COMMENTARY

This article is another example of development by means of a *combination* of expository devices. Almost every possible variety of detail contributes its share of information to this excerpt from a book-length report on the extent of the use of drugs on college and university campuses.

Your by-now-practiced eye may have already detected many of these devices, but let us run through some of them found herein. To begin with, there is *definition*—of *psychedelics*. Goldstein adopted the use of *classification* in naming and describing each of the various kinds of "pot" smokers— "dabblers," "users," and "heads." He makes careful distinctions between them in the light of student opinion, just as he does in explaining the *cause-and-effect* elements that govern these practices, especially the mental-physical results that they may produce, such as possible lung damage, possible brain damage, possible habit forming or turning to heroin, and possible danger to abnormal personalities, since these can do what pot-dream suggests they do. Numerous *examples* illustrate details by giving specific incidents and localities. *Analysis* of the reasons why marijuana is smoked across the nation and around the world includes the surprising number of names by which it is called.

Like that of "The New Pornography," this topic is a highly controversial one, and both call for the same kind of candid, well-informed *point of view* which is found in this article. As you may have concluded, this *combination* method of developing a subject is probably the best means of presenting a complex topic. However, it demands a planned sequence and a good sense of proportion to obtain desirable order and emphasis.

WHAT DOES IT SAY?

1. In its present context, what, to you, are the connotations of "turning on"? (This expression is derived from Dr. Timothy Leary's slogan: "Turn on, tune in, drop out.")

2. Is the name "marijuana" more or less appealing than the other names for the same drug: *cannabis savita, bhang, hashish, ma, kef?* Why?

3. What is there in a name? Why would you not so readily try smoking *hashish* as you would something, for example, called "Berkeley boo"?

4. Why are psychedelic drugs grouped with alcohol as "intoxicants"?

5. What do the following terms suggest regarding the nature of the English language: *dabblers, ethnics, foamies, folkies, fringies, heads, junkies, potheads, sickies, squares?*

6. An excessive user of marijuana is said to find "an entire personality in this solipsistic world." What is a *solipsistic world?*

7. How can a drug be termed both "nonaddictive" and "psychologically habit forming"? Isn't there a contradiction here?

8. What are "activist groups"?

WHAT DO YOU THINK?

1. Is the "T.G.I.F." social phenomenon restricted only to southern campuses? If you believe it observable in other areas, support your opinion by means of specific illustrations.

2. Which do you consider the lesser of two "evils," psychedelic drugs like marijuana or alcoholic beverages? Support your opinion by showing effects you have observed or read about and accept.

3. According to *Time,* the Haight-Ashbury district of San Francisco is a "psychedelphia" because a great number of its inhabitants demand "free freak-outs for all" and are high on such drugs as LSD, Methedrine, Dexedrine, and Benzedrine. It is also described as "the center of a new utopianism, compounded of drugs and dreams, free love and LSD." (*Time,* March 17, 1967, p. 27)
   What is your considered judgment of the values or dangers of such a "psychedelphia"?

4. Using *classification* and any combination of other devices, formulate and develop an opinion on any one of the following subjects on which you feel qualified to write:
   a) Types of alcoholic beverage users
   b) Types of cigarette smokers
   c) Types of Hippies
   d) Patterns of conservatism (old fears)
   e) New protests and groups
   f) Drugs and athletics
   g) Appeals of tranquilizers
   h) Effects of "pep" pills
   i) LSD "trips"

5. Express your approval or disapproval, in whole or in part, with reasons for your views concerning this statement:

Celebration is the real message coming out of San Francisco: celebration of the present and the possible. Of course, it is a gospel loaded with dangers, and already the movement has had many casualties, or "freak-outs," from drugs too freely taken or love too freely given away. The hippies would reply that our present system—with its "reasonable" wars, say, or its methodical peddling of violence—causes many more.—William K. Zinsser, "The Love Hippies," *Look,* April 18, 1967, p. 4.

Two Wars

1. *Do you see anything ironic in the Vietnam action photo?* 2. *What do the faces of each of these men tell you?* 3. *What other "war" is illustrated?*

Wide World Photos

Part 3

NATIONAL ISSUES AND THE CAMPUS

Wide World Photos

Logic,
Argument,
and Persuasion

As WE HAVE seen, skilled authors support their generalizations with evidence in the form of specific particulars. But it takes more than facts and evidence to make an article convincing; it requires *logic,* or correct reasoning, in presenting that data. To improve our own thinking and writing, let us examine some of the elements of sound, logical reasoning.

There are two types of reasoning: *deductive* and *inductive,* which also give their names to two kinds of order in presenting details. (See the introduction to Part 1.) Deductive reasoning is the process of beginning with a general principle and then applying it to a specific situation in order to reach a certain conclusion. Here is an example of deductive reasoning:

All who have served their term of military duty in Vietnam usually are glad to return home.
Corporal Smith has served his term of duty in Vietnam.
He very likely is glad to return home.

The conclusion, *deduced* or *inferred,* is *valid* because it follows correctly the laws of deductive reasoning.

This logical structure of deductive reasoning is called a *syllogism.* The first statement, which contains the general principle being applied, is termed

113

the *major premise*. The second, which does the applying to the specific situation, is the *minor premise;* and the inference which comes as a result is called the *conclusion*.

Although the reasoning in a syllogism may be valid, the conclusion reached may not necessarily be true. One or both of the premises may be faulty, as may be seen in this example:

Any nation that opposes the policies of the United States in Vietnam is communistic.
India opposes the policies of the United States in Vietnam.
Therefore, India is communistic.

Here, the major premise, which is always a generalization, consists of a *false assumption,* for it is clearly false to assume that any nation opposed to the policies of the United States in Vietnam is communistic. Therefore, the conclusion, though valid, is false. If you begin with a falsehood, you will end with another falsehood.

The minor premise in a syllogism can also be false. In the syllogism given above, the minor premise is accurate. India *has* opposed those policies. But let us take another simple illustration:

All fish are cold-blooded.
A whale is a fish.
Therefore, the whale is cold-blooded.

In this syllogism the generalization making up the major premise is accurate: fish *are* cold-blooded. However, the minor premise (the specific instance to which the generalization is applied) is false. A whale is not a fish, but a mammal. Consequently, the conclusion—that the whale is cold-blooded—is false.

Inductive reasoning is usually associated with scientific observation. It suggests a long series of experiments which finally lead to some laboratory-proven hypothesis that can be tested and found accurate by scientists throughout the world. Actually, it is a process of reasoning from particulars to universals—a conclusion based upon examined evidence.

A few years ago, Ralph Nader made a study of the construction of automobiles currently being manufactured, and from the evidence he gathered he made certain generalizations about the safety (or lack of safety) of the modern automobile. His was a good example of inductive reasoning based upon accurate observation, and the assumptions he reached were supported by such incontrovertible evidence that they led to a number of government regulations on automobile manufacturing.

Everyone, in fact, relies on inductive reasoning. When driving a car, for example, if we see a "Children–Caution" sign or youngsters playing near a curb, we slow down for the reason that we have read and heard of too many children darting in front of passing cars. Through repeated experience and observation we have reached the general principle: children are irresponsible. Thereafter, we apply that generalization each time such a traffic situation arises.

Automobile insurance companies follow the same inductive process on issuing policies. From statistical studies they have learned that certain individuals are accident-prone, so the companies keep a record of any accident involving a policyholder. When Mr. A.P. ("Accident-Prone") applies to his company for a policy renewal, the company reasons (deductively) in this way:

Accident-prone people are poor risks.
Mr. A.P. is accident prone.
Therefore, Mr. A.P. is a poor risk.

As a result, Mr. A.P. probably will pay much higher premiums than before.

By way of introduction, such are the elements of logical reasoning that are particular to *argument* and *persuasion*. The main difference between argument and exposition, or explanation, is in the point of view. In an argument, the writer realizes that he is engaged in a discussion involving differences of opinion and that he must persuade others to accept his particular belief. Argument can be strictly logical and stick to its clearly defined issues—the main points of difference requiring the main defense—or it can veer into illogical reasoning and lean heavily upon unfounded emotional appeals.

The various kinds of false logic, or "fallacies," have been given particular names. It is quite beyond the scope of this discussion to go into detail about any one of them, but we can mention a few of the most common. *Analogy* is faulty logic for the simple reason that A is not B no matter how much the two may resemble one another at times. Analogy is an excellent form of illustration, but it is illogical as argument. Another form of false logic is called "begging the question," which is assuming the truth of that which is being questioned. For example, if one argues that women should not be given responsible jobs because they are irresponsible, one is begging the question.

Any emotional appeal instead of sticking to the issues should be questioned in argument: name-calling, urging acceptance because "everyone else feels this way," appealing to vanity or prejudice, "slanting" one's language—for example, talking about the "intelligent minority" in comparison with the "poor fools who don't know any better"—all these attempts to influence without regard for logic ought to be eliminated from any argument.

Read the essays in this section paying particular attention to the kind and quality of the reasoning. And when you write, be sure that your topic or argument has been thought through logically. Above all, resist any temptation to adopt the sticky devices of false logic and unfounded emotional appeals, no matter how altruistic you may consider your motive.

THE AMERICAN DREAM

AND

THE AMERICAN NEGRO

JAMES BALDWIN

Note: On the anniversary of its founding 150 years ago, the Cambridge Union Society of Cambridge University invited James Baldwin to join others in debating the motion: "The American Dream is at the expense of the American Negro."

INTRODUCTION

Announcement of his role as speaker, warning of an incredible proposition and the false assumption on which it is based

The white man's ignorance of this assumption

I FIND myself, not for the first time, in the position of a kind of Jeremiah. It would seem to me that the question before the house is a proposition horribly loaded, that one's response to that question depends on where you find yourself in the world, what your sense of reality is. That is, it depends on assumptions we hold so deeply as to be scarcely aware of them.

The white South African or Mississippi sharecropper or Alabama sheriff has at bottom a system of reality which compels them really to believe when they face the Negro that this woman, this man, this child must be insane to attack the system to which he owes his entire identity. For such a person, the proposition which we are trying to discuss here does not exist.

On the other hand, I have to speak as one of the people who have been most attacked by the Western system of reality. It comes from Europe. That is how it got to America. It raises the question of whether or not civilizations can be considered equal, or whether one civilization has a right to subjugate—in fact, to destroy—another.

The proposition (thesis) stated

Now, leaving aside all the physical factors one can quote—leaving aside the rape or murder, leaving aside the bloody catalogue of oppression which we are too familiar with anyway—what the system does to the subjugated is to destroy his sense of reality. It destroys his father's authority over him. His father can no longer tell him anything because his past has disappeared.

BODY
The worst result of this blind view

In the case of the American Negro, from the moment you are born every stick and stone, every face is white. Since you have not yet seen a mirror, you suppose you are, too. It comes as a great shock around the age of 5, 6 or 7 to discover that the flag to which you have pledged allegiance, along with everybody else, has not pledged allegiance to you. It comes as a great shock to see Gary Cooper killing off the Indians and, although you are rooting for Gary Cooper, that the Indians are you.

His first discovery of it as a child

It comes as a great shock to discover that the country which is your birthplace and to which you owe your life and identity has not, in its whole system of reality, evolved any place for you. The disaffection and the gap between people, only on the basis of their skins, begins there and accelerates throughout your whole lifetime. You realize that you are 30 and you are having a terrible time. You have been through a certain kind of mill and the most serious effect is again not the catalogue of disaster—the policeman, the taxi driver, the waiters, the landlady, the banks, the insurance companies, the millions of details 24 hours of every day which spell out to you that you are a worthless human being. It is not that. By that time you have begun to see it happening in your daughter, your son or your niece or your nephew. You are 30 by now and nothing you have done has helped you to escape the trap. But

It traps him at 30

what is worse is that nothing you have done, and as far as you can tell nothing you *can* do, will save your son or your daughter from having the same disaster and from coming to the same end.

We speak about expense. There are several ways of addressing oneself to some attempt to find out what that word means here. From a very literal point of view, the harbors and the ports and the railroads of the country—the economy, especially in the South—could not conceivably be what they are if it had not been (and this is still so) for cheap labor. I am speaking very seriously, and this is not an overstatement: I picked cotton, I carried it to the market, I built the railroads under someone else's whip for nothing. For nothing.

The Southern oligarchy which has still today so very much power in Washington, and therefore some power in the world, was created by my labor and my sweat and the violation of my women and the murder of my children. This in the land of the free, the home of the brave. None can challenge that statement. It is a matter of historical record.

In the Deep South you are dealing with a sheriff or a landlord or a landlady or the girl at the Western Union desk. She doesn't know quite whom she is dealing with—by which I mean, if you are not part of a town and if you are a Northern nigger, it shows in millions of ways. She simply knows that it is an unknown quantity and she wants to have nothing to do with it. You have to wait a while to get your telegram. We have all been through it. By the time you get to be a man it is fairly easy to deal with.

But what happens to the poor white man's, the poor white woman's, mind? It is this: they have been raised to believe, and by now they helplessly believe, that no matter how terrible some of their lives may be and no matter what disaster overtakes them, there is one consolation like a heavenly revelation—at least they are not black. I suggest that of all the terrible things that could happen to a human being that is one of the worst. I suggest that what has happened to the white Southerner is in some ways much worse than what has happened to the Negroes there.

What he as a Negro has done for the South's economy
(Definition)

For the South's political power

Painful effects of this historic blindness on the modern Negro

Destructive effects on Whites

Sheriff Clark in Selma, Ala., cannot be dismissed as a total monster; I am sure he loves his wife and children and likes to get drunk. One has to assume that he is a man like me. But he does not know what drives him to use the club, to menace with the gun and to use the cattle prod. Something awful must have happened to a human being to be able to put a cattle prod against a woman's breasts. What happens to the woman is ghastly. What happens to the man who does it is in some ways much, much worse. Their moral lives have been destroyed by the plague called color.

Example

This is not being done 100 years ago, but in 1965 and in a country which is pleased with what we call prosperity, with a certain amount of social coherence, which calls itself a civilized nation and which espouses the notion of freedom in the world. If it were white people being murdered, the Government would find some way of doing something about it. We have a civil rights bill now. We had the 15th Amendment nearly 100 years ago. If it was not honored then, I have no reason to believe that the civil rights bill will be honored now.

Why the Negro mistrusts Civil Rights laws

The American soil is full of the corpses of my ancestors, through 400 years and at least three wars. Why is my freedom, my citizenship, in question now? What one begs the American people to do, for all our sakes, is simply to accept our history.

A plea for justice

It seems to me when I watch Americans in Europe that what they don't know about Europeans is what they don't know about me. They were not trying to be nasty to the French girl, rude to the French waiter. They did not know that they hurt their feelings; they didn't have any sense that this particular man and woman were human beings. They walked over them with the same sort of bland ignorance and condescension, the charm and cheerfulness, with which they had patted me on the head and which made them upset when I was upset.

Americans' attitude toward Europeans same as toward Negroes

When I was brought up I was taught in American history books that Africa had no history and that neither had I. I was a savage about whom the least said the better, who had been saved by Europe and who

His experience with this attitude

had been brought to America. Of course, I believed it. I didn't have much choice. These were the only books there were. Everyone else seemed to agree. If you went out of Harlem the whole world agreed. What you saw was much bigger, whiter, cleaner, safer. The garbage was collected, the children were happy. You would go back home and it would seem, of course, that this was an act of God. You belonged where white people put you.

It is only since World War II that there has been a counter-image in the world. That image has not come about because of any legislation by any American Government, but because Africa was suddenly on the stage of the world and Africans had to be dealt with in a way they had never been dealt with before. This gave the American Negro, for the first time, a sense of himself not as a savage. It has created and will create a great many conundrums.

One of the things the white world does not know, but I think I know, is that black people are just like everybody else. We are also mercenaries, dictators, murderers, liars. We are human, too. Unless we can establish some kind of dialogue between those people who enjoy the American dream and those other people who have not achieved it, we will be in terrible trouble. This is what concerns me most. We are sitting in this room and we are all civilized; we can talk to each other, at least on certain levels, so that we can walk out of here assuming that the measure of our politeness has some effect on the world.

I remember when the ex-Attorney General, Mr. Robert Kennedy, said it was conceivable that in 40 years in America we might have a Negro President. That sounded like a very emancipated statement to white people. They were not in Harlem when this statement was first heard. They did not hear the laughter and bitterness and scorn with which this statement was greeted. From the point of view of the man in the Harlem barber shop, Bobby Kennedy only got here yesterday and now he is already on his way to the Presidency. We were here for 400 years and now he tells us that maybe in 40 years, if you are good, we may let you become President.

Changed outlook since World War II

Sense of humanity shared with audience

But not shared with American Whites

Perhaps I can be reasoned with, but I don't know —neither does Martin Luther King—none of us knows how to deal with people whom the white world has so long ignored, who don't believe anything the white world says and don't entirely believe anything I or Martin say. You can't blame them.

CONCLUSION
Fear that lasting effects of their attitude may be fatal

It seems to me that the City of New York has had, for example, Negroes in it for a very long time. The City of New York was able in the last 15 years to reconstruct itself, to tear down buildings and raise great new ones and has done nothing whatever except build housing projects, mainly in the ghettoes, for the Negroes. And of course the Negroes hate it. The children can't bear it. They want to move out of the ghettoes. If American pretensions were based on more honest assessments of life, it would not mean for Negroes that when someone says "urban renewal" some Negroes are going to be thrown out into the streets, which is what it means now.

The just desires and hopes of Negroes

It is a terrible thing for an entire people to surrender to the notion that one-ninth of its population is beneath them. Until the moment comes when we, the Americans, are able to accept the fact that my ancestors are both black and white, that on that continent we are trying to forge a new identity, that we need each other, that I am not a ward of America, I am not an object of missionary charity, I am one of the people who built the country—until this moment comes there is scarcely any hope for the American dream. If the people are denied participation in it, by their very presence they will wreck it. And if that happens it is a very grave moment for the West.

Final dire warning of national disaster if false old assumption not discarded

OUTLINE

Outline or "brief" of the logic in the Baldwin argument as Mr. Baldwin may have prepared it prior to his presentation in the debate.
The proposition: "Yes, the American Dream is at the expense of the American Negro," for

      I. American Whites still are blind to the terrible, false assumption which governs their racial attitude; for

    A. They have derived their attitude of superiority from the old European civilization;

    B. It has led them to subjugate the Black civilization, and

II. It causes unspeakable suffering to Negroes, for

    A. Children are horrified by it;

    B. They are condemned to grow up coping with it daily;

    C. At the age of 30, they realize their future is a total trap, and

III. As subjugated people, Negroes have contributed to the Dream at their own expense, for

    A. They have built up the economy of the South with their cheap labor;

    B. Even I have worked for nothing;

    C. We have created the political power of the South through our work while being persecuted;

    D. Even now we grow up suffering the same old ills, and

IV. We helplessly witness what the Whites' assumption does to their minds, for

    A. It makes the poor Whites use it as a panacea;

    B. It makes Sheriff Clark of Selma capable of monstrous cruelties;

    C. It makes a mockery of their Civil Rights law;

    D. It also makes them mistreat Europeans;

    E. It has poisoned the minds of historians, and

V. It brought changes, that have made clear to the Negro his historic position and his real identity, for

    A. He realizes he shares a common humanity;

    B. He knows that even the most clear thinking Whites do not yet share this understanding;

    C. Negro leadership may not always continue to be "reasonable";

    D. If the assumption of White superiority is not dropped, national disaster threatens.

COMMENTARY

In his opening remarks, James Baldwin employs the technical terms of a debater to state the gist of his argument and to win the respect of his English university audience. His allusion to Jeremiah, the Old Testament prophet of doom, also sets the tone of his address. He then dramatically states in perhaps oversimplified terms the plight of both the Negro and the White man resulting from the fatal assumption of white supremacy. He carefully plays down details of violence suffered by the Negro in order to keep his discussion at first on a high level of sociological-psychological considerations.

    But then in the fifth and sixth paragraphs he tries to make the audience identify with the sufferings of the Negro by describing his own painful experiences with racism. Later in paragraphs 9 and 15 he again returns to this second-person viewpoint to arouse feelings of compassion.

He returns, in paragraph 10, to his higher philosophical level while telling of the acts of a brutal sheriff. He also shows a familiarity with the history of his proposition to show his scholarly competence. He uses various tones, playfully satiric as in the reference to Robert Kennedy, and then he resorts to the brutal force of *thrown-out-into-the-streets* language. Interspersed throughout his speech are pleas for justice and some forthright protests. He concludes with a mixed tone of compassion and jeremiad.

Underlying all of the persuasion of his rhetoric, he has constructed his argument upon one of the oldest and most formidable ploys of logic: the *dilemma*. He offers his audience only two alternative courses of action to choose from; they must either agree with his view or condone the further persecution of the Negro and the violence that will grow out of it. Anyone unsympathetic with his views would find himself in danger of being caught on the proverbial "horns of the dilemma." To escape being impaled, one would have to find other alternatives than the two he offers.

In Baldwin's speech you can find much to emulate and perhaps also a few things to avoid. His deep convictions and candor, his marshaling of facts and reasoning to form a basic dilemma did convince his English audience. In your own arguments, take care to follow Baldwin's example. Do not allow your emotions to trap you into making wild and illogical statements. Make your enthusiasm a help rather than a hindrance.

WHAT DOES IT SAY?

1. In what sense is the Negro father's authority over his children lost "because his past has disappeared"?

2. What is an *oligarchy*? For what reasons would Baldwin speak of "the Southern oligarchy" in Washington, D.C.?

3. Instead of stating simply that many of his ancestors have died for America, Baldwin says: "The American soil is full of the corpses of my ancestors, through 400 years and at least three wars." What effectiveness does he gain by this choice of words?

4. Does the expression "bland ignorance and condescension" suggest cruelty or indifference?

5. What are some of the connotations of the words in the statement "You belonged where white people put you"? What possible effect could they have on his audience?

6. Since World War II what changes in Africa have produced a "counter image" to the one earlier held?

7. How does his inclusion of "mercenaries, dictators, murderers, liars" among the black people prove his claim that "We are human, too"?

8. How do you see "the man in the Harlem barber shop"? Describe him and his viewpoint of Bobby Kennedy, who "only got here yesterday."

WHAT DO YOU THINK?

1. On the basis of your own observations and conclusions, write an argument addressed to your classmates on an aspect of one of the following controversial topics:

"Black ghetto"	Demonstrations
Neighborhood integration	"Black Power"
Social and club membership restrictions	Black Muslims
Busing of school children	Slum clearance
Trade union membership	Token integration

2. Here are some additional views on the subject of "The American Dream" and the Negro. In the light of your own thinking, formulate a thesis from among them and write an essay adequately developing it.

   a) I have criticized publicly the advocates of "black power." But I understand the bitterness and despair that lead many Negroes to embrace that destructive slogan. What I do not understand is that better-educated white Americans, who have so much more to lose by racial violence, should think that the answer to one stupid slogan is an equally stupid one called "white backlash."—Carl T. Rowan, syndicated columnist and first Negro to sit on the National Security Council, "The Negro's Place in the American Dream," *The Reader's Digest*, April 1967, p. 67.

   b) I'll still preach nonviolence with all my might, but I'm afraid it will fall on deaf ears.—The Rev. Martin Luther King, Jr., *New York Times* News Service, April 17, 1967.

   c) We've all been aware of the mad scramble to employ at least one Negro as "Exhibit A."—Whitney M. Young, Jr., "How We Integrated the Urban League," *Harper's Magazine*, December 1966, p. 114.

   d) Despite meetings, marches for open housing, big and little city riots against established authority and angry calls for "Black Power," the Negro masses made few wholesale gains in 1966. Defeat of the Civil Rights bill in Congress was only an indication of well-entrenched racism.—"Progress Report for 1966," *Ebony*, January 1967, pp. 34–35.

e) All (Negro area bookstores) reported that works by James Baldwin, LeRoi Jones and Ralph Ellison are widely read. In the case of Baldwin, everyone reads everything he writes. "In and Out of Books," *The New York Times Book Review,* April 1967, p. 8.

f) The best description of education by and for Negroes is found in Elliot Baker's *A Fine Madness:* "We have come a long way toward ignorance, and all uphill."—Lloyd T. Jones, *Time,* April 14, 1967, p. 21.

TRIAL

BY JURY

ERLE STANLEY GARDNER

RECENT COURT decisions, by the appellate courts, including the U.S. Supreme Court, may change the face of legal justice. These decisions bar confessions under certain circumstances from being admitted as courtroom evidence, prescribe that a person upon being arrested must be taken immediately before a judge and given counsel, and prevent the police from searching without evidence that a crime has been committed.

As a result of these decisions, and on the heels of such highly publicized trials as those of Dr. Sam Sheppard and Dr. Carl Coppolino, the public has been asking: Just how good is our jury system?

I think it is plenty good! But the answer to that question depends on whether the jury is given all the pertinent evidence.

Recently, society has had to face the fact that innocent men have been wrongfully convicted of crime while guilty men were being turned loose.

Great Britain has rather shamefacedly granted a posthumous pardon to Timothy Evans who was convicted of murder and hanged on the gallows.

I know of one case where New York State came within an inch of executing an innocent man.

I know of another where Canada sentenced a young boy (13-year-old Steven Truscott) to death. Because of his youth the sentence was commuted to life imprisonment. Then a crusading writer, Isabel Le Bourdais, examined all the evidence and wrote a book which had a terrific impact on the public, and the case was reopened.

Reprinted from *This Week* Magazine, January 22, 1967, by permission of Collins-Knowlton-Wing, Inc. Copyright © 1967 by Erle Stanley Gardner.

I could go on and on and on. But what must be apparent, by now, is that a review and reappraisal of the whole apparatus of our legal profession, an important element of which is our system of trial by jury, is necessary.

As one of the founders of the "Court of Last Resort," I investigated many cases in which innocent people had been convicted of murder.

In one case, where a man had been wrongfully imprisoned for some 16 years, the District Attorney of the County joined with us in our investigations and then walked into court and moved for a new trial on the ground that the wrong man had been convicted. When the Court granted a new trial, the District Attorney then dismissed the case. He felt the convicted man had been framed.

In a case in Washington where an innocent man served some 15 years of a life sentence for a murder he hadn't committed, it appeared that a "bushy-haired" man had been seen running from the premises. The prisoner told us that, at the time of trial, the police had let his hair grow long and just before entering the courtroom had rubbed some preparation on his head which caused his hair virtually to stand up on end so that the witnesses could see a bushy-haired defendant. The jury didn't know this.

There is no simple answer. It is a complex problem. Jurors should be given *all* the evidence, and the police should be given more cooperation in gathering that evidence.

Recently, appellate court decisions have given the suspect a two-edged sword; one is procedural. The defendant in federal courts must be taken forthwith before a magistrate. He must be advised of his rights. He must be given counsel if he requires it.

The other edge is directed against the police in gathering and presenting evidence. The police can't search a place without first having evidence of a crime. They can't eavesdrop on telephone conversations. If they make a search without "reasonable grounds" and uncover evidence of a dozen crimes, they would still be unable to do anything about it because the evidence wasn't admissible.

Now, this edge of the sword is of very little value in protecting the *innocent,* but it is a deadly weapon in the hands of the *guilty*—a terrific handicap for the police. I don't want a police state, but I don't want the police hamstrung in getting evidence. And when that evidence has been gathered, I feel that it should be presented to a jury.

Some years after Dr. Sheppard's conviction, my associates and I wanted to give polygraph—the so-called lie detector—tests to the parties involved.

Dr. Sam Sheppard was confined in prison and we couldn't give him a lie detector test without permission of the authorities; but the brothers and their wives were available. Those tests were conducted with the greatest care by a coalition of some of the greatest U.S. experts.

Dr. LeMoyne Snyder—a doctor of medicine, a doctor of law and an expert in the use of the polygraph—sat in on the tests. Alex Lee Gregory, in my opinion one of the best polygraph examiners in the U.S., helped give them. John E. Reid, universally conceded to be among the very top in his profession, participated. And so did C. B. Hanscom, in charge of security at the University of Minnesota. Hanscom is a pioneer in the field of narcoanalysis, with outstanding ability as a polygraph examiner.

Those tests were searching. The examiners wanted to know whether any of the parties had done anything in the way of a cover-up; whether they had withheld, doctored, destroyed or otherwise tampered with evidence; whether they had acted in good faith, whether they had, at any time, ever heard Dr. Sam Sheppard say he was guilty of the crime, or make any incriminating statements.

Each passed the tests with flying colors. We then wanted to give Dr. Sam Sheppard the same test. While we were trying to get permission, a convict in Florida startled the world with a confession, stating it was he who had murdered Marilyn Sheppard.

Alex Lee Gregory hurried to Florida and gave this man a polygraph test and, as a result of that test, it was his conclusion that the man either had murdered Mrs. Sheppard or believed that he had.

That last question presented a problem.

The convict, according to his story, had taken a shot of dope on the night that Marilyn Sheppard was murdered. He had a rather hazy idea of exactly what he had done. He said he found himself in possession of a big, blue automobile which presumably had been stolen. He went driving through Bay Village, the town where the Sheppards lived. He came to a house which looked good. He got out of the car, went to the house, found the door open, went in and found a man sleeping on a couch. He climbed to the second floor, was ransacking a bedroom when Mrs. Sheppard woke up and screamed.

He said he struck her several times, then started to run out, encountered a man on the stairs, struck him, ran out of the house, got in his automobile and drove away. Is it possible that while under the influence of dope he had heard a radio report of the crime, and upon regaining full consciousness thought that he had been the one who committed the crime?

There was no way of finding out. In some ways his story didn't ring true. Whoever killed Marilyn Sheppard had not only hit her a few times, he had literally pounded her to death in a frenzy.

However, here is the point I want to make. The governor of Ohio first gave us permission to give Dr. Sam Sheppard a lie detector test; and Harry Steeger (the publisher of "Argosy" Magazine), Dr. Lemoyne Snyder, Alex Lee Gregory, C. B. Hanscom, and I went to Ohio. While en route, the governor changed his mind and withdrew his permission.

For a short time, we stayed in the state marking time, hoping that the governor would change his mind. While we were there, I received a telephone call from a woman who lived in Bay Village. Her husband, a bartender, had been returning in the small hours of the morning, after having closed up his place of business. He had reached a point in front of the Sheppard house when he almost collided with a big, blue automobile, without lights, standing in the very center of the road. He had barely avoided it. Arriving home, he had wanted to telephone the police, but his wife had talked him out of it on the ground that he would be deprived of his much-needed sleep, that the police would be certain to find the car of their own initiative.

In the morning when the bartender had awakened, he had heard on the radio about the murder of Marilyn Sheppard. He had then, according to my informant, called the police and had been told to forget it, that the police knew the murderer.

This is a highly interesting partial corroboration of the story of the Florida convict; but it illustrates that too many times, having agreed upon a suspect, the police are interested only in evidence that points to that suspect. Jurors are entitled to *all* the facts.

I am strongly in favor of the jury system; but I believe that rules of procedure which can't possibly protect the innocent, but are designed to thwart the police in collecting and presenting evidence, should be removed.

I certainly don't believe that a man's house should be "bugged." But, on the other hand, if a man uses the long-distance telephone in connection with purchasing dope in a foreign country and having it delivered in this country, and if the governmental agents are able to intercept that phone message at some point, I see no reason why their hands should be held behind their backs with legalistic handcuffs so they can't act and intercept the shipment.

I dislike the so-called "box score" by which the efficiency of a prosecutor is rated by his percentage of convictions on the number of cases tried.

If we had a few more prosecutors like the late Gerald K. O'Brien, the district attorney in Detroit who joined with us in our investigation of the man who had been wrongfully convicted, and had the courage to stand up in court and move for a new trial, the public would give the prosecutors everywhere greater support.

Years ago when James Davis was the district attorney of Siskiyou County, he courageously refused to prosecute the Brite brothers for first-degree murder on the grounds that the evidence as it had first been presented to him showed the brothers had acted in justifiable self-defense.

Because two very popular officers had been killed in the resulting fight, because the public sentiment was inflamed to the point of a lynching, District Attorney Davis committed political hari-kari by his courageous stand. He knew he was doing it at the time, but he did it because that was the way that he felt. He said in part: "He (the district attorney) must view the situation in the light of substantial justice and whoever might be killed, whatever might be the roar of the mob, if a district attorney cannot withstand the onslaught of apparent injustice, although he may stand alone in his convictions, that district attorney is not worthy of his job."

Davis was pushed to one side. A special prosecutor took over the case against the Brite brothers. They were convicted of first-degree murder and sentenced to be hanged. Later on the sentence was commuted to life imprisonment, but it took us years to bring about their actual release from prison.

This country is badly in need of a better understanding of what law enforcement means and, above all, what law *obedience* means.

The citizens need to learn to respect the law, to obey the law, and to have a greater respect for the police officer who is called upon to enforce the law.

Personally, I want the jury system left as it is. But I certainly hope that the jurors can be given all the pertinent evidence and that legalistic doctrines, which are of no value to the innocent but of such great value to the guilty, can be abrogated.

The innocent man earnestly hopes that the police will discover *all* of the evidence.

The guilty man is equally hopeful that the police will discover *none* of it.

COMMENTARY

As the author of the Perry Mason defense lawyer stories, Erle Stanley Gardner should be knowledgeable about the effective arrangement of evidence and the use of logic in presenting a *persuasive argument*. In this article he demonstrates some of that proficiency in the way he attempts to convince his readers.

His opening statements arouse interest by linking recent, important U. S. Supreme Court rulings with two notorious murder trials. He immediately then raises the debatable question, or *proposition*, to which he will reply: "Just how good is our jury system?" His reply states his *thesis*: "I think it is plenty good! But the answer to that question depends on whether the jury is given all the pertinent evidence."

Ahead of him now lies the task of convincing his readers on two basic *issues* on which he fears he may be opposed: (1) juries are not often given all the evidence they require for reaching just verdicts; (2) police and district attorneys now more than ever before need cooperation in gathering evidence. Perhaps to overwhelm the reader on the first issue, Gardner quickly lists six murder cases wherein jury verdicts were later overturned because of the discovery of new evidence. Having proven this issue to his satisfaction, he repeats his thesis: "Jurors should be given *all* the evidence, and the police should be given more cooperation in gathering that evidence."

His second issue, dealing with increased difficulties of police and attorneys, now follows. To support his views on this issue, he describes emotion-arousing developments in the Dr. Sam Sheppard case. Then once more he repeats his thesis: "I am strongly in favor of the jury system. . . ." He further supports this issue with two appealing examples of the conscientiousness of heroic district attorneys. Finally, in his conclusion, wherein he appeals to his readers' sense of justice, he repeats his thesis for a fourth time: "Personally, I want the jury system left as it is. But I certainly hope. . . ." He ends with two dramatic sentences expressing antithetical hopes.

Like James Baldwin's in his persuasive speech on the Negro, Gardner's *point of view* reveals how argument differs from exposition. Both writers are too involved in iterating their theses to be merely explaining an opinion.

It is this quality of sincere, well-reasoned presentation that distinguishes argumentation. Since it requires strong convictions as well as clear and honest thinking, make certain that in your own choice of debatable topics you choose one that affects you deeply enough to make the necessary effort to do well by it. Your readers will thank you for your pains.

WHAT DOES IT SAY?

1. What does Gardner mean by saying that recent court decisions may change "the face of legal justice"? Can you express in your own words the protection these new decisions give everyone?

2. Why should the trials of Dr. Sam Sheppard and Dr. Carl Coppolino have raised questions concerning the jury system?

3. What is a *posthumous pardon*? Why would one be desired or granted?

4. From the context of the article can you describe what the "Court of Last Resort" consists of and what it does?

5. What is the difference between a *polygraph* and a *lie detector*?

6. If a man's house has been "bugged," what has been done to it?

7. Define *law obedience* as Gardner uses the term.

WHAT DO YOU THINK?

1. On the question of jurors, former U.S. Attorney General Nicholas de B. Katzenbach is quoted as saying: "I think it would be just fine if we could guarantee common sense in all jurors. It is a little difficult to know exactly how one guarantees a jury with common sense." Define the kind of "common sense" thinking and attitudes you would hope to demonstrate were you chosen to be a juror in an important court

trial. (You may even assume that you have been selected as a juror in a case presently receiving attention in the newspapers.)

2. It took more than four weeks and the examination of over four hundred potential jurors before a jury was finally impaneled for the trial of the seaman accused and later found guilty of the murder of eight student nurses in Chicago. The presiding judge allowed such care in the selection of the jury in order to avoid the possibility of having the verdict upset by a higher court on grounds of "prejudicial press coverage." Do you think that news media "try the case" before the accused person is actually brought to trial? If so, what are the grave issues involved? What should be done to insure a fair trial and maintain freedom of the press?

3. "Justice requires that jurors make their decisions solely on the facts properly presented to them. Ways must be found to block those who would put before them material which does not belong there. Only then can we really guarantee the constitutional right to a fair trial." In the light of this opinion expressed by a prominent criminal attorney, explain in detail just what facts you would want presented to jurors *if you were on trial on a serious charge* but were, of course, innocent.

4. If you were charged with an infraction of the law, would you prefer to be tried by a jury of your peers or by a judge alone? Give reasons for your answer, and try to base them upon cases you have known or read about.

5. How does Perry Mason handle juries in the fiction of Erle Stanley Gardner? Based on specific cases, what is your opinion of the quality of Gardner juries?

CAR
AS HERO

DEREK JEWELL

MODERN MAN is, of course, enamoured of the automobile. It is a strange love affair when you consider that the car kills something like 150,000 people each year around the globe and often makes cities hell to live in. It is all becoming, perhaps, more of a love-hate relationship.

But there is no doubt which element in the dichotomy predominates. It is love. And its expressions are so bizarre and various that the chief problem in preparing my book on the affair was the agonizing one of deciding what to leave out—that, and getting through the writing of something like 1,000 letters around the world seeking out facts, figures, copyrights and the rest.

There is no space here to *prove* that the love affair exists, and it is scarcely necessary. The evidence (car-polishing, car-decoration, desirable girls and phallic symbols in car and petrol ads) is all around us, while most people know something of the psychologists' explanations of how, through the car, men fulfil their desires for freedom, power, superiority, virility. The car has become both a part of man's personality and an expression of it.

Women aren't left out of the affair, either. The difference is that they see the car as an extension of home—carpet on the floor, colour-schemes and all that—instead of a fantasy vehicle which transforms the male into James Bond or Superman.

Reprinted from *Books and Bookmen*, January 1967 by permission of author and publisher. Copyright © 1967 by Derek Jewell.

The car as loved one . . . gets into every corner of our lives—into, among other things, religion, movies, love-making, painting, sculpture, poetry, music, pop songs and novels. Above all, perhaps, novels. From Kipling all the way through to Fleming, Leasor and Braine there runs this obsession with cars. What to leave out? Ultimately I had to content myself with extracts from 14 novelists as representative.

No other generation had been able to speed into the sunset, wrote Sir Osbert Sitwell in *Great Morning,* the third volume of his autobiography, during a magnificent description of open-car motoring around the turn of the century, and this feeling of sheer lyricism also dominates early fictional writing about the car.

In his story *Steam Tactics,* Kipling describes how a Lanchester, disguised as "The Octopod," drove through the countryside and *sang like a six-inch shell.* Later he says that *she turned her broad black bows to the westering light, and lifted us high upon hills that we might see and rejoice with her.* The car has already become a *character,* and a woman at that—which nicely parallels the fact that one of the great marques, Mercedes, was named after the daughter of its creator.

The process of humanizing the car was being taken even further at the same time by the husband-and-wife team of C. N. and A. M. Williamson, who wove best-selling romantic novels around their own motoring experiences, beginning with *The Lightning Conductor.* In one of its sequels, *The Lightning Conductress,* they go further: *I told you about the high-powered French car. Well, there's an even higher-powered French maid . . . The car . . . 40 horse-power, I believe; whereas I'm much mistaken if Angèle isn't about 100 demon-power. She's geared terribly high, can "crank" herself I should imagine, and has the smartest new type of body, all glittering paint and varnish.*

Galsworthy (the Model T Ford in *To Let,* part of *The Forsyte Saga*), Conan Doyle, Ian Hay (*Knight on Wheels*) and Dornford Yates were others deeply involved in the early part of the century with using the car as a character. By the 1920s the convention was so well established that in *Those Barren Leaves,* Aldous Huxley could remarkably extend the Williamsons' technique of using the car to describe or illustrate human traits.

Huxley's hero, Lord Hovenden, is confident and cool-headed inside his 30/98 Vauxhall Velox, shy and diffident outside it. The car transforms him. *Lord Hovenden's spirits rose with the mounting speed. His lips curved into a smile of fixed and permanent rapture. Behind the glass of his goggles his eyes were very bright.* He sighs, not surprisingly: *"If only one could spend all one's life in the Velox."*

Another of these ecstatic descriptions of fast driving occurs in *Peter Jackson, Cigar Merchant,* one of the many books in which Gilbert Frankau turned motoring knowledge into fiction. He uses a staccato language of speed. *Couple behind felt the car gather herself as if for a great leap; saw passing hedgerows fade out to a continuous blur. Speedometer needle clicked to 60; held there for three and a half ecstatic minutes.*

The car there was a Crossley—and other marques made much of during the 1920s and 1930s were the Hispano-Suiza (Michael Arlen's *The Green Hat*), the Isotta-Fraschini (Eric Linklater's *Poet's Pub*), the Daimler (Lord Peter Wimsey had a whole string in Dorothy L. Sayers's thrillers) and the Duesenberg (Scott Fitzgerald). The principle seems to be that the car must be *special*—in performance or luxury or rarity—to get into books. But not always.

The aged Morris staggered in its gait like an old lady in the rain, wheezing a little, anxious about her umbrella which the wind was bullying, runs one passage in *Poet's Pub*. And in America, the home of mass-production, it was to be expected that the more ordinary marques would get a look in. John Steinbeck (*The Grapes of Wrath* and *Cannery Row*) dealt with cars, especially the Model T, in loving *technical* detail as well as using them, like Huxley, to reflect human character. By contrast, Henry Miller's approach in his delightful *Automotive Passacaglia,* contained in *The Air-Conditioned Nightmare,* is supremely non-technical. Miller (yes, *the* Henry Miller), describes a car engine thus: *It was rather beautiful, in a mechanical way. Reminded me of a steam calliope playing Chopin in a tub of grease.*

The automobile, though, is more likely to be described in terms of jewellery, as a symbol of wealth and status, than as a grease-tub. Since the last war this has been the theme with John Braine, Kingsley Amis and others. Ian Fleming, like Braine, chose the Aston-Martin as the best-known instrument of his Bond-fantasy, and used other aficionado's cars like the Bentley and the rare old American Cord. An exotic variation is the car imagery employed by J. P. Donleavy for one very funny bedroom scene in *A Singular Man.*

The game is never-ending. The automobile has become quite human. A passage in Roger Vailland's *The Law* runs: *The car had found its balance: these sighs, like those of a human chest or abdomen, had still not lost their power to delight him.* It is so human that with some writers it is difficult to separate fact from fiction.

Jason Love, hero of a continuing series of thrillers by James Leasor, drives his Cord through every book. *It was impossible for him to look at the horizontal radiator louvres, the four chrome-steel outside exhausts, the raked V-windscreen fitted with faintly tinted glass against the tropical sun, without feeling the same absurd, irrational thrill of pleasure that the sight of his own Cord always roused in him.*

The passage comes from *Passport to Peril* and is typical of many in these books. Leasor himself owns a Cord, and describes in my book how he tracked down this rarity. He says he thinks best while sitting in it. Could a love affair ever have been more usefully consummated?

COMMENTARY

Derek Jewell wastes no time in announcing the *general principle* that is to govern his line of thought in this persuasive essay. At the outset he tells us, "Modern man is, of course, enamoured of the automobile," and by *modern man* he means everybody, but especially, as we soon learn, novelists. He also informs us that he is going to *apply* this principle to "extracts from 14 novelists." So if we accept the *major premise*—Modern man is in love with automobiles—and also agree to accept the *minor premise*—Novelists are certainly "modern"—we have to accept the *conclusion*—Novelists are in love with automobiles.

Note that Jewell holds it unnecessary to "prove" the truth of the *assumption* that he has framed as his general principle: "There is no space here to *prove* that the love affair exists, and it is scarcely necessary." We may be willing to grant that principle, especially if we have just recently finished polishing up our own "pride and joy." But we may not be quite prepared to admit that novelists have also been obsessed with cars. Jewell himself seems to have been surprised to learn how much "the car as loved one" has meant to novelists, for he devotes most of his essay to discussing extracts of novels showing this affection.

One of the most delightful features of this essay is its use of *analogy* as a colorful means of comparison. Since every reader knows that a car is, after all, only a machine and a woman is a human being, he is willing to accept this particular analogy, which identifies cars as "heroes" or "heroines" and "loved ones," at its face value and smile at its gentle absurdity, as the author intended him to do.

Do not overlook the fact, however, that the main interest and substance of this mild argument lie in the painfully collected and carefully ordered extracts from the novels.

WHAT DOES IT SAY?

1. Is a "love-hate" relationship generally to be found in a "love-affair"? What is the source of such a dichotomy?

2. Phallic symbols are ones representing the male generative power. Do American car and gasoline advertisments often feature such symbols? Can you give examples?

3. What is the difference between *liking* cars and having an *obsession* with them?

4. How does one come to humanize a car? Do you know someone who does? What characteristic things does he say and do?

5. What movies have you enjoyed that showed cars as being "part of man's personality and an expression of it"?

6. For some readers the car models mentioned by Derek Jewell may have special connotations. How about these?

Model T Ford	Duesenberg
Vauxhall Velox	Morris
Crossley	Aston-Martin
Hispano-Suiza	Bentley
	Cord

WHAT DO YOU THINK?

1. Describe the feelings and the line of reasoning in detail of a person who would deliberately choose to buy *one* of the following kinds of automobiles:

Foreign-made sports car	American-made sports car
American antique	American compact
Camper	European compact
Four-wheel drive	Station wagon
Luxury sedan	Medium-priced sedan

2. Do you agree that "modern man is enamoured of the automobile"? If you or someone in your family or circle of friends has treated his car with pride and affection, you have the material for an interesting essay. Write it, using specific incidents, expressions associated with it, care given it, and so forth.

3. Discuss the problems besides the ones mentioned in the first paragraph that can make owning a car what Jewell calls a "love-hate relationship."

4. Prepare a list of the names that automobile makers give to their various models, for example, "Falcon," "Barracuda," and "Jaguar." Then after deciding what connotations these names have and what they appeal to in prospective buyers, write an essay on "Images Meant to Sell Cars."

5. Describe in an essay the kind of logic and analogies a neighbor might use to justify his wanting to trade in a still very good automobile on a new model when really all he wants is to improve his "status" in the neighborhood.

FAMINE

IS HERE

T. R. B.

PEOPLE KEEP SAYING that something must be done before population out-strips food supply. Reiteration makes it tedious. But we have a new version. We say that the thing has already happened. World population has passed food supply. The famine has started.

Famine isn't like a satellite countdown; you don't say "Three-two-one, it's here!" What happens is like the New York water shortage: It develops slowly; experts wring hands; public pays no attention; then, suddenly, it's headlined. That's what's happening in world food. "Malnutrition" becomes "famine" any time the headline writer wants. Our estimate is that the thing is here and will get a lot worse before it gets better. Even the most dramatic counter-measures aren't likely to reverse things for several generations. That's why we think world hunger will be the single most important fact in the final third of the 20th Century.

Don't take our word for it. There have been dozens—scores—of surveys. In fact, the subject has been surveyed to death. Here, for example, is the report of the National Council of Churches of Christ in the U.S., as of last June: Two billion persons *now* live in areas of nutritional deficiency. (That's two-thirds of the world's population.) They are the ones with the highest birth-rates. Half of these people, the report says, (i.e., one billion) "suffer daily or recurrent crippling hunger." The report ends with the usual conventional warnings; unless something is done quickly "the predicted widespread, acute

Reprinted from *The New Republic*, September 18, 1965, by permission of *The New Republic*, copyright 1965, Harrison-Blaine of New Jersey, Inc.

famine in some parts of the world in the next few years will become more grim."

It is a typical report; you probably never heard of it. And here is Gunnar Myrdal, eminent Swedish economist. He foresees a "world calamity." Time? In "five or 10 years." To interviewers he says," "It makes me afraid." He still thinks we have a little time. Well, maybe.

The World Food and Agriculture Organization estimates that maybe 10,000 people a day die of hunger *now*. But of course most victims don't die directly of starvation but of some side-effect: the children in parts of India, Africa, Latin America are frail, stunted, hollow-eyed, with distended stomachs: a touch of sickness and they're gone! Always a couple more, though, to take their place. It's a fecund earth.

War is of course one way to check population; the U.S. has helped Malthus in the India-Pakistan situation, by selling guns to both sides.

Here's a fact: Only three-and-a-half percent of the world's surface is arable. Another fact: World population in 35 years will double. Famine? Of course.

Experts are "substantially less optimistic" now than they were a few years ago about heading off world famine, Lester Brown, staff economist of the Department of Agriculture, told a symposium recently. Chester Bowles testified to a Senate subcommittee in June that the approaching world famine threatens "the most colossal catastrophe in history." He, too, put it in the future, as though something would be done about it. Perhaps. But read a little further: Here is Thomas M. Ware, chairman of the Freedom From Hunger Foundation, himself a practical industrialist.

"Very few grasp the magnitude of the danger that confronts us," he said. He offered an illustration. The new Aswan Dam will add 2 million arable acres on either side of the Nile. But while the dam is being built enough new people will be added to Egypt's population to eat up all the food the dam produces. Result: same hunger, more people.

It is doubtful if Americans understand the population problem. If so, how could the House pass its version of the new "nondiscriminatory" immigration bill? (It does not end discrimination, it just juggles it about.) Latin America, for example, with the highest birth rate in the world, has no quota restrictions at all on immigration to the U.S. The Senate may change this. But the House majority still quaintly believes that immigration can solve over-population.

As Mr. Ware puts it, "The catastrophe is not something that *may* happen (his italics); on the contrary it is a mathematical certainty that it *will* happen" unless action is immediately forthcoming.

What action? Ten years ago the compassionate U.S. started a food export program: It was wonderful to feed the starving, but population kept growing. Next the U.S. tried a new approach; the soil of hungry lands is good so America sent fertilizer abroad as well as food. Fine. And population kept on growing. Then in the last couple of years came the third effort—give them cash and credit to build their own fertilizer plants. Fine. Population kept growing.

Now comes the fourth phase. Food, fertilizer, hybrids, insecticides, factories, know-how: These are all good. But they won't work unless the recipient nations limit births at the same time. The point will be stressed, we understand, in a report from an inter-agency task force named by Mr. Johnson. It finds, incidentally, that half the preschool children in "developing" countries are seriously undernourished, amounting to mental and physical retardation for 10 percent to 25 percent.

President Johnson had the courage to mention family planning in both his State of the Union speech, and the one before the UN at San Francisco. It is all the more discouraging that Archbishop O'Boyle of Baltimore delivered his recent anti-birth control tirade. He implied that there is somehow a kind of conspiracy against the poor. Well, the hierarchy in Latin America knows better; it knows that the most generally accepted means of birth control in the world today is abortion. The poor use it; the rich know about birth control.

Barbara Ward describes the widening gap "between a white, complacent, highly bourgeois, very wealthy, very small North Atlantic elite, and everybody else." Yet man can now for the first time feed himself adequately, and he can control the birthrate, too, with the new intra-uterine device. Alas, we guess that the gap will widen and hunger grow, for a time anyway. You can't reverse gears suddenly in a situation that involves most of the earth.

COMMENTARY

Underlying this persuasive editorial is the mournful *general principle* stated clearly in the first paragraph: When population outstrips food supply, the deadly consequence is famine. This general principle is applied to the situation in the world today, and the conclusion reached is that "The famine has started."

Putting this argument into a syllogism would result in something like this:

Major Premise: When population outstrips food supply, famine results.
Minor Premise: World population has now outstripped food supply.
Conclusion: The famine has started.

Mr. T. R. B. spends no time "proving" his major premise. He takes for granted that this assumption is valid. All his attention is centered upon bringing in evidence to support his minor premise: that world population today has increased to the point that it has passed food supply.

The evidence that he relies upon to prove his minor premise is the following: (1) the conclusion of a survey by the National Council of Churches of Christ in the United States (T. R. B. *states* that there have been scores of surveys, all presumably arriving at the same conclusion, but he gives only the one, which he insists is "typical"); (2) an estimate by the World Food and Agriculture Organization (possibly the conclusion of another survey); (3) the testimony of an eminent Swedish economist and three United States experts on food resources. In addition, he offers two "facts" in support of the assertion that conditions will grow steadily worse: (1) only three and one-half percent of the world's surface is arable, and (2) world population will double in 35 years.

Once his case has been established to his satisfaction, T. R. B. goes ahead to discuss the remedies. He first discusses those so-called remedies that he regards as failures: The Aswan Dam will offer only temporary help, "nondiscriminatory" immigration bills passed by the United States House of Representatives are a naive solution, feeding the hungry hordes from U.S. surplus, or sending fertilizer, capital to construct fertilizer plants, insecticides, trained experts—these are only stopgaps.

He sees only one solution: Stop the rapid growth of population. War, he notes in passing, does check population growth. But the logical method is birth control. This solution is stated succinctly in the final paragraph: "Yet man can now for the first time feed himself adequately, and he can control the birthrate, too, with the new intra-uterine device."

This editorial, then, is concerned with both argument and persuasion. T. R. B. argues that world famine has started, and we either accept or reject his conclusion on the basis of the evidence he presents. His attempt to persuade his readers that birth control is the only logical solution to the situation must also rest upon the strength of his evidence that other methods have failed and that this method can succeed.

When you, in turn, write to convince your readers of something, or to persuade them to do as you suggest, be sure that your assumptions are valid and your arguments sound.

WHAT DOES IT SAY?

1. What is a *euphemism*? Why would a headline writer choose *malnutrition* rather than *famine*?

2. What to you are some of the realistic images or associations suggested to you by this statement: "Two billion persons now live in areas of nutritional deficiency"?

3. In what vein or mood does T. R. B. remark, "It's a fecund earth"?

4. Who is Malthus and how can it be said that "the U.S. has helped Malthus in the India-Pakistan situation, by selling guns to both sides"?

5. What are "developing" countries? Is there any irony in the application of the term "developing" to countries wherein "half the preschool children . . . are seriously undernourished"?

6. Which countries would you include in Barbara Ward's category of "a white, complacent, highly bourgeois, very wealthy, very small North Atlantic elite"?

7. "Family planning" is a euphemism for what more blunt term?

8. List three assumptions you find in T. R. B.'s argument.

WHAT DO YOU THINK?

1. Are you convinced from this article that "it is a mathematical certainty" that world famine will occur, that, in fact, the famine has already started? Or do you believe that this is merely a "scare" article? Write a logical defense or attack.

2. Ten years ago, articles such as the one from which the following excerpt is taken would never have appeared in a "family" magazine. What is your considered opinion of the facts it states as well as those you can infer from it?

Nobody can say which of these experiments will be fully successful. But to judge from progress to date, the new methods that are likely to be developed far enough for public use over the next ten years fall into these categories (roughly in order of their possible appearance): (1) Refinements of the Pill, to further reduce side effects. (2) An every-day pill, which will eliminate calendar-watching and finger-counting. (3) Long-acting versions, some of them in injectable forms. (4) A morning-after pill. (5) A super IUD (intrauterine device) for women who must not, or choose not to, take drugs. (6) Reversible surgical sterilization for both women and men. (7) Male shots and pills. (8) An antifertility vaccine.—Warren R. Young, "Beyond the Pill," *McCall's,* March 1967, p. 91.

3. Amidst all of the debate among Catholic theologians all over the world, the official position of the Roman Catholic Church in 1967 was still the one described below. What is the present position? What arguments have been advanced for changes from the historic view?

For present purposes, the Catholic condemnation of contraceptives dates from December 31, 1930, when Pope Pius XI wrote in his encyclical *Casti Connubii,*

"Any use whatever of marriage, in the exercise of which the act by human effort is deprived of its natural power of procreating life, violates the law of God and nature, and those who do such a thing are stained by a grave and mortal flaw."—Joseph Roddy, "The Pope's Unsolvable Problem," *Look,* December 13, 1966, p. 124.

4. Do you agree or disagree with a statement such as the following made by a prominent Catholic woman?

I share what, according to rumor, is the majority view in the papal commission's report: Any physically harmless birth-control means, short of sterilization (which is sexual suicide) and abortion (which is self-violence and infanticide) should be accepted by the Church.

How will the problem be solved? No one knows.—Clare Boothe Luce, "Birth Control and the Catholic Church," *McCall's,* February 1967, p. 198.

5. Controversy perhaps even more heated than that arising from the use of the Pill by married women is the one brought to light by reports such as the following one. What fundamental question is raised here? What are its implications from the point of view of morality? Health? The colleges and universities?

Pullman, Wash. (I.P.)—Findings, based on returns from 315 member institutions of the American College Health Association, revealed that nearly half the nation's college health services now will prescribe contraceptive pills, but only one in 25 will do so for single women who do not intend to marry in the near future.

Returns of the national survey, compiled early last year by Dr. Ralph Buttermore, director of the Student Health Service at Washington State University, showed:

174 (55 percent) do not prescribe contraceptive pills;
77 (26 percent) prescribed only to married women students;
23 (7 percent) prescribed only for medical purposes;
28 (8 percent) will prescribe for a single woman who intends to take a pre-marital exam or show other intent to marry in the near future;
13 (4 percent) will prescribe for single, unmarried women; and
12 of the latter group will prescribe for women under 21.

No individual institutions were identified by Dr. Buttermore.

Most institutions which would not prescribe the pill said this was an appropriate function of a college health service, but required continued, careful supervision by a personal physician, Dr. Buttermore reported. "Others thought prescribing the pill would express (tacit) approval for pre-marital relations, implying that the college accept a responsibility that does not properly belong to it and runs counter to the great majority of parents."

Those health services prescribing contraceptive pills felt they should be treated the same as any other drug. Most prescribed for unmarried women in conjunction with a pre-marital examination.

Some indicated that parental approval was required for unmarried minors, even when the prescription was made solely for medical reasons.—*The Vanguard,* Portland State College, April 5, 1967.

6. Were you as a high school student required to take a course in sex and marriage? What is your considered opinion of such instruction? Would you favor classes in such subjects for your own children if you were a parent?

THE INFORMATION
WAR
IN SAIGON

HANSON W. BALDWIN

"IT'S A Madison Avenue war," the harried public information officer complained. "We are supposed to fight an immaculate war—never kill civilians, never be ambushed, never make mistakes. Hell! We're human; we're bound to make mistakes. We'd be a damn sight better off if we were allowed to be more frank, more honest."

His comments emphasize a major factor, largely ignored, that may ultimately determine the outcome of the war: the factor of public opinion. For the government's reputation for credibility or lack of it—its relationships with the press, the reporting of the war, and the effect of the whole upon the American public in particular and world public opinion in general—could win or lose the war, regardless of what happens in the jungle battles.

Public information officers in Vietnam sometimes compare their problems with the French experience in Algeria. There is little doubt that France had won the Algerian war in a military sense: the guerrillas were stalemated. But it lost the war at home because the French public had wearied of the fight. The influence of public opinion upon contemporary history has already been of major importance in our Vietnamese policies. It is certain to become more important now that Hanoi has once again rejected the President's persistent peace overtures and a long war of attrition appears probable.

In every insurgency conflict, public opinion is a major and often the dominant factor in the outcome. In Vietnam, Hanoi's hopes are keyed to winning the battle of public opinion. Encouraged by the anti-war demonstrations, editorials, and columns in this country, and by de Gaulle's open criticisms and Britain's luke-warm attitude, Hanoi clearly believes that the United States will not have the fortitude or the patience to stay the course. Unfortunately—and for reasons that are in part remediable—the enemy appears to have made some gains in his efforts to capitalize upon these elements.

There are three major weaknesses in our public-relations apparatus in Washington and in Vietnam. The first and by far the most damaging is what has been described as the "credibility gap"—the lack of belief of far too many people in the government's word. The second is the failure of some of our officials in Vietnam to present their case as honestly, as rapidly, and as effectively as they might have done. The third is the failure of some of the press, television, and other media representatives in Vietnam to provide a balanced and factual picture of the war.

The credibility gap has not developed overnight, nor is it the fault of any one man or any one department of the government. The atomic age, with its emphasis on secrecy and its encouragement of evasion, has tarnished the government's reputation for truthfulness. News management and news suppression—particularly in the Pentagon under Secretary Robert S. McNamara and Assistant Secretary for Public Affairs Arthur Sylvester—have served to increase public skepticism. Yet, to be fair to McNamara and Sylvester, they have served two Presidents of widely different personalities, each intensely sensitive about his public image.

This sensitivity has been one of the causes during the Kennedy administration, and even more during the Johnson administration, for the over-control of military operations by Washington. Detailed and continuous supervision of operations seven thousand miles away is at least theoretically possible, thanks to the development of high-speed communications facilities and the tightly centralized control of the Defense Department that has been one of McNamara's principal "achievements." In the Vietnam war and in the Dominican intervention—as in the Cuban missile crisis—Washington instructed military commanders in detail not only what to do but how to do it. In effect, even tactical command has at times been transferred to Washington.

Like everything else, public-relations policies in Vietnam are tightly controlled from Washington. "Rockets" about a story appearing in some newspaper, queries, and requests for clarification flow in a constant stream from the Pentagon to Saigon; a telephone call from a White House assistant to the Marine Corps Commandant's office is apt to cause an earthquake in Da Nang.

Because press and public have become aware of a tendency to give the best version of the conflict, because of past evasions, distortions, or half-truths in Washington, and particularly because of vivid memories of government public relations in Saigon under Diem and General Paul D. Harkins, a considerable credibility gap remains. A number of important and able correspondents who were bruised by official antagonism and denunciation during the stormy period leading to Diem's overthrow are still reporting the war in Saigon. They have a built-in skepticism and mistrust of government announcements and government figures that date back to the days when Secretary McNamara was claiming that we were winning the war at the same time the correspondents were reporting—with far greater accuracy—that we were in deep trouble.

Much of the skepticism of these reporters today focuses on the Army. "The Army just hasn't established its credibility," one correspondent told me, "or at least not to the same extent that Barry Zorthian [Minister Counselor for Information of the U.S. embassy in Saigon] and the political-civilian side of the embassy country team have done. We believe that Zorthian is trying to tell us the truth; we are not so sure about the Army."

There is reason for this doubt. Too many of the current generation of military PIOS—especially those trained in the last decade—no longer believe that they serve two masters, the Executive branch of the government (in the form of their own superiors) and the public. This change in attitude and concept is epitomized by the current teachings of the Defense Information School, which in its new Indianapolis home trains the services' public information personnel.

The concepts of the school were well expressed by two of its current lecturers. Captain Gary Werner of the Army (as quoted in the New York *Times*) said: "Our task is to prepare the students for their primary obligation, which will be to the people they work for, the Executive branch. The public's right to know is not the controlling factor as far as the individual information officer is concerned."

Martin F. Nolan, who worked for the Boston *Globe* before he taught at the school as a draftee (and has since rejoined the newspaper) commented: "The course's main aim is to further goals of the brass and not the public's right to know. The spirit of public relations prevails while democratic ideals get lip service."

The Army's PIOS are dealing with more security information than the civilians are and they can't be as free as the civilian PIOS. But I am convinced, along with many other correspondents, that the Army is now making an honest attempt to depict the war accurately—particularly as judged by the controversial "body count" yardstick.

The Vietnam war is the only war in which body count has become a major yardstick of victory or defeat. It should never have assumed such significance. Body count became important for two reasons—first, because it was emphasized by the frequently apocryphal Vietnamese accounts of "victories" in the Diem days; second, because McNamara's computer-minded assistants seized upon these statistics as one of the important measurements of success.

But in a guerrilla war, the seizure of the enemy's ammunition and rice supplies is perhaps more important than the number of guerrillas killed. Second, body count, especially in the jungles against an enemy who carries away his dead, can never be completely accurate. And third, if measured against our own casualties, which are given not in numbers but in terms of "light," "moderate," or "heavy," with their widely different interpretations, body count carries no comparable significance. All things considered, it would be much better if Vietcong casualties were described as our own are.

The second factor that has hampered the transmission of the fullest and frankest possible picture of the war is in considerable measure the fault of the Army and its public-relations apparatus in Saigon. There, each afternoon, in a briefing for correspondents, the Army attempts to round up and present a balanced picture of the operations of the preceding twenty-four hours. This attempt is complicated and sometimes compromised by the fact that the South Vietnamese government now provides its own separate briefing, which is handicapped by language difficulties, a mental gulf, and inadequate or distorted information.

Until recently the U.S. briefings also left much to be desired. Information was inadequate, late, or inaccurate. Correspondents who had returned from a battle area found they often knew more about what was actually happening than the briefing officer. He, in turn, was often miscast for his role—undoubtedly an excellent combat officer, but unable to reply effectively to some of the loaded questions of the press. Without meaning to, he could give the impression of withholding information. Last summer and fall the situation between the press and the Saigon PIOs was often near the boiling point. Correspondents complained that some of the PIOs were misleading, inefficient, and even dishonest; the PIOs complained that some of the journalists were arrogant, untrustworthy, and sensational.

Fortunately, the Army, with the help of Barry Zorthian and other embassy officials, has attempted to remedy some of its own shortcomings. Public-relations communications systems from Saigon to the various combat units and corps areas are being improved and gradually the briefing information will be more up to date, although the gap between the front lines and headquarters can never be completely closed. A new briefing officer with more of the extrovert qualities the job demands is now on the stage in the little press auditorium. This month or next, Rodger R. Bankson, an Army colonel who has been one of Sylvester's assistants, will become the military PIO in Saigon. The job will be elevated to one-star rank to symbolize its importance and to give Bankson more prestige and power.

The press, too, appears to be cleaning house in Saigon. In the opinion of both the Army and many of the more mature correspondents in Saigon, it is high time. For there is no doubt that the third problem that has handicapped the presentation of an honest and comprehensive picture of the war is the fault of the media themselves.

The Vietnamese war is probably the most complex and difficult war to interpret and present that the American press has ever covered. Yet there are very few editors who are willing or able to allocate the space or the time required for real in-depth reporting. Too often the day-by-day reporting is brief, episodic, and partial. For this, the editors and publishers and television producers, not the correspondents in Saigon, deserve the blame.

But the Army PIOs and many of the correspondents themselves have rightly complained of distorted, biased, and sensational reporting by a few of the younger members of the press and TV corps based in Vietnam. The Army and some correspondents in Saigon say that the press associations and some of the broadcasting companies have been the worst offenders; the same competition for "exclusives" and "beats" and for headlines that marred some of the Associated Press and United Press coverage during the Second World War has been a factor in Vietnam. Moreover, some of the correspondents in Saigon simply are not capable of adequately reporting military operations. And some of the TV reporters have delivered generalized editorial judgments that they have neither the competence nor the knowledge to sustain.

During the Ia Drang Valley and Chuprong Mountain fighting of the 1st Cavalry Division (Airmobile) last fall, some of the accounts that appeared in the American press were greatly distorted. Indeed, General Westmoreland felt called upon to deny headlines or accounts that implied that the 1st Cavalry had been defeated or had been forced to abandon the battlefield. Squad and platoon actions, he asserted, had been taken out of the context of the entire battle.

Fortunately for the reputation of the press and the good of the country, the quality of reporting in Vietnam has improved. Mature and responsible correspondents head all the major bureaus of press associations, broadcasting companies, and major newspapers, and the worst offenders have departed.

A good thing, too, for the Vietnamese war is at a crisis, and what we do, how we do it, and how we report the situation will color the history of all our tomorrows. For unless the American public feels the war is worth winning and must be won, we face ultimate defeat no matter how many military victories we win.

COMMENTARY

Since the first appearance of this article, there have been many changes in the Vietnam war and the political situations connected with it. But Hanson Baldwin's *thesis* and the *evidence* he advanced to support it still deserve analysis.

By definition, *evidence* means anything that tends to prove or give grounds for belief; it may consist of an indication, a sign, the statement of a witness, or anything else that bears on or establishes a fact in question. The *thesis* that Baldwin's evidence tries to prove appears in substance in the second paragraph: the largely ignored factor of public opinion may ultimately determine the outcome of the war, regardless of what happens in the jungle battles. It is repeated in the final sentence of the essay: "For unless the American public feels the war is worth winning and must be won, we face ultimate defeat no matter how many military victories we win."

As *evidence,* Hanson Baldwin discusses the "three major weaknesses in our public-relations apparatus in Washington and in Vietnam." These are the "credibility gap" in Washington, the failure of U.S. public-information officers in Vietnam, and the shortcomings of news media reporters trying to cover a difficult war. He outlines the bad effects of these "weaknesses," and although hopeful of improvements, he sticks to his warning thesis.

We come now to the key questions to ask regarding this evidence. Is each of the "three major weaknesses" really the dangerous thing he says it is? How reliable are the witnesses he cites? How valid is their testimony? How unquestionable are the "facts" he draws upon to convince us? Certainly, in the first place, we need to inquire as to his own competency as a reporter, for he writes with a tone of authority.

It is just such questions that readers of your arguments may raise about your work. Like Baldwin, you will, therefore, want to take great care in choosing the details that you offer as *evidence* in your next essay on a debatable proposition or question.

WHAT DOES IT SAY?

1. What is implied in the complaint—"It's a Madison Avenue war"?

2. What is the difference between "propaganda" and the press releases handed out by such PIOS as those in Vietnam?

3. Why is almost any U.S. President "intensely sensitive about his public image"?

4. What do "evasions, distortions, halftruths" have in common?

5. What do "mature and responsible correspondents" have to avoid if they wish to present a "balanced and factual picture" of events in a Vietnamese kind of war?

6. What, if any, are your own personal associations with the term "body count" as applied to the Asiatic war?

WHAT DO YOU THINK?

1. Speaking for The American Society of Newspaper Editors, a committee of editors at the 1967 convention made the following comment on President Johnson's handling of the news from Vietnam. How do you view now what was called the "credibility gap" in Washington, D.C.?

. . . The war has escalated to the accompaniment of an almost unbroken succession of pronouncements that it was going in the opposite direction, or at least that something else was happening. . . . President Johnson continues to hurt his image and his credibility by consistently trying to make the news sound or seem better than it is.—*Time,* April 28, 1967, p. 88.

2. Write an analysis comparing and contrasting two different television treatments of the same general event in Vietnam. Point out in detail the qualities of reporting that you liked or disliked in each.

3. To discover any special publishing "slant" or style, write up your discoveries in analyzing the reporting of a Vietnam incident as reported in *Time, Newsweek,* and *U.S. News and World Report.*

4. Besides military censorship, what further difficulties do we encounter in securing reliable news from critical events happening abroad? Does the fact that a great city like New York now having only three daily newspapers in any way stifle news gathering and publishing? How many local newspapers do you have access to daily? What is their editorial policy on American involvements abroad? Who owns these newspapers?

5. In reviewing two recent books on the fighting in Vietnam, Neil Sheehan relates the following anecdote regarding President John F. Kennedy:

At a National Security Council meeting in September of 1963 the President listened to a Marine general and a State Department officer, both of whom had just returned from Vietnam, give two opposing estimates of the situation there. "Are you gentlemen sure," the President asked, "that you visited the same country?"—*The New York Times Book Review,* May 14, 1967, p. 3.

6. Write your own notion of the kind of "reporting" that two people whom you know to have different views of our affairs in Asia would produce if sent there to investigate our activities.

THE ATTACK

BILL MAULDIN

Pleiku, South Vietnam

THE MORTAR barrage on Camp Holloway and the 52nd aviation battalion began at exactly 2 A.M. It was intense and murderous, some 80 rounds in five minutes saturating a bivouac area perhaps two blocks square. They were using captured 81 millimeter weapons of our own manufacture.

I was sleeping in the east half of a hut house or "hooch" of Lt. Col. John C. Hughes, of Herrin, Ill. My son, Bruce, a warrant officer and helicopter pilot in the battalion, whom I had come to visit, is billeted in the town of Pleiku, near Second Corps Headquarters which was also hit. I had just spent the evening in Pleiku having a reunion celebration with Bruce and had left him at his billet.

My first awakening thought at the roar of the mortar barrage was that Chinese New Year was still being celebrated. When a round hit nearby, I realized what was going on and began to worry about Bruce, assuming (correctly) that he would try to get back to his outfit and worrying that the attack might be general in scope, in which case the road to camp would be a bad place for him.

Any further speculation on my part was cut off by Colonel Hughes who roared at me to get myself into the bunker out back, as he tore out of the front door to take charge of his battalion. So emphatic was his order and so positive was my response that I found myself arriving at the bunker barefoot and in my underwear.

The barrage was at its height as I started down the earthen steps to the sand-bagged shelter. By the light of the drumming explosions I could see the

153

barbed wire of the southern edge of camp a few feet away, and I fully expected to see hostile faces on the other side moving up under cover of the mortars. It turned out that the only infantry penetration was to the east, where the parked aircraft were attacked.

A young soldier from headquarters company came up to me at the bunker entrance. He was also in his underwear, but mine was white and his was red. He was holding both hands over a large wound in his right side and was covered with blood from several lesser cuts. Mortar shells are designed to cut people up and apparently we make good ones.

"Help me," he said, "I've got to lie down." I tried to help him into the bunker but he refused to come down those dark steps. He said he had decided he was going to die and he wanted to lie down on something comfortable. From the looks of his wound, I felt in no position to question his prognosis, so I helped him into the hut and put him on my cot, where I found a small light and took a closer look at his side. I couldn't tell whether the large fragment had gone into his guts or had simply cut him open in passing but hoped for the latter. At this time, the mortar barrage had been going on for about four minutes, interspersed with grenades and some recoilless rifle fire. Again I asked my friend to let me take him into the bunker but he was adamant about staying above ground. "I'm pretty sure I'm going to die in a minute," he said in a real tone of apology, "and I would appreciate it if you would let me hold onto your hand and say my prayers."

What can you do? I let him hold my hand. He recited the Lord's Prayer.

As he finished, the mortars let up and Colonel Hughes came in, as mad as a hornet. He had seen our light and wanted to know what the hell I was doing upstairs.

"Oh," he said, looking at the cot, "I'll send some litter bearers back." Shortly, four soldiers with carbines came in on the colonel's orders, to help me move the wounded man. Lacking a stretcher, we carried him on my mattress for the two-block walk to the dispensary.

For some reason, I had stupidly assumed that my boy, who had made his peace with his Maker and was now uncomplainingly enduring the rather bumpy ride we were giving him, was the only casualty in the area. Now, as we made our way among the riddled hooches, we found ourselves part of a regular gory procession with hurt men stumbling out of practically every tent, each leaving his special trail of splatters, so that next morning there were scores of little red trails converging into one big one leading to the medical hut. Most of the wounded were being supported or carried. Few had only one cut and some had dozens. Of the initial five dozen casualties treated, only 18 were walking wounded.

Although the mortars had stopped, the war was still on, with a fire fight at the air strip, where the Viet Cong were going after the parked helicopters and twin-engine Caribou troop carriers. There was the thump of TNT, as some of the attackers managed to get charges under the machines. The dispensary was at the edge of the strip, and when we got there, we could see several aircraft burning.

At no time did I see any sign of panic, even though there was every excuse for panic. An enclosed garrison in a hostile environment had been hit suddenly and hard and there was no way of knowing if we were going to be overrun. But our new army seems to be a bunch of pros. Those who weren't hit had their weapons in hand and were going quickly but calmly about their business, and it is worth noting that later in the morning a number of these were surprised to find blood had run down into their own shoes from punctures they didn't know they had. The first casualty count was seven dead in the battalion and 43 wounded. A later count showed seven killed and 103 hurt.

Inside, the dispensary looked like a Technicolor scene out of *Gone With the Wind*. Badly wounded men were sprawled over every bit of floor and huddled on every piece of furniture. Blood was pooled and splattered everywhere and I kept slipping in it as I made my way through barefooted. Our boy had to give up his mattress because there wasn't room for it. He didn't mind. I believe, at this point, he had begun to believe he was going to make it after all, and this turned out to be right. I told him goodbye, he smiled a trifle wanly, and I headed back for the colonel's hut to get my pants.

I believe this was my worst time in the whole affair, because it suddenly occurred to me that in my state of undress I resembled a montagnard, local Vietnamese hillbilly, who runs around in shirttails and not much else. This could lead to a misunderstanding in the dark with an armed soldier on the alert for infiltrators, so every time I passed one, I made a point of pretending to stumble, then uttering a four-letter word in unmistakable English.

Back at the hut, I got dressed, found my camera and sketchbook, and went out to cover the war like a gentleman correspondent. At 2:35 A.M. the firing had stopped. At 2:45, I heard a loud commotion at the front gate, angry voices, and a shot. I never did learn what the shot was about, but the ruckus was created by my son, Bruce, who had come to save his beloved helicopters and was having trouble getting past the sentries.

Later, I watched him help direct operations as the wounded were evacuated by air and told him he was doing a fair job for a man who couldn't even get to his own war on time. He told me to go to hell.

COMMENTARY

On a first reading, "The Attack" appears to be only a lively account of what happened during the Vietcong mortar attack that Bill Mauldin underwent while visiting his son at Pleiku. In chronological order, one dramatic detail of action and reaction follows the other. It is only when we are about three-fourths through the report that we discover we are being asked to accept a *thesis* based upon these details. We learn that Mauldin's point of view is argumentative rather than explanatory when he reaches the proud judgment: "But our new army seems to be a bunch of pros." To reach this conclusion he has obviously employed *inductive logic.*

Not until Mauldin had witnessed the exemplary behavior of the battalion commander, the wounded young soldier, and all of the others who gave no sign of panic under the severe shelling and possibility of being overrun, did he reach the evaluation he wants his readers to believe and respect: "But our new army seems to be a bunch of pros." He has proceeded from individual points of evidence to a conclusion, and he has adopted the inductive order of development also.

He further persuades us to accept this complimentary view of the army by ending with the incident of his son's effort "to save his beloved helicopters." The final sentence rings not only with paternal pride but also with confidence in the bravery and capability of the American soldier in Vietnam.

By avoiding almost all editorial or value judgments and stressing dramatic incidents leading to his thesis, Mauldin has written a most effective argument. He lets the events speak almost entirely for themselves. This method of reporting and at the same time evaluating a situation is one that you may also find suitable in trying quietly to persuade your readers to accept a conclusion you have reached as a result of some illuminating experience.

WHAT DOES IT SAY?

1. What images does the opening statement suggest: "It was intense and murderous, some 80 rounds in five minutes saturating a bivouac area perhaps two blocks square"?

2. In paragraph 3 is there anything unusual about Mauldin's first reactions and speculations?

3. Why is the term "drumming explosions" appropriate in the description of the mortar firing?

4. What are the implications of the young, wounded soldier's request: " 'I'm pretty sure I'm going to die in a minute,' he said in a real tone of apology, 'and I would appreciate it if you would let me hold onto your hand and say my prayers' "?

5. Explain the effectiveness of the following sentence in contributing to the desired impression of the whole essay: "Blood was pooled and

splattered everywhere and I kept slipping in it as I made my way through barefooted."

6. Is there anything significant concerning the American character in the fact that Mauldin says he pretended to stumble and uttered "a four-letter word in unmistakable English"?

7. What is Mauldin trying to suggest regarding the "ruckus" his son raised at the front gate?

8. Ordinarily, would a father be proud to report—"He told me to go to hell"?

9. What are the characteristics of military "old pros"?

WHAT DO YOU THINK?

1. Presume the following report is accurate, and then describe in Mauldin fashion "the eve" and the actual taking of "a tough college exam."

A new study indicates that today's fighting man, far from flooding himself with such hormones (as adrenalin) in times of stress, actually finds sub-conscious ways to suppress them. . . . In all probability, any of the men studied would have had a higher stress-hormone level back home on the eve of a tough college exam than they showed in Vietnam.—*Time*, April 14, 1967, p. 57.

2. How does the following excerpt from a letter written by Joe Jacobs, a former Stanford University student who was fatally wounded in February 1967, measure up with Mauldin's description of the American soldier in Vietnam?

You said people wanted to know what I think about the war. I think the U.S. had no business getting involved in Vietnam in the first place, when the French pulled out. But we are here now in a position of commitment so great that we could not simply pull out. As for the concensus, I would say that most of the guys here think it's a hot, dirty, stinking war and cannot wait to get home. But they feel that they have a job to do and must do it as well as they can. Does that help any?—*Time*, March 31, 1967, p. 19.

3. After some consultation of library sources, write a brief description in chronological order of the various events that could have led Arthur M. Schlesinger, Jr. to the following *inductive* conclusion: "In retrospect, Vietnam is a triumph of the politics of inadvertance. . . . We have achieved our present entanglement, not after due and de-

liberate considerations, but through a series of small decisions." (*The New York Times Book Review,* April 1967, p. 7.) Also point out whether you agree or not with this conclusion.

4. Here are two other conclusions arrived at inductively from the listing of somewhat the same items of evidence. Choose one of these two, and write the essay supplying the kind of data and reasoning that will best fit it.

   a) General Maxwell Taylor: The United States "can no longer be a one-eyed Cyclops, but must partake of the many-eyed vigilance of Argus—constantly watching in all directions in anticipation of the emergence of forces inimical to our national purpose." (*The New York Times Book Review,* April 1967, p. 28.)

   b) Senator Mark Hatfield (R—Ore.): "We've become world police-men. . . . We are going to fight other people's wars. We are determined to establish little Americas all over the world." (Associated Press, April 4, 1967.)

IT'S HALFWAY
TO 1984

JOHN LUKACS

FOR A long time the term "1984" evoked, to me, the image of a police state of the Eastern European type. But when I think of 1984 now, the image that swims into my mind is that of a gigantic shopping center and industrial complex—something like the one which has been erected a few miles from where I live in eastern Pennsylvania.

The undulating rural landscape around Valley Forge, with its bright dots of houses and its crossroads, has been transformed. There is now the eerie vastness of the General Electric Space Center whose square edifices spread across hundreds of acres. Beyond it stand other flat windowless blocks of buildings—the King of Prussia shopping center, around the trembling edges of which bulldozers roar from morning to night, boring their brutal tracks into the clayey soil which they must churn to mud before it can be covered by concrete. The predominant material is concrete, horizontal and vertical concrete. Twice a day, thousands of people pour into and out of this compound, in a tremendous metallic flow. But no one lives there. At night and on Sundays, these hundreds of acres resemble a deserted airport, with a few automobiles clustering here and there, or slowly cruising on one of the airstrips, occasionally peered at by uniformed guards. Why fly to the moon? Stand on a cold January night in the middle of a parking lot in a large shopping center in the American North. It is a man-made moonscape. This is how the moon will look after our Herculean efforts, after we reach it, colonize it, pour concrete over it.

This is how 1984 looks to me, in the middle sixties, but I know and feel that this view is neither solitary nor unusual. There are millions of Americans who, passing a similar space-age complex of buildings, will say "1984," covering up their resignation with a thin coat of defensive humor. What strikes us is not just the ugliness of the buildings but something else, something that is not so much the reaction of middle-aged earthmen against brave new worlds as it is the expression of a feeling which is, alas, close to the Orwellian nightmare vision: a sense of impersonality together with a sense of powerlessness.

The impersonality is there, in the hugeness of the organization and in the anonymous myriads of the interchangeable human beings who make up most of their personnel. The powerlessness is the feeling which I share with so many of my neighbors—that we cannot stop what in America is called the March of Progress, the cement trucks coming toward us any day from across the hill; the knowledge that our voices, our votes, our appeals, our petitions amount to near-nothing at a time when people have become accustomed to accepting the decisions of planners, experts and faraway powerful agencies. It is a sickening inward feeling that the essence of self-government is becoming more and more meaningless at the very time when the outward and legal forms of democracy are still kept up.

Let us not fool ourselves: Now, halfway to 1984, with all of the recent advances of civil rights, with all of the recent juridical extensions of constitutional freedoms, we *are* facing the erosion of privacy, of property and—yes —even of liberty. This has nothing to do with the Communist Conspiracy or with Ambitious Government Bureaucrats—that is where our New Conservatives go wrong. It has nothing to do with Creeping Socialism. It has very much to do with Booming Technology. The dangers which our modern societies in the West, and particularly the United States, face now, halfway to 1984, are often new kinds of dangers, growing out of newly developing conditions. What ought to concern us is the rootlessness of a modern, technological, impersonal society, with interchangeable jobs and interchangeable people, on all levels of education.

We ought to dwell less on the possibility of unemployment arising out of automation, in a society which, after all, feels obligated to produce full employment; rather, we ought to consider the growing purposelessness of occupations in a society where by now more people are employed in administration than in production. And in such a society we ought to prattle less about the need for more "creative leisure" when the problem is that work becomes less and less creative. We ought to worry not about the insufficient availability of products but about the increasing impermanence of possessions. We ought to think deeply not so much about the growth of the public sectors of the public economy at the expense of private enterprise (which, at any rate, is no longer very "private"), but rather, about the cancerous growth of the public sectors of our existence at the expense of the private autonomy of our personal lives.

We ought to concern ourselves less with the depreciation of money and more with the depreciation of language; with the breakdown of interior, even more than with the state of exterior, communications—or, in other words, with the increasing practices of Orwell's Doubletalk and Doublethink, and with their growing promotion not so much by political tyrannies as by all kinds of techniques, in the name of Progress.

I cannot—and, perhaps, I need not—explain or illustrate these concerns in greater detail. They are, in any event, 1966 concerns about the future, not 1948 ones. Still, while many of the phantoms that haunted Orwell's readers 18 years ago have not materialized, the public currency of the term 1984 has lost none of its poignancy. The tone of our literature, indeed of our entire cultural atmosphere, is far more pessimistic than it was 18 years ago. "Alienation" and "hopelessness" are no longer Central European words; they are very American. This broad, and often near-nihilistic, cultural apathy and despair is relatively new on the American (and also on the British) scene. Its existence suggests that, despite the errors of Orwell's visions, the nightmare quality of "1984" continues to obsess our imagination, and not merely as the sickly titillation of a horror story. It haunts millions who fear that life may become an Orwellian nightmare even without the political tyranny that Orwell had predicted.

"It is by his political writings," Bertrand Russell once wrote, "that Orwell will be remembered." If this is so—and at this moment, halfway to 1984, it still seems so—he will be remembered for the wrong reasons, and one can only hope that the slow corrective tides of public opinion in the long run will redress the balance.

Orwell was not so much concerned with the degeneration of justice as with the degeneration of truth. For Orwell, both in the beginning and in the end was The Word. This is true of "1984," too, which had three levels. On the top level there is the "plot," the love affair of Winston and Julia, which is really flat and inconsequential. On the second level there is the political vision which, as we have seen, sometimes holds up, sometimes not. It is the third level, of what is happening to words and to print, to speech and to truth in 1984, which agitated Orwell the most. Indeed, this spare and economical writer chose to end the novel "1984" by adding an appendix on "The Principles of Newspeak." Orwell was frightened less by the prospects of censorship than by the potential falsification of history, and by the mechanization of speech.

The first of these protracted practices would mean that the only possible basis for a comparison with conditions other than the present would disappear; the second, that the degeneration of traditional language would lead to a new kind of mechanical talk and print which would destroy the meaning of private communications between persons. This prospect haunted Orwell throughout the last 12 years of his life. Some of his best essays dealt with this theme of falsifications of truth—even more than totalitarianism, this was his main concern. As long as people can talk to one another meaningfully, as long as they have private beliefs, as long as people retain some of the qualities of Winston Smith's mother (she had not been an "unusual woman, still less an intelligent one; and yet she had possessed a kind of nobility, a kind of purity, simply because the standards she obeyed were private ones. Her feelings were her own, and could not be altered from the outside . . ."), tyranny was vulnerable; it could not become total.

Orwell was wrong in believing that the development of science was incompatible with totalitarianism (by 1984, "science, in the old sense, has almost ceased to exist. In Newspeak there is no word for science"). As we have seen, he foresaw a decay of technology ("the fields are cultivated by horse-ploughs while books are written by machinery"). This is not what has happened; now, halfway to 1984, the fields are cultivated by bulldozers while books are written by machine-men. But Orwell was right in drawing attention to Doublethink, "the power of holding two contradictory beliefs in one's mind simultaneously, and accepting both of them," and to the desperate prospects of Doubletalk, of the degeneration of standards of language through varieties of super-modern jargon, practiced by political pitchmen as well as by professional intellectuals. There is reason to believe that, were he alive today, Orwell would have modified his views on the nature of the totalitarian menace; and that, at the same time, he would be appalled by many of the present standards and practices in mass communications, literature and publishing, even in the West, and perhaps especially in the United States.

In short, the 1984 that we ought to fear is now, in 1966, different from the 1948 version. Politically speaking, Tocqueville saw further in the eighteen-thirties than Orwell in the nineteen-forties. The despotism which democratic nations had to fear, Tocqueville wrote, would be different from tyranny: "It would be more extensive and more mild; it would degrade men without tormenting them. . . . The same principle of equality which facilitates despotism tempers its rigor." In an eloquent passage Tocqueville described some of the features of such a society: Above the milling crowds "stands an immense and tutelary power, which takes upon itself alone to secure their gratifications and to watch over their fate. That power is absolute, minute, regular, provident and mild. . . ." But when such a government, no matter how provident and mild, becomes omnipotent, "what remains but to spare [people] all the care of thinking and all the trouble of living?"

Orwell's writing is as timely as Tocqueville's not when he is concerned with forms of polity but when he is concerned with evil communication. In this regard the motives of this English Socialist were not at all different from the noble exhortation with which Tocqueville closed one of his chapters in "'Democracy in America": "Let us, then, look forward to the future with that salutary fear which makes men keep watch and ward for freedom, not with that faint and idle terror which depresses and enervates the heart." Present and future readers of "1984" may well keep this distinction in mind.

Newspeak

In George Orwell's "1984," standard English (Oldspeak) has been replaced by Newspeak, "a language designed to diminish the range of thought." Below is a sample "1984" lexicon:

bellyfeel—Blind, enthusiastic acceptance.

blackwhite—Contradiction of plain facts. (Also used to mean a loyal willingness to say that black is white when discipline demands it.)

crimestop—Faculty of stopping short at the threshold of a dangerous thought.

crimethink—Thought-crime.

doublethink—Power of holding two contradictory beliefs simultaneously, and accepting both.

duckspeak—To quack like a duck; implies praise if opinions quacked are orthodox ones.

goodsex—Normal intercourse between man and wife for the sole purpose of begetting children, and without physical pleasure on the part of the woman.

goodthinkful—Orthodox.

joycamp—Forced-labor camp.

Minipax—Ministry of Peace— i.e., Ministry of War.

oldthink—Wickedness and decadence.

prolefeed—Entertainment and news.

COMMENTARY

By means of analogy and analysis, John Lukacs has drawn an effective argument of protest and warning against certain nationwide practices endangering traditional American values. He begins with pointing out parallels between George Orwell's grim novel, *1984,* and some aspects of life in America as he sees it in 1966, "halfway" to Orwell's projected date.

At once we need to raise the question one must always ask of the use of *analogy:* Does the author argue from analogy and maintain that because *A* resembles *B, A* must be *B?* Does Lukacs hold that because there are certain similarities to be found between present conditions and those fictional ones portrayed in *1984,* we are arriving at a period when all of Orwell's prophecies will come true?

No, on the contrary, Lukacs employs the device of analogy most properly; he limits it carefully to its powerful and right purpose of making striking comparisons to illustrate and explain his thesis. He takes great pains to show just which of Orwell's fears and projections have not and cannot become realities; for example, he considers Orwell wrong in thinking that totalitarianism and a growth of science are incompatible, and notes that Orwell's political nightmare is not ours. But Lukacs does regard Orwell as having been a man of insight who first saw what "doublethink" and "doubletalk" would do to harm mass communications. Also, in contrasting Orwell with the earlier critic, Tocqueville, Lukacs seeks to correct any possible tendency the reader may have to identify all of the nightmarish conditions of *1984* with those of the present.

In leading up to his *inductive* generalization and the appeal with which the argument ends, Lukacs presents these details of evidence: the increasing erosions of dignity and liberty; the growing purposelessness of occupations, depreciation of language, and pessimism of literature; the Orwellian warnings regarding degeneration of language and private standards as affecting also the reliability of mass communications; the Tocqueville earlier warnings being still applicable. This body of evidence supports his generalization or *thesis,* which can be stated thus: "Every democracy must fear and oppose some very possible future degradation of the rights of its citizens."

Analogy, as Lukacs employs it, provides another means of interesting and convincing your readers. Only don't try to force relationships of similarity onto situations that really have little in common with one another.

WHAT DOES IT SAY?

1. What is Lukacs trying to suggest by linking together in the second paragraph "Valley Forge," "General Electric Space Center," "King of Prussia shopping center," and the "moon"?

2. Have you had any experiences with the "Orwellian nightmare" of impersonality and powerlessness? Describe them.

3. How can our "modern society" be termed "rootless"?

4. Who or what are "the Communist Conspiracy," "Ambitious Government Bureaucrats," "our New Conservatives," "Creeping Socialism," and "Booming Technology"?

5. How does "creative leisure" differ from "days off" or "free time"?

6. What is meant by "the increasing impermanence of possessions," and why should we "worry" about it?

7. Can you coin some additional "Newspeak" expressions applicable to present social "rules" or "codes" you consider "undemocratic"?

8. What kind of books is Lukacs referring to when he says that now "books are written by machine men"?

WHAT DO YOU THINK?

1. Here are some suggested theses and the analogous items that could possibly be used to support and illustrate them. Choose one and write your essay, having care for the proper use of analogy.
   a) Society makes us all something of a hypocrite. (*Main Street* by Sinclair Lewis)
   b) The Hippies are nothing new. (*Huckleberry Finn* by Mark Twain)
   c) Tragedy strikes when you least expect it. (*The Death of a President* by William Manchester)
   d) It takes great courage to face the unknown. (*The Red Badge of Courage* by Stephen Crane)

2. Do you agree at all with Lukacs that the "March of Progress" is becoming almost overwhelming? Relate the occasions and the conditions that give rise to such feelings.

3. Lukacs maintains that too many of our families suffer from *rootlessness*. Define and exemplify this painful state. John Steinbeck's *The Grapes of Wrath* or a John Dos Passos novel might provide you with some analogies.

4. Have you read any novel dealing with the theme of *alienation* or *hopelessness*? Discuss the book in the light of such a theme.

1. *What does this photograph represent? What are the objects these people are viewing?* 2. *Why have the people come here? What do they expect?* 3. *What will the people do after they leave here? Why?* 4. *How would you feel living in a world dominated by these objects?*

Sky and Telescope photo by Peter A. Leavens

Part 4

ISSUES
IN SCIENCE

Paragraphs
and Their Sentences

It MUST BE obvious by now that whether it is for exposition or argument, paragraphs are developed by details that are carefully selected for their appropriateness and relevance. Paragraphs become little essays in miniature, with a generalization or topic sentence of their own, and fit into the larger pattern of the essay as logical divisions. As self-sufficient units, the paragraphs should have unity and an orderly development or coherence.

Earlier, we discussed the sequence of paragraphs in an essay and commented briefly on the transitional devices that serve to link paragraphs together. Paragraph sequence was also indicated in many of the commentaries accompanying the essays in the three previous sections, and will be taken up in detail in the analysis of L. Jerome Stanton's "The Final Word on Flying Saucers?" appearing in this section. On the whole, however, the aim of Part 4 is to concentrate on the paragraph as a unit by itself, and on the role of the sentences that compose it.

The difficulties usually encountered in trying to write a good paragraph lie in the very nature of writing as opposed to speaking. In college you may find those difficulties especially trying since your instructor naturally demands that you observe the conventions currently recognized for "good" or "standard" prose. Needless to say, no writing is easy. Everyone finds himself at a loss from time to time as he attempts to think through the effective expression of an idea.

As we have suggested before, one of the most effective aids in writing is to formulate a clear and succinct topic sentence. Once you have that down on the page you know in which direction you are headed, what idea you intend to develop in this particular unit of your essay. If you find you have written no such direction-pointing statement, you will want to form one, or at least be clear in your mind about your aim if you are writing inductively. Then you can check each sentence you write to be sure you are not wandering away from the point. When you have jotted down sufficient details to develop your topic generalization adequately, you can go on to your next paragraph in the chain of little units that make up your essay.

All this is not as easy as it sounds. You may have the right topic sentence as well as the most effective details to make it clear and acceptable to your reader, but the ordering of those details and the transitions from sentence to sentence may still pose a problem. Sometimes paragraphs seem almost to write themselves, as ideas flow smoothly. But even so, the relationship of sentence to sentence, which may seem clear to you as you write, may not be so clear to your reader unless you guide him carefully by means of transitional words or phrases which make the relationship instantly obvious. In the first essay in Part 1, the author, Kelman, opened his final paragraph as follows: "These are only random examples. The point is this." The first sentence is an example of *retrospective reference*—calling the reader's attention to what has just been said. The second is *prospective reference*—calling the reader's attention to what is going to be said, something to be noted particularly. Kelman, as we saw, also carefully introduced his illustrations by saying things like "For instance . . ." or "Take this example from Hoover's book."

Indeed, an examination of any of the essays printed in this book will reveal how careful the authors are to take their readers from sentence to sentence. All of the devices used to tie paragraphs together, such as transitional words or sentences, or the repetition of key words, can also be used to smooth the transitions and clarify the relationships between sentences within the paragraph. Transitional words or phrases are particularly helpful in showing the relationship between sentences. Words like *then, also, moreover, in the same category,* indicate to the reader that you are proceeding along the same line of thought. Expressions such as *however, nevertheless, but, still, on the other hand* show that you are taking a divergent path. Try removing helpful transitional devices like these from the essays you have studied and note the resulting loss in clarity.

One important hindrance to coherence in a paragraph is a needless shift in subject from sentence to sentence. We can see, for instance, that when Leo Rosten was writing about Miss O'Neill, he constantly used her as the subject of the sentences in a paragraph, repeating *she,* time after time, as he referred to the various ways in which she was a taskmaster. And when he turned his attention to the students in her class, he was just as careful to keep *we* as the subject of the sentences. In the concluding essay of Part 3, "It's Halfway to 1984," John Lukacs also carefully observed this procedure. Examine especially his sixth paragraph. He is talking about "we" people, and he keeps *we* constantly as the subject of his sentences: "We ought to dwell . . . we ought to consider . . . we ought to prattle less . . . we ought to worry . . . we ought to think deeply. . . ." This kind of repetition of similar syntactical, or grammatical, forms is known as the rhetorical device of *parallelism,* which is another natural and effective way of tying sentences together. You will find that in his fifth paragraph Lukacs again effectively uses parallelism to tie two sentences together: "It has nothing to do with Creeping Socialism. It has very much to do with Booming Technology." The sentences are even kept to much the same length to emphasize the relationship.

THE SENTENCE IN THE PARAGRAPH

Just as the paragraph is a unit of the whole composition, so is the sentence a unit of the paragraph. It is so because our English language forces us to think in terms of sentences. From earliest childhood, we are taught, both in and out of school, to put words into a basic word pattern: subject—verb—complement (S—V—C). We call any such self-sufficient word pattern a *sentence.*

Linguistics scholars think of a sentence as a group of words (meaningful sounds) followed by a distinct pause—a pause longer than any other made within that group of words. If you were to listen to yourself reading aloud this sentence, for example, you would notice that you paused slightly at the commas, but certainly not so long as you did on reaching the period and before beginning the next sentence. This explains why the beginning and end of a sentence are the parts most likely to attract the reader's attention. Of the two, the end position is the more emphatic.

The *periodic sentence,* which holds off stating or completing its main idea until the end, capitalizes upon this end-position emphasis. In the first essay of this section, George Stade phrases three *rhetorical questions*—ones asked without expecting direct replies—in periodic form. Here is one of them: "Who else but a people whose deepest social dream is of a condition in which prodigies of individualism are still teamwork, in which the fiercest acquisitiveness of any individual advances all the members of the group, could see in football the testing of their national aspirations?" Note how we are kept in suspense until we reach the "complement" part of the S—V—C statement.

The *loose sentence,* on the contrary, places the main idea near the beginning, and lets modifying elements string out toward the end. Bentley Glass in "The Ethical Basis of Science" has some very long loose sentences; here is one of the shorter ones: "Ethics is a philosophy of morals, a moral system that defines duty and labels conduct as right or wrong, better or worse." This sentence form is the one on which we most frequently depend, since in it the S—V—C judgment immediately appears. It probably most closely approximates our daily speech habits, wherein we tend to blurt out what we think or feel without much concern for the manner of saying it, as in a common S—V—C statement like "I'll meet you over at the house soon's I get through here."

Do not overlook the strength and economy that the *balanced sentence* can give a paragraph. Whenever you wish to place two similar or contrasting ideas side by side, you can rely upon the close parallelism of the balanced sentence to make your comparison or contrast clear and dramatic. Bentley Glass's essay offers, among others, this example: "High mortality or sterility led to extinction; good viability and fertility enabled a gene or a trait, an individual or a species, to be perpetuated."

The fourth sentence form, the *short, wiry sentence,* differs from all the others in that it is brief and strikingly terse in expression. Loren Eiseley employs this form as an ironic conclusion in one of the paragraphs of "How Natural Is 'Natural'?": "In man, I know now, there is no such thing as wisdom." This one is also periodic, but then, all sentences have to be essentially either periodic or loose.

Taken together, these four rhetorical sentence forms provide the writer with means of varying his statements so that the reader will not tire of any one monotonous S—V—C pattern. Needless to say, you may not find occasion to experiment with all of them until you have finished the first draft of your essay and are revising and rewriting its paragraphs.

In the essays now coming up, you will find more of these same sentence forms at work helping to give their paragraphs grace as well as clarity and tensile strength. In Part 5, which deals with *style,* we shall view once more many of these same matters, but from another viewpoint. Meanwhile try to become proficient in at least the mechanics of good paragraphing so far presented.

GAME
THEORY
GEORGE STADE

1. THERE ARE many ways in which football is unique among sports, and as many others in which it is the fullest expression of what is at the heart of all sports. There is no other major sport so dependent upon raw force, nor any so dependent on a complex and delicate strategy; none so wide in the range of specialized functions demanded from its players; none so dependent upon the undifferentiated athletic *sine qua non*, a quick-witted body; none so primitive; none so futuristic; none so American.

2. Football is first of all a form of play, something one engages in instinctively and only for the sake of performing the activity in question. Among forms of play, football is a game, which means that it is built on communal needs, rather than on private evasions, like mountain climbing. Among games it is a sport; it requires athletic ability, unlike checkers. And among sports, it is one whose mode is violence and whose violence is its special glory.

3. In some sports—basketball, baseball, soccer—violence is occasional (and usually illegal); in others, like hockey, it is incidental; in others still, car racing, for example, it is accidental. Definitive violence football shares alone with boxing and bullfighting, among major sports. But in bullfighting a man is pitted not against another man, but against an animal, and boxing is a competition between individuals, not teams, and that makes a great difference.

4. If shame is the proper and usual penalty for failures in sporting competitions between individuals, guilt is the consequence of failing not only oneself and one's fans, but also one's teammates. Failure in football, moreover, seems more related to a failure of courage, seems more unmanning than in any other sport outside of bullfighting. In other sports one loses a knack, is outsmarted, or is merely inferior in ability, but in football, on top of these, a player fails because he "lacks desire," or "can't take it anymore," or "hears footsteps," as his teammates will put it.

5. These physical and mental risks, the fact that pain and injury are not only commonplace but inevitable, dignify the game, give the playing of it gravity and the watching of it zest. For in sports, as in gambling, and as in most of the activities that we think of as peculiarly masculine, the greater the risk, the more serious the play, the keener the fun. But what the football player risks and the activity in which he risks it are not in the first place symbolic, like the risks and activities of gamblers, captains of industry, and intellectual explorers. These stand to lose or gain money, or power, or communicable truth, and take their risks through verbal and human intermediaries. The football player, on the other hand, risks the violation of his being, and risks it in public. Every forty-five seconds or so he must endure the intimacy of a violent collision with another man; he must pit his skill, courage, and strength, the qualities that define him, against another's, and then consult his flesh and emotions to see whether he has been diminished or increased in the process.

6. Many sports, especially those in which there is a goal to be defended, seem enactments of the games animals play under the stimulus of what ethologists, students of animal behavior, call *territory*—"the drive to gain, maintain, and defend the exclusive right to a piece of property," as Robert Ardrey puts it. The most striking symptom of this drive is aggressiveness, but among social animals, such as primates, it leads to "amity for the social partner, hostility for the territorial neighbor." The territorial instinct is closely related to whatever makes animals establish pecking orders: the tangible sign of one's status within the orders is the size and value of the territory one is able to command. Individuals fight over status, groups over *lebensraum* and a bit more. These instincts, some ethologists have claimed, are behind patriotism and private property; and also, I would add, codes of honor, as among ancient Greeks, modern Sicilians, primitive hunters, teen-age gangs, soldiers, aristocrats, and athletes, especially football players.

7. The territorial basis of certain kinds of sports is closest to the surface in football, whose plays are all attempts to gain and defend property through aggression. Does this not make football *par excellence* the game of instinctual satisfactions, especially for Americans, who are notorious as violent patriots and instinctive defenders of private property? (At the same time, in football this drive is more elaborated than in other sports

by whatever turns instinct into art; football is more richly patterned, more formal, more complex, in the functions of its parts, which makes football *par excellence* the game of esthetic satisfactions.) Even the unusual amity, if that is the word, that exists among football players has been remarked upon, notably by Norman Mailer. And what is it that corresponds in football to the various feathers, furs, fins, gorgeous colors by means of which animals puff themselves into exaggerated gestures of masculine potency? The football player's equipment, of course. His cleats raise him an inch off the ground. Knee and thigh pads thrust the force lines of his legs forward. His pants are tight against his rump and the back of his thighs, portions of his body which the requirements of the game stuff with muscle. Even the tubby guard looks slim of waist by comparison with his shoulders, extended half a foot on each side by padding. Finally the helmet, which from the esthetic point of view most clearly expresses the genius of the sport. Not only does the helmet make the player inches taller and give his head a size proportionate to the rest of him; it makes him anonymous, inscrutable, more serviceable as a symbol. The football player in uniform strikes the eye in a succession of gestalt shifts: first a hooded phantom out of the paleolithic past of the species; then a premonition of a future of spacemen.

8. In sum, and I am almost serious about this, football players are to America what tragic actors were to ancient Athens and gladiators to Rome: models of perennially heroic, aggressive, violent humanity, but adapted to the social realities of the times and places that formed them.

9. For only American money, only the American educational system, only the American life-style could have produced football or created an audience capable of responding to its unique beauty. Who else but a people now grown sedentary on profits from the violence that continues to be their national habit are likely to feel the psycho-social relevance of football with any sort of poignancy? Who else but a people whose deepest social dream is of a condition in which prodigies of individualism are still teamwork, in which the fiercest acquisitiveness of any individual advances all the members of his group, could see in football the testing of their national aspirations? Who but such a people could be absorbed enough in the visible strategies of the game to take in, enjoy, thrive on the instinctual, the sub-social gratifications that inform the social ones? Only Americans could. And that is why, every year from July through January, American men neglect their wives and daydream at their jobs.

10. And so they should; nothing so easily pursued is as good for a man as football. I take it as axiomatic that play is good, whether one participates in it directly or as a spectator. And I take it as self-evident that anything which allows a man to take an unabashed delight in masculine display is for the good. But football is good for us in other ways. Freud noticed that humans have what seems like a species-characteristic way of dealing

with realities too painful—too immense, too chaotic, too revealing—for them to be confronted directly. They return again and again to analogies of the painful situations through forms created by the individual and social imaginations. They confront and master in dreams, rituals, works of art, and games the transpersonal and unconscious forces that are otherwise as much resistant to the hopes of reason as intractable to the instruments of science. Football, in the course of giving pleasure, allows us Americans to domesticate and for the moment to bear those keenly felt but elusive forces that have largely made us what we are without quite being either what we are or what we want to be. Football is at once the expression of what has made us Americans and our human response to what has made us Americans. It is the product of a perfect fusion of our human nature with our national character.

11. So there is no use asking whether football is immoral or brutal or costly. No use asking whether it is a sign of health or disease in our civilization. It is a part of things as here and now they necessarily are. And it is one of the few things of that sort that can make you feel good.

PARAGRAPH OUTLINE

The *paragraph outline* is not a practicable one for planning an essay you intend to write, for it indicates none of the details you will want to include as you go along. It is useful mainly to show that in your reading you have caught the step-by-step sequence of the paragraphs in their development of the essay topic. This outline form merely lists the topic sentence for each paragraph, except those of the introduction and the conclusion. If no topic sentence is stated, a summary sentence, giving the gist of what you consider to be the essence of the paragraph idea, is substituted.

For your own essay planning and writing purposes (especially for rewriting!), you will find most helpful the *sentence outline* form as it is shown in the outline accompanying the first essay in each of the first three sections of this book. The convenient *topic outline,* which uses phrases instead of complete sentences, can also help you in organizing or reorganizing your ideas. Unlike the *paragraph outline,* exemplified below, both the topic and sentence outlines reveal not only the main ideas but also their relationship to their supporting facts and ideas. The outline of "Game Theory" which follows will point out the importance of the topic sentence as a guide in paragraphing.

PARAGRAPH OUTLINE
OF "GAME THEORY"

1. *Generalization* or *thesis:* "There is no other major sport so dependent upon raw force, nor any so dependent on a complex and delicate strategy . . . none so American."

2. "Football is first of all a form of play . . . ." (deductive)
3. "In some sports . . . violence is occasional . . . ." (deductive)
4. "If shame is the proper and usual penalty . . . ." (deductive)
5. "These physical and mental risks . . . dignify the game. . . ." (deductive)
6. "Many sports . . . seem enactments of the game animals play. . . ." (deductive)
7. "The territorial basis of certain kinds of sports . . . ." (deductive)
8. Summary, transition
9. "For only American money . . . could have produced football. . . ." (deductive)
10. "And so they should; nothing so easily pursued . . . ." (deductive)
11. Conclusion

COMMENTARY

After reading "Game Theory" no one can doubt that George Stade believes that football, as played in the United States, is not only the best game in the world, but also the one most characteristic of the American culture. In his two-sentence *introduction* (the first paragraph) he lists the main reasons why he believes as he does, and in the rest of his persuasive essay he gives the details that support his belief.

As the paragraph outline has pointed out, each paragraph has a clear-cut topic sentence with which it begins. Paragraph 2, which opens the *body* of the essay, is devoted to a definition of football as a "form of play," which is then distinguished as a particular kind of play, a "game," and, among games, as a "sport." Finally the definition is narrowed down to a sport that glorifies violence.

At this point, paragraph 3 goes on, distinguishing the violence of football from the violence of other sports, where it is occasional, incidental, or accidental, and introduces the important distinction of violent competition between teams, not individuals: an idea the fourth paragraph develops with the emphasis upon guilt as the consequence of failure.

As each paragraph develops its own topic idea, it also builds Stade's central thesis. The paragraphs as "building blocks" are neatly joined to each other. Paragraph 6, for instance, takes off from 5 by its initial reference to "many sports," and 7 ties in with 6 by its initial reference to the "territorial basis of certain kinds of sports," which was the subject of paragraph 6.

Within the paragraph we see also how careful Stade is to take the reader from sentence to sentence. He uses the repetition of *key words* as a principal device. See the second paragraph, for example. He first calls football a "form of play." The second sentence begins, "Among forms of play," and goes on to indicate that football is a game. The third sentence then begins, "Among games it is a sport," and the final sentence picks up those words by beginning,

"And among sports." This repetition of key words to link sentences as well as paragraphs together is carried out throughout the article. Note the repetition of *failure,* of *drive,* of *territory,* of *instinct,* of *gain,* and of *defend* in succeeding paragraphs. Note also transitional words and phrases like *finally* and *in sum.*

"Never forget your reader" is a writer's axiom that George Stade exemplifies in the care he has taken to develop his paragraphs as miniature essays and to take his reader from sentence to sentence and from paragraph to paragraph. What is more, whether you wholly agree with his thesis or not, you will have to admit his unified, coherent paragraphs are packed with interesting details.

WHAT DOES IT SAY?

1. Name and briefly describe three different acts or movements in football that justify George Stade's contention that "no other major sport" is "so dependent upon raw force."

2. What does he mean in saying of football in the introduction that no other sport is "so dependent upon the undifferentiated athletic *sine qua non,* a quick-witted body"?

3. What are typical outward signs of a player's feelings of "shame" and "guilt"?

4. Is it generally visible how a player "consults his flesh and emotions to see whether he has been diminished or increased in the process" of doing his part in a particular play or "down"?

5. How has the ethologists' term "pecking order" been adopted as being descriptive of some forms of social behavior?

6. Who is Norman Mailer and why is it remarkable that he has called attention to the "unusual amity . . . that exists among football players"?

7. What does Stade mean in saying Americans are "a people now grown sedentary on profits from the violence that continues to be their national habit"?

8. What were "tragic actors" to Athens and "gladiators" to Rome that perhaps football players are to America?

WHAT DO YOU THINK?

1. Write a 500-word essay of not more than four paragraphs, including those of the introduction and the conclusion, expressing your thoughts

and feelings regarding one of the following of George Stade's views as found in the context of his article. Be sure to underline the topic sentence of your main paragraphs. (Do not use the topic as a title, but make up an interesting one of your own.)

a) Football appeals to the primitive in man.
b) Mountain climbing is a sport of "private evasion."
c) Pain and injury dignify the game of football.
d) Football is always a gamble for the players.
e) Americans are "instinctive defenders of private property."
f) All men battle over "status."
g) "Esthetic satisfactions" are great in football.
h) Only America could have produced football.

2. Following the same directions as in assignment 1, choose one of these topics.
a) Why women go to football games (or professional wrestling or boxing matches)
b) My favorite game
c) Implications of television violence
d) Car-driving as a "game"
e) The "game" of being popular
f) The psycho-social aspects of—(supply your own game or sport)

3. Some psychologists and sociologists hold that TV news reports on war violence tend to make the viewers think of battles and "fire fights" as "games" in the sense that American football is herein described as a "sport." In an essay having at least two well-developed paragraphs with topic sentences underlined, analyze and judge this analogy between a typical TV war correspondent's report and a football game.

4. Using examples and other details to support your paragraphs of analysis and judgment, discuss your views on "little league" sports in the light of Stade's article and your own experiences.

THE FINAL WORD
ON FLYING SAUCERS?

L. JEROME STANTON

ARE WE being spied upon and studied by intelligent beings from outer space, as we study the primitive aborigines of central Australia and New Guinea? Is the U.S. Air Force deliberately withholding information about flying saucers, for fear that releasing the truth would trigger a panic? Why do we still know so little about the true nature of unidentified flying objects? In this time when science says other intelligent life almost surely exists elsewhere in our galaxy, these questions are being asked by a great many people who formerly would have laughed off such thoughts as pure fantasy.

Almost 20 years ago a news story about "flying saucers" flashed over the press wires, startling our nation and much of the civilized world. From that moment, a world-wide interest in unidentified flying objects has stubbornly stayed alive, despite efforts of authorities and others to refute and debunk them.

Fortunately one new factor has entered the picture that bids fair to resolve some of our doubts and puzzlement. On October 7, 1966, a contract was awarded to the University of Colorado to conduct a scientific investigation of UFO sightings and report findings to the U.S. Air Force, with recommendations for future operation of the Air Force's own Project Blue Book UFO inquiry. The Colorado report will then be reviewed by the National Academy of Sciences. Funded at somewhat more than $300,000, the study will analyze UFO reports, and actually assign scientists to the field to study UFOs at first hand, if that proves feasible. Guaranteed a completely free hand by the Air Force, the inquiry should do much to quiet the louder critics of Project Blue Book, and also to allay any public doubts and fears. It is, in fact, the first really scientific attack on the UFO enigma yet set in motion in the United States.

The critical problem of national security makes an all-out scientific attack on the UFO puzzle seem long overdue. But since the first reports of modern times, the subject has been beset by unstable notoriety-seekers, hoaxers and plain crack-pots, so that most serious scientists have shied away from the problem. The nearest approach to a scientific investigation, the 20-year USAF study called Project Blue Book, has been extremely limited. Indeed, with a staff limited most of the time to one commissioned officer, one noncom and two clerks, it's amazing that Project Blue Book could do any job effectively.

The first modern sighting of a UFO occurred June 24th, 1947, near Mt. Rainier in Washington. A veteran private pilot named Kenneth Arnold, while flying his own light aircraft, saw nine large, silvery objects shaped like inverted plates or saucers, flying in a reversed-echelon formation. Arnold had described the objects as moving "like a saucer skipped across a pond," and from this a reporter devised the name "flying saucer."

In the two decades since that episode, literally thousands of UFO sightings have been reported from all parts of the world.

In January, 1950, Major Donald E. Keyhoe, a retired Marine Corps officer, authored an article for *True* magazine, in which he insisted that flying saucers were real, physical objects, and that they came from some place not on our own planet Earth. The article touched off a sensation. But solid evidence such as good, close-up photographs or motion pictures (or debris of a crashed saucer!) proved impossible to get, and conclusions had to be based solely on the accounts of eye-witnesses.

The Air Force began the first official investigation of the more impressive reports a few weeks after the Arnold sighting, but the effort was reduced to practically nothing early in 1950. Then in 1951 a renewed surge of nationwide interest and publicity compelled a widening of the inquiry.

By 1952, reports reached a dizzying peak. But time passed and public interest dwindled. In the following eight years UFOs continued to be reported over the U.S. and many other parts of the world. Press and radio now gave more attention to "contactee" accounts than to soberly factual episodes. Project Blue Book plodded on, although proposals to put a team of scientists in the field with instruments for direct observation of a UFO were never actually put into effect. So matters stood until 1965, when a book *Anatomy of a Phenomenon*, by Jacques Vallee, a French scientist living in the U.S., was published.

Soberly scientific in tone, it gave an unusually complete and authoritative summary of the entire history of the flying saucer-UFO phenomenon. It also opened the eyes of many people to the fact that sightings were world-wide.

Then in the early hours of August 2, 1965, authorities in adjacent parts of Texas, New Mexico, Oklahoma and Kansas were flooded with calls reporting UFOs, many of the reports coming from police officers in highway patrol cars. One group of objects was seen for about 30 minutes flying in a diamond formation over the area around Shawnee, Okla. They were lights of indefinite shape, that changed color randomly from orange-red to white to blue-green and back again. Radar at Tinker and Carswell Air Force Bases in the area tracked four objects that coincided with objects seen by eye-witnesses, according to a statement issued by the Oklahoma Highway Patrol. The radar tracking was later denied by the Air Force, but the denial was contradicted by a nine-page report from the Oklahoma Department of Public Safety. The confusion was only increased when the Project Blue Book officer later reported solemnly that the stars Rigel, Capella and Aldebaran, and the planet Jupiter, seen under peculiar local weather conditions, had been the cause.

The celebrated incident at Exeter, N.H., occurred during the early morning hours of September 3, 1965. Norman Muscarello, an 18-year-old Exeter resident, was badly frightened by a large object that swooped silently over the highway. He informed the local police and was driven back to the spot by Officer Bertrand. The object returned and was seen at close range and low level by both Muscarello and Bertrand, and by Officer David Hunt, in another patrol car. The object was circular, about 100 feet in diameter, and in addition to the over-all orange-red glow, showed a pattern of smaller, brighter lights that waxed and waned in regular rhythm.

The Exeter incident brought to light the case of the Halls. While undergoing treatment for a period of amnesia, Mr. and Mrs. Hall told their psychoanalyst a strange story of having been captured and interrogated by beings in a weird flying vehicle some two years before.

During 1966, in addition to many other reports from more remote parts of the world, a persistent series of peculiar lights was seen over Wanaque reservoir in Northern New Jersey. Similar lights were reported near Hillsdale, Mich., by many residents of the area, who loudly contradicted semi-official statements that marsh gas was responsible. Still more odd-shaped glowing lights were seen and photographed over Long Island. This time the official explanation put the blame on the star Sirius.

In January, 1967, two youngsters, Daniel and Grant Jaroslaw, in Harrison Township, northeast of Detroit, snapped photos of something that looked like a big hamburger and was the size of a helicopter. The photos were sent to Dr. J. Allen Hynek, chairman of the Astronomy Department at Northwestern University, who has investigated reported sightings for the Air Force. His comment at the time was that the photos did not "indicate an obvious hoax," but that they required analysis. Undoubtedly, the photos will also be shown to the University of Colorado group.

As matters now stand, there is anything but agreement, either within the body of the general public, or among various groups of UFO buffs. At one extreme of the organized UFO groups are the clubs and individuals who swear they have had actual contact with intelligent beings who come in flying saucers.

At the other end of the gamut of UFO groups is NICAP, the National Investigations Committee on Aerial Phenomena, of Washington, D.C., with Major Keyhoe as Director, and Richard Hall as Assistant Director. With a membership of about 11,000 claimed, NICAP is the largest organization and has a hefty percentage of scientific, technical, military and law-enforcement personnel.

Somewhere in the middle is the Saucer and Unexplained Celestial Events Research Society, of Ft. Lee, N.J., and New York City. SAUCERS was founded in 1954, claims about 7,000 members and holds a broader view of UFO phenomena than does NICAP.

At present, NICAP scorns the contactees and their claims and believes that UFOs are real physical objects and that they are under the control of intelligent beings. NICAP has had a long-term disagreement with the Air Force Project Blue Book method of investigation, but is now cooperating with the University of Colorado inquiry.

The SAUCERS organization believes that there is overwhelming evidence that so-called flying saucers are probably of extraterrestrial origin and most likely come from the planet Mars.

Beliefs of the farther-out saucer fans are more diffuse, but all agree that they are real. Many consider that UFOs come from planets of other suns than ours, and are operated by beings more advanced than we. Many insist that the Visitors mean only Infinite Good, have visited earth many times in the past, and are the cause of many of our religious beliefs in gods, miracles and legends.

Is it possible to choose between these differing views? For many the answer apparently is "No!", and it will probably remain so until a saucer crashes in Central Park, or the University of Colorado presents its report. Unfortunately, UFOs seem to be far more reliable than earthly aircraft, for no authenticated debris of a crashed saucer has come to light.

Nevertheless, if you answer the door some night and find yourself confronted by a small, greenish individual who politely asks for the loan of a cup of uranium, don't slam the door; it may be the Martian ambassador— victim of the interplanetary equivalent of an empty gas tank.

COMMENTARY

A report such as this 1800-word one, consisting of 23 fact-filled paragraphs, attracts the kind of casual reader for whom L. Jerome Stanton was writing. In length, these journalistic-style paragraphs are generally very short (they average eighty words). Many of these sets of sentences which are indented as paragraphs do not deal with a new subtopic, as we expect a paragraph should do. Instead they merely continue the same topic sentence idea found in the previous indentation. This manner of breaking up a subtopic paragraph development may be a mass media concession to what is called "the twelve-year-old-mind" of the general reading public.

Before looking into the *paragraph sequence* of this article, let us examine in a little more detail this business of paragraph length. How long should a paragraph be? How many words should a *good* paragraph have? (We must italicize *good* for the reason that we all assume there are definite standards still governing the written language on its more formal levels.) Usually the length of any paragraph depends upon two things: (1) the scope or complexity of the judgment or generalization to be found either stated in the topic sentence or implied by the sentence context; (2) the number and kinds of details needed to make that paragraph idea adequately clear, or to satisfy the reader's expectations aroused by the claims or promises made by the topic sentence idea.

Since you are supposed to be writing for far more mature and intellectually demanding readers than was Stanton, you will not write down to them by chopping up what should be a single paragraph into easily devoured tidbits. You will try to give a paragraph as many sentences of details as its topic requires. If it takes 200 or more words of concise information and analysis, you will try to arrange the sentences to say what each must say in the best order you can find for them. If, on the other hand, you can complete the paragraph topic in 100 words or less, well and good. Leave it and go on to the next.

Now we can run through the *paragraph sequence* of "The Final Word on Flying Saucers?" to see how despite the multiplicity of short paragraphs, Stanton has arranged them in a good order. He opens the article with three *rhetorical questions* which indicate the wide interest that "flying saucers" continue to arouse. The sketchy second paragraph on the beginning of the UFO problem leads to the basic *generalization* of the article in the third paragraph: "Fortunately one new factor has entered the picture that bids fair to resolve some of our doubts and puzzlement." This is also the topic sentence of this detail-filled, six-sentence paragraph, which runs twice the length of the average one. There follows a brief summary of the inadequacy of the investigations prior to the contract award to the University of Colorado.

As may be expected, the rest of the article tells in *chronological sequence* the history of UFO sightings and the reactions to them, beginning with the first one in 1947, and continuing up to 1967, as described in the next ten paragraphs. Then another group of seven very brief paragraphs introduces the various schools of thought on UFO sightings. The concluding paragraph ends with a humorous possibility.

All in all, after an introduction that states the repercussions to UFO reports and the announcement of the Colorado project, Stanton outlines according to their time sequence the significant UFO news stories and the schools of thought arising concerning them. This historic survey reinforces the importance of the task assigned to the University of Colorado research staff. Despite its chopped up paragraphs, the article displays, on the whole, a well-unified sequence, and shows how historic summary can be made very interesting by focusing that history upon some decisive new development. But there must always be a worthy "new development" to justify such a historic survey.

WHAT DOES IT SAY?

1. Which of our human abilities would you consider that "beings from outer space" must possess to merit being called "intelligent"?

2. What objectionable traits do these three have in common: "unstable notoriety-seekers, hoaxers, and plain crack-pots"?

3. If you were sceptical about the existence of "flying saucers," would you *debunk* them or *refute* them? What is the difference?

4. What kind of "solid evidence" would be necessary to prove conclusively to you the real existence of "flying saucers" as being extraplanetary space ships?

5. If some people whom you knew personally would "swear they have had actual contact with intelligent beings who come in flying saucers," how would you react to such informants?

6. What is a *buff*? Which are the three types of "UFO buffs"?

7. Why in the third from the last paragraph does Stanton use the expression "farther-out saucer fans" instead of "further-out saucer fans"? Is he correct in choosing "farther" instead of "further"?

8. Why is a Martian described as "a small, greenish individual"?

WHAT DO YOU THINK?

1. Summarized below are two more sets of reactions to UFO: the first taken from an American source and the second from an Associated Press report with the Moscow dateline, April 24, 1967. Study them in the light of Stanton's article, and then write an essay stating and explaining your agreement with one or the other of these viewpoints. Should you disagree with all of them, explain in detail—also in an appropriate paragraph sequence—just why you do so.

    A. 1. "They are nonsense, the result of hoaxes or hallucinations."

        2. "They are some kind of military weapon being tested in secret. . . . Why should any country test them in scores of nations?

        3. "They come from outer space. . . . It would be foolish to rule out the possibility."

        4. "We are dealing with some natural phenomenon we cannot even conceive of as yet."—Dr. J. Allen Hynek, "Flying Saucers —Are They Real?" *The Reader's Digest,* March 1967, pp. 64–65.

    B. 1. All such reports are either "nonsense or inventions."

        2. They are "optical illusions related to the distribution of light in the earth's atmosphere, such as a rainbow."

        3. They are "a new secret flying apparatus of one of the military powers on earth. 'No one holds this view now'."

        4. They are "an unknown phenomena of nature, just as radio-activity was unknown until the end of the last century. In this context, ionized particles and charged particles of dust in the atmosphere" may be the answer.

        5. They may be "spaceships from an advanced civilization on another planet. . . . The speed of UFOs supports this theory."

2. The eminent atomic physicist, Dr. Edward U. Condon of the University of Colorado, who is in charge of the Colorado investigation of UFOs, is quoted as having made the following announcement: "I won't believe in outer-space saucers until I see one, touch one, get inside one, haul it into a laboratory and get some competent people to

go over it with me."—Warren Rodger, "Flying Saucers?" *Look,* March 21, 1967, p. 78.

Write your projection of what you think would be the reactions of the three schools of UFO thought if the outcome of Dr. Condon's investigations should be one of the following:

a) Dr. Condon fails to see, touch, or haul a "saucer" into a laboratory.

b) Dr. Condon does make the discovery of the century and does bring in an outer-space "saucer."

c) Dr. Condon finally is able to disprove the existence of all such "saucers."

3. Some psychologists hold that popular belief in the "flying saucer myth" is a kind of substitute for the religious faiths lost in recent years. What do you think of this hypothesis? Discuss in an orderly sequence of paragraphs the reasons why you find it reasonable or unreasonable. (Perhaps you will have to decide first on how you would answer this question: "Do I really want the UFOs to turn out to be outer-space saucers?")

THE ETHICAL BASIS
OF SCIENCE

BENTLEY GLASS

IT HAS been said that science has no ethical basis, that it is no more than a cold, impersonal way of arriving at the objective truth about natural phenomena. This view I wish to challenge, since it is my belief that by examining critically the nature, origins, and methods of science we may logically arrive at a conclusion that science is ineluctably involved in questions of values, is inescapably committed to standards of right and wrong, and unavoidably moves in the large toward social aims.

Human values have themselves evolved. Man arose after some two billions of years of organic evolution, during which species after species originated, flourished, and fell, or occasionally became the progenitors of species that were new and better adapted, on the basis of the evolutionary scheme of values. Fitness, like it or not, in the long run meant simply the contribution of each trait and its underlying genes to survival. High mortality or sterility led to extinction; good viability and fertility enabled a gene or a trait, an individual or a species, to be perpetuated. Man's own values grew out of his evolutionary origins and his struggle against a hostile environment for survival. His loss of certain unnecessary structures, such as bodily hair once clothing was invented; the homeostatic regulation of his body temperature and blood pressure, breathing, and predominant direction of blood flow; his embryonic and fetal growth inside the mother and his prolonged dependence

Reprinted from *Science,* vol. 50, December 1965, pp. 1254–1255, by permission of University of North Carolina Press. This article is part of Mr. Glass's *Science and Ethical Values.*

upon maternal lactation; the slow maturation that enabled his brain to enlarge so greatly; the keen vision so necessary to the hunter using his weapons—all of these and many other important human characteristics that contributed to the social nature of man and cemented the bonds of family and tribe arose adventitiously, were improved step by step, and endured because they promoted human survival. Our highest ethical values—the love of the mother for her child and of the man for his mate, the willingness to sacrifice one's own life for the safety of the family or tribe, and the impulse to care for the weak, the suffering, the helpless—all of these too had the same primitive beginnings.

But these ethical values are always, in the evolutionary scheme of things, relative, and never absolute. Whenever the environment becomes changed, the adaptiveness of existing traits becomes maladjusted, and the forces of natural selection lead to a realignment of the genotype, an alteration of the external features and modes of behavior, a modification of the species. What was once good is so no longer. Something else, in terms of reproductive fitness, has become better.

Finally, a crude, embryonic form of science entered the scheme of things, a method of observing and reporting accurately to other persons the movements of the stars, the planets, and the sun and moon, the behavior and migrations of the food animals, the usefulness of certain seeds for food and of certain stems for fibers, the poisonous properties of others. For generations all such practical lore was transmitted only by word of mouth, but the day came when useful knowledge could be written down and preserved inviolate from the forgetfulness and the twists of memory. These were the first simple steps in the development of science: observation, reporting, written records, communication. To such must be added the processes of human reasoning, at first mostly by analogy, so often wrong; then by improved analysis, by deduction from an established truth, or by induction of an established truth from a multitude of observations.

Seen aright, science is more than the instrument of man's increasing power and progress. It is also an instrument, the finest yet developed in the evolution of any species, for the malleable adaptation of man to his environment and the adjustment of his environment to man. If the human species is to remain successful, this instrument must be used more and more to control the nature and the rate of social and technological change, as well as to promote it. In this sense, at least, science is far more than a new sense organ for comprehending the real relations of natural phenomena and the regularities we call "laws of nature." It is also man's means of adjustment to nature, man's instrument for the creation of an ideal environment. Since it is preeminently an achievement of social man, its primary function is not simply that of appeasing the individual scientist's curiosity about his environment—on the contrary it is that of adjusting man to man, and of adjusting social groups in their entirety to nature, to both the restrictions and the resources of the human environment.

Ethics is a philosophy of morals, a moral system that defines duty and labels conduct as right or wrong, better or worse. The evolutionist is quite prepared to admit the existence of right and wrong in terms of the simple functions of biological structures and processes. The eye is for seeing, an evolutionary adaptation that enables an animal to perceive objects at a distance by means of reflected light rays. Sight conveys information about food, water, danger, companionship, mating, the whereabouts and doings of the young ones, and other vitally important matters. Should one not then say, "To see is right; not to see is wrong"? Similarly, the mind reasons as it does because in the countless ages of evolutionary development its characteristic mental processes led to successful coping with the exigencies of life. Humans whose mental processes, because of different genes, too often led them to wildly erroneous conclusions did not so often leave children to reason in similar ways. It is thus right to be guided by reason, wrong to distrust it. Does it not follow, finally, from consideration of the social role and function of science, that it is *right* to utilize science to develop and regulate human social life, adjustment to change, and rate of social transformation? Conversely, it is *wrong*—morally and ethically wrong—not to do so. We must use whatever light and whatever reason we have to chart our course into the unknown.

Those who distrust science as a guide to conduct, whether individual or social, seem to overlook its pragmatic nature, or perhaps they scorn it for that very reason. Rightly understood, science can point out to us only probabilities of varying degrees of certainty. So, of course, do our eyes and ears, and so does our reason. What science can do for us that otherwise we may be too blind or self-willed to recognize is to help us to see that what is right enough for the individual may be wrong for him as a member of a social group, such as a family; that what is right for the family may be wrong for the nation; and that what is right for the nation may be wrong for the great brotherhood of man. Nor should one stop at that point. Man as a species is a member—only one of many members—of a terrestrial community and an even greater totality of life upon earth. Ultimately, what is right for man is what is right for the entire community of life on earth. If he wrecks that community, he destroys his own livelihood. In this sense, coexistence is not only necessary but also right, and science can reveal to us the best ways to harbor our resources and to exploit our opportunities wisely.

COMMENTARY

To express fresh thinking in standard sentence forms and paragraphs is as natural as to put new wine in old bottles, as European vintners still do. In asking recognition for the close relationship he has discovered existing between science and ethical values, Dr. Bentley Glass chose just such traditional sentence forms for his new ideas. Perhaps we can learn something from his practices that will help us make our sentences more effective.

As Glass shows us, one of the best ways to say a great deal in a few words is to adopt the principle of *parallelism,* which means giving similar ideas similar constructions. It is often parallelism that gives *loose, periodic,* and *balanced* sentence forms their economy of words and force. Here are five sentences selected from "The Ethical Basis of Science" exemplifying five different uses of parallelism in these sentence types. An analysis of each sentence follows the quoted sentence, which has the parallel elements numbered or lettered.

1. "Sight conveys information about food, water, danger, companionship, mating, the whereabouts and doings of the young ones, and other vitally important matters."

This is a *simple sentence* (having only one independent clause—one S—V—C) and also rhetorically a *loose* sentence. Its eight parallel elements are all tied to the preposition *about.* In drawing up any list or giving items of a series, make every part grammatically alike; if the first one is a noun, as in this example, then all the others should be nouns or substantives.

2. "Our highest ethical values—[the love of the mother for her child and of man for his mate,] [the willingness to sacrifice one's own life for the safety of the family or tribe,] and [the impulse to care for the weak, the suffering, the helpless]—all of these too had the same primitive beginnings."

Long and involved as this sentence appears to be, it is still a *simple* one but *periodic* because of holding off its main idea to the end. Each of the three parallel elements contains also other parallel units. Again we have a list, this time of noun phrases; they are in apposition to "ethical values."

3. "It has been said [that science has no ethical basis], [that it is no more than a cold, impersonal way of arriving at the objective truth about natural phenomena]."

Here the two parallel units are noun clauses in a *complex* sentence (having one independent clause and one or more dependent clauses). How many words would it have taken you to say as much as these twenty-nine words do?

4. "If [he wrecks that community], [he destroys his own livelihood]."

Another *periodic* sentence and a strong one because of the exact matching of S—V—C elements in the two clauses: *he wrecks community, he destroys livelihood* despite the subordinating *if.*

5. "Ultimately, [what is right for man] is [what is right for the entire
community of life on earth]."

Note how the two halves of this *balanced* sentence equate and complete
one another: S—V—C = S—V—C.

If you turn to examining the paragraphs in which these sentences are
developing units, you will find that each also contributes important details
to the subtopic idea governing its paragraph. Should you experiment with
parallelism and these sentence forms, do so in the process of rewriting and
revising. Otherwise, you may become so involved with your experiments that
you may get lost in what you are trying to say effectively through such devices.

WHAT DOES IT SAY?

1. What particular places and things do you think of on reading that
   science is "a cold, impersonal way of arriving at objective truth"?

2. What are "values" and what do they have to do with "standards of
   right and wrong"?

3. Glass maintains that all of the characteristics that make man a social
   and family animal "arose adventitiously." What in this context does
   adventitiously mean?

4. Science, Glass says, has a "pragmatic nature." What does he mean?

5. How does Glass define *deduction* and *induction* as forms of reasoning?

6. What "social and technological changes" can you think of that Glass
   argues are needed and that only science can bring about?

7. Glass concludes by defining in general terms what is in the light of
   science ethically *right* and what is *wrong*. What do the words apply
   to as he uses them here?

8. What is "the unknown" that Glass says "We must use whatever light
   and whatever reason we have to chart our course into"?

WHAT DO YOU THINK?

1. Write one well-developed paragraph to experiment with parallelism
   and rhetorical sentence forms on a topic derived from your agreement
   or disagreement with one of the following statements:

a) "Our highest ethical values . . . had the same primitive beginnings" as did our bodies.—Bentley Glass

b) "A finer instrument [than science] for the malleable adaptation of man to his environment is love."—R. W. Kraft

c) Conscience is "man's instrument for the creation of an ideal environment."—Bentley Glass

2. We cannot always know enough about subjects we need to form opinions on. Choose one of the following general topics, and explain why you would like to know more about it and why more knowledge of it might help solve an especially critical problem that you have often wondered about.

Anthropology	Humanities
Archeology	Meteorology
Astronomy	Oceanography
Biology	Physics
Chemistry	Psychology
Ethics	Sociology

3. Formulate a thesis in reply to one of the following propositions, and write a persuasive essay supporting that thesis:

a) Has science changed for the better mankind's views and behavior concerning crime and violence?

b) Is science hostile to religion?

c) Is science being too much occupied with war weaponry?

THE FIRMAMENT
OF TIME

LOREN EISELEY

MANY YEARS AGO I was once, by accident, locked in a museum with which I had some association. In the evening twilight I found myself in a lengthy hall containing nothing but Crustacea of all varieties. I used to think they were a rather limited order of life, but as I walked about impatiently in my search for a guard, the sight began to impress, not to say overawe, me.

The last light of sunset, coming through a window, gilded with red a huge Japanese crab on a pedestal at one end of the room. It was one of the stilt-walkers of the nightmare deeps, with a body the size of a human head carried tiptoe on three-foot legs like fire tongs. In the cases beside him there were crabs built and riveted like Sherman tanks, and there were crabs whose claws had been flattened into plates that clapped over their faces and left them shut up inside with little secrets. There were crabs covered with chitinous thorns that would have made them indigestible; there were crabs drawn out and thin, with delicate elongated pinchers like the tools men use to manipulate at a distance in dangerous atomic furnaces.

There were crabs that planted sea growths on their backs and marched about like restless gardens. There were crabs as ragged as waterweed or as smooth as beach pebbles; there were crabs that climbed trees and crabs from beneath the polar ice. But the sea change was on them all. They were one, one great plan that flamed there on its pedestal in the sinister evening light, but they were also many and the touch of Maya, of illusion, lay upon them.

I was shivering a little by the time the guard came to me. Around us in the museum cases was an old pattern, out of the remote sea depths. It was alien to man. I would never underestimate it again. It is not the individual that matters; it is the Plan and the incredible potentialities within it. The forms within the Form are endless and their emergence into time is endless. I leaned there, gazing at that monster from whom the forms seemed flowing, like the last vertebrate on a world whose sun was dying. It was plain that they wanted the planet and meant to have it. One could feel the massed threat of them in this hall.

"It looks alive, Doctor," said the guard at my elbow.

"Davis," I said with relief, "you're a vertebrate. I never appreciated it before, but I do now. You're a vertebrate, and whatever else you are or will be, you'll never be like that thing in there. Never in ten million years. I believe I'm right in congratulating you. Just remember that we're both vertebrates and we've got to stick together. Keep an eye on them now—all of them. I'll spell you in the morning."

Davis did something then that restored my confidence in man. He laughed, and touched my shoulder lightly. I have never heard a crab laugh and I never expect to hear one. It is not in the pattern of the arthropods.

Yet those crabs taught me a lesson really. They reminded me that an order of life is like a diamond of many reflecting surfaces, each with its own pinpoint of light contributing to the total effect. It is a troubling thought, contend some, to be a man and a God-created creature, and at the same time to see animals which mimic our faces in the forest. It is not a good thing to take the center of the stage and to feel at one's back the amused little eyes from the bush. It is not a good thing, someone maintained to me only recently, that animals should stand so close to man.

It depends, I suppose, on the point of view.

On my office wall is a beautiful photograph of a slow loris with round, enormous eyes set in the spectral face of a night-haunter. From a great bundle of fur a small hand protrudes to clasp a branch. Only a specialist would see in that body the far-off simulacrum of our own. Sometimes when I am very tired I can think myself into the picture until I am wrapped securely in a warm coat with a fine black stripe down my spine. And my hands would still grasp a stick as they do today.

At such times a great peace settles on me, and with the office door closed, I can sleep as lemurs sleep tonight, huddled high in the great trees of two continents. Let the storms blow through the streets of cities; the root is safe, the many-faced animal of which we are one flashing and evanescent facet will not pass with us. When the last seared hand has flung the last grenade, an older version of that hand will be stroking a clinging youngster hidden in its fur, high up under some autumn moon. I will think of beginning again, I say to myself then, sleepily. I will think of beginning again, in a different way. . . .

COMMENTARY

Since Loren Eiseley is not only a scientist but also a poetic thinker, we can hope to find the narration of an unusual experience almost anywhere in his work written for the general public. Like William Wordsworth, the famous English poet who defined poetry as "the recollection of emotion in tranquility," Eiseley recalls the strange feelings and thoughts he has had in memorable moments when his senses were keenly awake and led him to some illuminating discovery concerning the world of everyday reality that surrounds us all. He begins this essay with such a narrative, and it leads us to share his great moments of insight.

He begins quietly by telling us of the mischance whereby he found himself locked within a museum full of zoological specimens. What he saw and thought as he looked at the extensive display of Crustacea under the red light of sunset makes up most of the essay; the second incident concerning the photograph of "a slow loris" in his office supplements and somehow completes the thesis or basic generalization: "The many-faced animal of which we are one flashing and evanescent facet will not pass with us." These "stories" have somewhat the same effect on us as does John Updike's "Eclipse," which opens our following section, Part 5.

Eiseley's paragraphs gain much of their effective *emphasis* from the *sentence patterns* he weaves within them. For example, beginning in the second paragraph and continuing into the third, he has seven consecutive clauses opening with "there were crabs." His repetition of "there were crabs" is followed each time by vivid descriptive details which build the impression of an awesome determination that he senses in this seemingly endless variety of adaptations made by these Crustacea to their many environments. The final two sentences of the essay also evoke this charmlike mood through a similar repetition of sentence elements: "I will think of beginning again, I say to myself then, sleepily. I will think of beginning again, in a different way. . . ." But that last prepositional phrase, "in a different way," shocks us out of any drowsiness we may have been lulled into, for it implies that next time the evolutionary process would, if Eiseley had any control over it, not end with man as a creature of war and violence.

In the fourth paragraph, the succession of very *short, dramatic* sentences hits the reader hard: "It was alien to man. I would never underestimate it again. It is not the individual that matters. . . ." And at the very end of this inductive paragraph stands this dramatic topic sentence: "One could feel the massed threat of them in this hall."

Parallelism through repetition of similar sentence forms appears again to create something of a hypnotic effect also in the third paragraph from the end. We find a sequence of three "It is" and "It is not" sentences, wherein the pronoun *it* is used as an expletive, or introductory word, to make the sentence *periodic*.

Eiseley's essay is also an excellent illustration of how a skilled writer ties his sentences together. All of the devices that a writer has at hand to take his reader smoothly along from sentence to sentence are in evidence.

He begins in a very informal, personal fashion, writing: "Many years ago I was once, by accident, locked in a museum. . . ." During the rest of the paragraph he is careful to keep *I* the subject of his successive statements: "*I* found myself. . . . *I* used to think. . . . *I* walked about. . . ." Then, as we have already noted, he ties his sentences in the second and the third paragraphs together by the repetition of the key word *crab* and a series of parallel statements. In all, there are seven successive statements beginning "there were crabs." After listing these various crabs in this carefully maintained parallelism, he introduces a divergent idea with the transitional conjunction *but*: "But the sea change was on them all."

WHAT DOES IT SAY?

1. Why does the word *crabs* have more connotations for most of us than does the term *Crustacea*?

2. What is the meaning of *order* in the phrase "a limited order of life" as applied to Crustacea?

3. Eiseley's language is rich in imaginative comparisons known as *similes* —comparisons beginning with words such as *like, as if, as,* and *as though.* Find four of his similes and comment on their appropriateness.

4. "But sea change was on them all"—what scientific fact is Eiseley poetically expressing herein?

5. What does he mean by "the Plan"? Why the capitalization?

6. Who or what is "Maya"? This kind of reference to a myth is called "an allusion." What does this one contribute to the description?

7. Why is the statement "The forms within the Form are endless" awe-inspiring?

8. And what is Eiseley trying to say in this expression: "the many-faced animal of which we are one flashing and evanescent facet"?

WHAT DO YOU THINK?

1. Write a brief account of an experience that you have had which impressed you with some revealing fact about nature. Suggested topics: What I learned during:

A walk	A swim
A hike	A plane flight
A camp-out	An automobile ride
A field trip	A job in the country

2. Relate a significant experience and the feelings and thoughts it suggested while you were taking care of a pet.

3. To test your own powers of observation and imagination, explore one of the following places, meanwhile taking notes on what your ears, eyes, and other senses detect as having some special meaning for you. Then write a unified, coherent report on one aspect of your experience. You might visit one of the following places:

Zoo	Back alley
Museum	Country meadow
City park	Strip of ocean beach
Vacant lot	City riverbank

4. Develop a thesis in reply to the following question: "Is man by nature a warlike animal given to violence?"

1. *What possibly are these two young people discussing?* 2. *Do they belong to this world of hazy outlines pictured in the paintings behind them?*

Photograph by Edmund Y. Lee

Part 5

ISSUES
IN LITERATURE
AND ART

Style

ANYONE WHO writes well must constantly make choices. From moment to moment he has to decide which word or phrase best expresses what he has to say, which detail most adequately will make his topic generalization clear and interesting to his readers. Indeed, all the many elements of composition that we have discussed so far become matters of deliberate choice and must constantly be kept in mind.

The more practiced and the better informed in these matters a writer becomes, the less difficulty he generally has in making such decisions. Gradually, in fact, he can rely upon his good working habits to make many of these decisions for him, almost without his thinking about them. When a writer has arrived at this stage of development he can be said to have developed "a style"; that is, a manner of writing by which his work can readily be recognized by readers accustomed to it. Part of that style will naturally be a reflection of the writer as a person: his education, his social background, his basic values. But a good deal of this style will be craftsmanship—the technique of expression that he has carefully mastered. It is this combination of personal qualities and acquired techniques that identifies a Philip Wylie, a Loren Eiseley, or a John Updike and an Ernest Hemingway, writers whose work we have already examined, or soon will.

In this final section we want to call your attention to some of those techniques, those tools of the craft, that will make your prose most effective. Many of these techniques we have already discussed, inevitably, in earlier sections of this book. No text on writing is going to alter your personality, or change you as an individual, but it can help you write with skill and even with distinction.

Style as craftsmanship is a matter of *diction* (choice of words) and *rhythm* (the arrangement of words in a sentence). Let us examine diction first.

Clarity is obviously the most important consideration, for *clarity* involves choosing the word with the exact shade of meaning that you want. But finding the precise word is not always easy. Dictionaries are an invaluable aid in that they mark two aspects of a word that contribute to its meaning: its *denotation* and its *connotation*. The *denotation* of a word is its literal meaning without any overtones; the *connotation* is the suggestion, the associated meanings, that it has acquired through wide usage. *Kid, child,* and *youngster* all have the same literal meaning—offspring of a human being. But they could not be used interchangeably because they carry different associated meanings. One would scarcely write that the former Grace Kelly recently gave birth to her fourth kid. Loren Eiseley wrote, in the essay which we have examined: "There were crabs as ragged as waterweed or as smooth as beach pebbles." *Ragged, waterweed, smooth,* and *beach pebbles* are all both accurate in their literal meaning, or denotation, and wonderfully suggestive in their associated meanings, or connotation.

This sentence of Eiseley's illustrates another important technique in the choice of words: *concreteness.* A concrete word is a sense word, one which names something that can be directly seen or heard or felt or smelled or tasted. Since readers find sense words easier to understand than abstractions, it would be wise for you to strive for the concrete expression wherever possible. That is why illustrations—examples and analogies—are so effective. Furthermore, in choosing the exact word, besides considering both its denotation and connotation or deciding whether it is concrete or abstract, always choose the most *specific* word you can find. Vague, general words leave a vague, general impression with the reader. If we look once more at Eiseley's sentence, we can see that nothing could be more specific, as well as concrete and suggestive, than his description of those crabs.

One effective way to be suggestive and concrete with words that stir the imagination is to use figurative language, such as *similes, metaphors, personifications, allusions,* and *symbols.* These figures of speech are alike in that they involve some degree of comparison between two unlike things. In the *simile,* as we have seen, the comparison is introduced by words suggesting similarity: *like, as, as if, as though.* Eiseley used a simile to help the reader see what certain crabs looked like. He called them "ragged as waterweed or as smooth as beach pebbles." In a *metaphor* these introductory words are omitted, and the comparison is expressed baldly by speaking of one thing in terms of another. In describing another type of crab Eiseley used a metaphor as well as a simile. He spoke of "crabs built and riveted like Sherman tanks." *Built* and *riveted* are metaphors—the comparison with a tank is expressed directly. Let us look at two other examples from Eiseley's essay. He wrote that these crabs remind him "that an order of life is like a diamond of many reflecting surfaces, each with its own pinpoints of light" (simile). And a sentence or two later he wrote: "It is not a good thing to take the center of the stage" (metaphor), directly comparing the relation of man and other forms of life to an actor in a theater in view of an audience.

In a *personification,* as the term suggests, an inanimate or abstract thing is given human qualities: "Time rides roughshod over us all." In an *allusion,* indirect or passing reference is made to something generally familiar, like a quotation, a historic name, or an ancient myth: "He will never be a Hemingway." A *symbol* is a word or expression that is so rich in connotation that it represents the thing with which it has become identified. Almost all imaginative writing relies upon symbols to awaken emotions by drawing upon associations that the reader readily supplies. For example, the Japanese crab that first drew the attention of Eiseley to the crabs in the museum became for him a symbol of all the awesome mystery of things in nature struggling to survive by adapting themselves to changing environments.

These figures especially help create the *tone* of a work. They reinforce the author's point of view toward his subject and his readers by eliciting a desired response from them. Tone, for instance, in Eiseley's essay is the sense of wonder and awe; in Wylie's "Generation of Zeros" it is abusive anger; and in Kelman's "You Force Kids to Rebel" it is honest indignation.

Sound is also an important consideration. You know how sound can influence one's impressions, and this is also true in the use of words. Choose words, if possible, that sound like their meaning. The English language is rich in such words. Some words are purely imitative sounds, as in *clang* and *bubble* and *hiss* and *chug.* This direct imitation of sound is called *onomatopoeia.* Other words, alone or in context, suggest by their sound the idea they represent: *snub-nosed,* for example, or *frisky* or *quick* (compare with *slow*). Sounds in combination help to support an idea. Poets know this and reinforce a harsh idea by the use of harsh words, *cacophony,* or a quiet, calm idea by the use of melodious words, *euphony.* Prose writers employ the same technique. Look at Eiseley again, how sound enforces the description here: "crabs whose claws had been flattened into plates that clapped over their faces."

And finally, learn the principle of economy. Don't use more words than are necessary. Good writing is sparse writing, not verbose, wordy, nor tautological.

The rhythm of the words and groups of words comprising one's sentences also markedly contributes to tone and style. Rhythm flows from the pattern of word and syllable stresses built into a sentence. Unlike verse, prose should not have a regular beat or measure of stress, yet all smooth-flowing paragraphs have some satisfying rhythm arising from the arrangement of stresses in the sentences forming the paragraph group.

We have discussed sentence structure without specifically mentioning sentence rhythm, but you will note that *loose* sentences have a much more informal rhythm than do periodic ones, because the loose come closer to the normal rhythm of speech. Again, a balanced sentence, in which one part is set off against another by being phrased in a similar grammatical fashion, has a distinctive rhythm that calls attention to antithetical ideas.

Parallelism within the sentence, as we noted when looking at Eiseley's essay, can be extremely effective, not only in putting ideas in the proper relationship (parallel ideas should be expressed in parallel form) but in achieving a rhythm pleasing to the ear, and, with Eiseley in the particular passage about crabs, an almost hypnotic effect. In matters of sentence rhythm your ear has to be your guide. Sometimes effective rhythm is achieved simply by choosing a three-syllable word (*however*) in place of a one-syllable word (*but*) or a word accented on the first syllable (*really*) in place of one accented upon the second (*indeed*). There are, of course, some things to avoid, such as stringy sentences. Robert Louis Stevenson said of rhythm that "the one rule is to be infinitely various," and this principle is perhaps a good one to follow. Vary the length of your sentences. Use a short, wiry sentence for emphasis after a long, detailed one. Never allow your sentences to fall into identical patterns, one identical one following another, unless you are doing so deliberately for the sake of balance.

Do not expect to develop an effective style immediately. As we said at the beginning of this discussion, good writing is a matter of making choices. And this inevitably means that style comes about through revision. Stevenson also said when talking about style that a writer is like a juggler trying to keep his eye on a number of colored balls at one time. As soon as he takes his eyes from one, the rest will come tumbling down around his head.

You will find it difficult to keep in mind all of these suggestions about writing at one time, but remember: it is much better to know what are the possibilities of making you an effective writer than not to know. Without that knowledge writing becomes nothing but a matter of trial and error.

ECLIPSE

JOHN UPDIKE

I WENT OUT into the backyard and the usually roundish spots of dappled sunlight underneath the trees were all shaped like feathers, crescent in the same direction, from left to right. Though it was five o'clock on a summer afternoon, the birds were singing good-bye to the day, and their merged song seemed to soak the strange air in an additional strangeness. A kind of silence prevailed. Few cars were moving on the streets of the town. Of my children only the baby dared come into the yard with me. She wore only underpants, and as she stood beneath a tree, bulging her belly toward me in the mood of jolly flirtation she has grown into at the age of two, her bare skin was awash with pale crescents. It crossed my mind that she might be harmed, but I couldn't think how. *Cancer?*

First person viewpoint
Informal narrative tone
Mood of "strangeness"

The eclipse was to be over 90 percent in our latitude and the newspapers and television for days had been warning us not to look at it. I looked up, a split-second Prometheus, and looked away. The bitten silhouette of the sun lingered redly on my retinas. The day was half-cloudy, and my impression had been of the sun struggling, amid a furious knotted huddle of black and silver clouds, with an enemy too dreadful to be seen, with an eater as ghostly and hungry as time.

The dramatic situation
Details increasing mood
of apprehension

Every blade of grass cast a long bluish-brown shadow, as at dawn.

My wife shouted from behind the kitchen screen door that as long as I was out there I might as well burn the wastepaper. She darted from the house, eyes downcast, with the wastebasket, and darted back again, leaving the naked baby and me to wander up through the strained sunlight to the wire trash barrel. After my forbidden peek at the sun, the flames dancing transparently from the blackening paper—yesterday's Boston *Globe,* a milk carton, a Hi-Ho cracker box—seemed dimmer than shadows, and in the teeth of all the warnings I looked up again. The clouds seemed bunched and twirled as if to plug a hole in the sky, and the burning afterimage was the shape of a near-new moon, horns pointed down. It was gigantically unnatural, and I lingered in the yard under the vague apprehension that in some future life I might be called before a cosmic court to testify to this assault. I seemed to be the sole witness. The town around my yard was hushed, all but the singing of the birds, who were invisible. The feathers under the trees had changed direction, and curved from right to left.

Then I saw my neighbor sitting on her porch. My neighbor is a widow, with white hair and brown skin; she has in her yard an aluminum-and-nylon-net chaise longue on which she lies at every opportunity, head back, arms spread, prostrate under the sun. Now she hunched dismally on her porch steps in the shade, which was scarcely darker than the light. I walked toward her and hailed her as a visitor to the moon might salute a survivor of a previous expedition. "How do you like the eclipse?" I called over the fence that distinguished our holdings on this suddenly lunar earth.

"I don't like it," she answered, shading her face with a hand. "They say you shouldn't go out in it."

"I thought it was just you shouldn't look at it."

"There's something in the rays," she explained, in a voice far louder than it needed to be, for silence framed us. "I shut all the windows on that side of the house and had to come out for some air."

"I think it'll pass," I told her.

"Don't let the baby look up," she warned, and

Vivid images of wife, trash burning, and clouds

Eerie behavior and warnings of neighbor

turned away from talking to me, as if the open use of her voice exposed her more fatally to rays.

Superstition, I thought, walking back through my yard, clutching my child's hand as tightly as a good-luck token. There was no question in her touch. Day, night, twilight, noon were all wonders to her, un-scheduled, free from all bondage of prediction. The sun was being restored to itself and soon would radiate influence as brazenly as ever—and in this sense my daughter's blind trust was vindicated. Nevertheless, I was glad that the eclipse had passed, as it were, over her head; for in my own life I felt a certain assurance evaporate forever under the reality of the sun's disgrace.

Superstition as the thematic word

Resolution of the tensions aroused by the experience

COMMENTARY

A seemingly forgotten incident, as Loren Eiseley has shown us, can suddenly come into the focus of memory and occupy hours of present time teasing us with hints of some great significance hidden in its details. The memory promises a revelation, a crystallization of some long bewildering puzzle. James Joyce called his short stories based on such remembered incidents with sub-sequent illumination "epiphanies." John Updike in "Eclipse" gives us a similar intuitive discovery, and in the selection from Ernest Hemingway's "Death in the Afternoon," which follows next, we shall find still another.

What distinguishes Updike's prose from that of Eiseley? Its main distinc-tion must be that "Eclipse" is primarily a narrative, revealing a theme or a sudden insight, whereas Eiseley's is mainly an expository essay featuring two brief narratives to support its generalization. Both display figurative lan-guage, but Updike's figures are far more plentiful and complex. Both also create a mood of strange uneasiness in the reader, but Updike's mood is far more unified and intense. Eiseley's details are dramatic, but Updike builds his to a climax without any letup or return to the beginning midway, as does Eiseley when he begins the second incident. We shall compare the styles of Updike and Hemingway later.

There are several specific features that mark "Eclipse" as a work of imaginative literary art. First, as the marginalia suggest, it is a narrative of short length, telling of the position in which the narrator found himself, what he felt and did during the exigencies of that situation, and how he had changed at the end of it. The mood of eerie strangeness, summarized by the theme-word *superstition,* increases with everything he sees, hears, and does once the narrator begins, saying, "I went out into the backyard and the usually roundish spots of dappled sunlight underneath the trees were all shaped like feathers. . . ."

The mood of awesome fearfulness which begins at the sight of those shadow "feathers" is never dissipated even at the end. The narrator (the first-person "I") is slightly relieved to find that his little daughter seems not to have suffered the harm he at one time feared she might: "It crossed my mind that she might be harmed, but I couldn't think how. *Cancer?*" But *he* remains disturbed at having witnessed the "sun's disgrace": "for in my own life I felt a certain assurance evaporate forever under the reality of the sun's disgrace." His trust in something he had always considered reliable and unchanging—the sun—was shaken; he has glimpsed mankind's plight as terrestrial beings on a solar planet.

It is in Updike's diction, his choice of words, that we see how his imagination and his ability to observe things accurately enable him to build a mood. The *simile* we find in the first sentence, "the spots of dappled sunlight . . . like feathers" later becomes a *metaphor*, "The feathers under the trees had changed direction." Since these direction-changing "crescents" of "feathers" register the course of the eclipse and mark all the incidents taking place during it, they become a *symbol* of the disturbing elements an eclipse evokes and the superstitions it gives rise to. This symbolism becomes even more evident when we properly associate the "crescents" of the "feathers" and "the bitten silhouette of the sun" with the narrator's fears for his little girl. The mood is intensified also by such *personifications* as these: "the sun struggling . . . with an enemy too fearful to be seen, with an eater as ghostly and hungry as time" (simile); "flames dancing transparently from the blackening paper"; "near-new moon, horns pointed down"; "the sun was being restored to itself." The whole narrative abounds with many other similes. We cannot overlook the *allusion* to the myth of Prometheus, the immortal who defied the commands of the gods and stole fire as a gift for mankind.

Finally, Updike's sentence forms contribute their effects to the pervading mood which this story generates. To study their variety and sequence takes more space than is available here, but some most obvious examples can be mentioned. In the first paragraph, consider how the three short, dramatic sentences punctuate the scene, and note the impact of the one-word final sentence. The short exchanges of conversation in the manner that Hemingway made memorable also add drama in contrast to the longer loose *sentences* devoted to description.

Notice, also, how specific and concrete Updike is, how sharp are his images. Instead of speaking, for example, about burning trash, he writes of "flames dancing transparently from the blackening paper." And the paper itself is pictured in specific terms: "yesterday's Boston *Globe,* a milk carton, a Hi-Ho cracker box." He pictures his neighbor, who normally would lie "head back, arms spread, prostrate under the sun" on her "aluminum-and-nylon-net chaise longue" now "hunched dismally on her porch steps in the shade."

From this effective treatment of an incident, you can find much to imitate to improve the forcefulness of your own work. But make sure that you have *felt* the experience you describe as deeply as John Updike seems to have felt this one, for "epiphanies" come only to those who seek meaning in their experiences.

WHAT DOES IT SAY?

1. What events that took place before the opening of the narrative does the word "dared" imply in the sentence "Of my children only the baby dared come into the yard with me"?

2. Is the expression "mood of jolly flirtation" appropriate when applied to a two-year-old child?

3. Why does the allusion to Prometheus add to the tension of the mood?

4. Why would the fast burning paper in the trash barrel have flames that "seemed dimmer than shadows"?

5. "Yesterday's Boston *Globe,* a milk carton, a Hi-Ho cracker box"— what are the connotations of each in their context?

6. What does her "aluminum-and-nylon-net chaise longue" tell you about the neighbor?

7. What is the narrator telling us about the little girl when he says "There was no question in her touch"?

8. What is the daughter's "blind trust" which is "vindicated"?

WHAT DO YOU THINK?

1. It took Updike only about 800 well-chosen words to recreate for us his vivid experience. Using your imagination and experiences, try to create an appropriate mood in writing of some experience of your own. Here are some suggestions:

Fire in the neighborhood	Desolate hallway
Danger in the dark	Alien yard or street
Sudden storm	Daytime nightmare
Contagious illness	Joyless picnic
Drive-in movie	Ill-omened game
Blind date	Longest afternoon

2. Stanley Kauffmann, a noted critic, quotes Updike as saying: "My subject is the American, Protestant, small-town middle class. I like 'middles'. It is in middles that extremes clash, where ambiguity restlessly rules." (*Life*, November 4, 1966, p. 74c). Can you show in what respects "Eclipse" is one of these special kinds of subjects?

3. Keep a consistent tone and mood in describing the events of a typical family or other social group gathering on an occasion such as one of these:

Thanksgiving dinner	Wedding shower
Christmas Eve	Funeral
Birthday celebration	Sunday evening meal
Mother's Day	Week-end party
Father's Day	Church bazaar

DEATH

IN THE AFTERNOON

ERNEST HEMINGWAY

ONE TIME in Madrid I remember we went to a novillada in the middle of the summer on a very hot Sunday when every one who could afford it had left the city for the beaches of the north or the mountains and the bullfight was not advertised to start until six o'clock in the evening, to see six Tovar bulls killed by three aspirant matadors who have all since failed in their profession. We sat in the first row behind the wooden barrier and when the first bull came out it was clear that Domingo Hernandorena, a short, thick-ankled, graceless Basque with a pale face who looked nervous and incompletely fed in a cheap rented suit, if he was to kill this bull would either make a fool of himself or be gored. Hernandorena could not control the nervousness of his feet. He wanted to stand quietly and play the bull with the cape with a slow movement of his arms, but when he tried to stand still as the bull charged his feet jumped away in short, nervous jerks. His feet were obviously not under his personal control and his effort to be statuesque while his feet jittered him away out of danger was very funny to the crowd. It was funny to them because many of them knew that was how their own feet would behave if they saw the horns coming toward them, and as always, they resented any one else being in there in the ring, making money, who had the same physical defects which barred them, the spectators, from that supposedly highly paid way of making a living. In their turn the other two matadors were very fancy with the cape and Hernandorena's nervous jerking was even worse after their performance. He had not been in the ring with a bull for over a year and he was altogether unable to control his nervousness. When the banderillas were in and it was time for him to go out with the red cloth and the sword to prepare the bull for killing and to kill, the crowd which had applauded ironically at every nervous move he had made knew something very funny would happen. Below us, as he took the muleta and the sword and rinsed his mouth out with water I could see the muscles of his cheeks twitching. The bull stood against the barrier watching him. Hernandorena could not trust his legs to carry him slowly toward the bull. He knew there was only one way he could stay in one place in the ring. He ran out toward the bull, and ten yards in front of him dropped to both knees on the sand. In that position he was safe from ridicule. He spread the red cloth with his sword and jerked himself forward on his knees toward the bull. The bull was watching the man and the triangle of red cloth, his ears pointed, his eyes fixed, and Hernandorena knee-ed himself a yard closer and shook the cloth. The bull's tail rose, his head lowered and he charged and, as he reached the man, Hernandorena rose solidly from his knees into the air, swung over like a bundle, his legs in all directions now, and then dropped to the ground. The bull looked for him, found a wide-spread moving cape held by another bullfighter instead, charged it, and Hernandorena stood up with sand on his white face and looked for his sword and the cloth. As he stood up I saw the heavy, soiled gray silk of his rented trousers open cleanly and deeply to show the thigh bone from the hip almost to the knee. He saw it too and looked very surprised and put his hand on it while people jumped over the barrier and ran toward him to carry him to the infirmary. The technical error that he had committed was in not keeping the red cloth of the muleta between himself and the bull until the charge; then at the moment of jurisdiction as it is called, when the bull's lowered head reaches the cloth, swaying back while he held the cloth, spread by the stick and the sword, far enough forward so that the bull following it would be clear of his body. It was a simple technical error.

That night at the café I heard no word of sympathy for him. He was ignorant, he was torpid, and he was out of training. Why did he insist on being a bullfighter? Why did he go down on both knees? Because he was a coward, they said. The knees are for cowards. If he was a coward why did he insist on being a bullfighter? There was no natural sympathy for un-controllable nervousness because he was a paid public performer. It was preferable that he be gored rather than run from the bull. To be gored was honorable; they would have sympathized with him had he been caught in one of his nervous uncontrollable jerky retreats, which, although they mocked, they knew were from lack of training, rather than for him to have gone down on his knees. Because the hardest thing when frightened by the bull is to control the feet and let the bull come, and any attempt to control the feet was honorable even though they jeered at it because it looked ridiculous. But when he went on both knees, without the technique to fight from that position; the technique that Marcial Lalanda, the most scientific of living bullfighters, has, and which alone makes that position honorable; then Hernandorena admitted his nervousness. To show his nervousness was not shameful; only to admit it. When, lacking the technique and thereby admitting his inability to control his feet, the matador went down on both knees before the bull the crowd had no more sympathy with him than with a suicide.

For myself, not being a bullfighter, and being much interested in suicides, the problem was one of depiction and waking in the night I tried to remember what it was that seemed just out of my remembering and that was the thing that I had really seen and, finally, remembering all around it, I got it. When he stood up, his face white and dirty and the silk of his breeches opened from waist to knee, it was the dirtiness of the rented breeches, the dirtiness of his slit underwear and the clean, clean, unbearably clean whiteness of the thigh bone that I had seen, and it was that which was important.

COMMENTARY

"Where are the similes, the metaphors, the personifications?" you may be asking yourself. "Hemingway is supposed to be a great artist. Where's his imagination?" The style of this episode from one of his finest works does seem to differ greatly from that of John Updike, yet it displays some of the features that have made Hemingway admired and imitated the world over. Without intruding on the analysis of Hemingway's style which Wright Morris gives us in the following selection, we can point out some very obvious features of the style found in this story of a remembered Sunday afternoon in a Madrid bullring.

This three-paragraph narrative about what happened to a nervous aspirant matador serves only as an illustration in a chapter explaining some of the rules of bullfighting that sophisticated Madrid fans know and apply in judging the acts of a bullfighter who can expect death or terrible injury by goring if he violates those rules. As an illustration of how a matador should not act, this incident beautifully serves its purpose. In typical Hemingway fashion, it makes fresh and lively reading because through its *images* it presents a whole picture of an action composed of vivid descriptive details. We see Domingo Hernandorena, the "short, thick-ankled, graceless Basque" in his "cheap rented suit." We are given the *prospective* note of forewarning as to his fate: ". . . it was clear that Domingo . . . if he was to kill this bull would either make a fool of himself or be gored." (No pity from the narrator, is there?) We see "the muscles of his cheeks twitching" and then how in desperation he "knee-ed himself a yard closer and shook the cloth." We see with the narrator: ". . . the heavy, soiled gray silk of his rented trousers open cleanly and deeply to show the thigh bone from the hip almost to the knee." (How close the recording "eye" has come, but then we must remember Hemingway always took binoculars with him to a bullfight.)

Yet, as the second paragraph reveals, that scene could not be dismissed by the narrator as being only "a simple technical error" by a bumbling matador lucky to have escaped death. We are told in objective detail why the crowd felt as it did about the unforgivable act of the matador who had "admitted his nervousness." But note the comparison with which the paragraph ends: "no more sympathy with him than with a suicide."

It is the phrase "being much interested in suicides" in the third paragraph that illuminates the direction of this well-planned episode. We discover here how to interpret the significant details of that revelation in the bullring of the "clean, clean, unbearably clean whiteness of the thigh bone" showing through the horn-ripped dirty silk breeches. Why should this be "that which was important" to the narrator? We can surmise that "clean, clean, unbearably clean whiteness of the thigh bone" is a *symbol*. But again we ask, "A symbol of what? Death-bleached bones of all the many dead matadors killed in rings? The narrator's own eventual death?" And why the *"unbearably clean whiteness"*?

Hemingway's diction is deceptively simple. The brief one-syllable words joined together create a forward movement, a rhythm of mounting suspense. Let us look at one more sentence, a *periodic* one: "When the banderillas were in and it was time for him to go out with the red cloth and the sword to prepare the bull for killing and to kill, the crowd which had applauded ironically at every nervous move he had made knew something very funny would happen." The choice of words here is the kind one might expect of a writer who at the age of 18 started as a cub newspaper reporter for the *Kansas City Star*. Only the phrase "applauded ironically" may be unusual in that it describes the total response of the crowd in two words. Yet these simple words lead us on and create suspense because their movement is periodic: the sentence begins with our seeing the gayly festooned barbs set painfully deep in the bull's shoulders, but we are not told what we want to know about that nervous matador and that bull; our attention is turned to the crowd and its mocking applause, and only in the last few words do we see the matador as the crowd does: one to whom "something very funny would happen." The bull, the matador, the crowd—all three are fused into the first-person narrator's intense mood of concentration upon all the details of that one engagement in the sanded ring. It is that same intenseness that awakens the narrator during the night and reveals to him "that which was important."

Do not be deceived, however, by this apparently artless language and think that you can equal it by writing exactly the way you talk. If you miss the obvious fact that Hemingway chose each one of those simple words with deliberate care and with a vivid image of what he was seeing in his mind, you are sadly misreading him. Imitate his economy of forceful detail, his respect for the strength of everyday, idiomatic language, and you will learn how the apparently unadorned style can still be a result of carefully planned self-expression.

WHAT DOES IT SAY?

1. List all of the facts given in the opening sentence of 74 words. Is it overloaded, cluttered, difficult to understand?

2. What do you see on reading in context the expression ". . . the other two matadors were very fancy with the cape"?

3. What makes a sentence such as the following one effective? Analyze it word by word as was done with another in the commentary. "The bull's tail rose, his head lowered and he charged and, as he reached the man, Hernandorena rose solidly from his knees into the air, swung over like a bundle, his legs in all directions now, and then dropped to the ground."

4. Why is the above sentence typical of others in this episode?

5. "He was ignorant, he was torpid, he was out of training"—what is the meaning of *torpid*?

6. What is the Madrid crowd's interpretation of *shameful*? Is it also your definition? If not, why not?

7. What does the narrator mean when in the final paragraph he says "the problem was one of depiction"?

8. "That which was important"—what does *important* in this context suggest to you?

WHAT DO YOU THINK?

1. Describe in a way which is similar to Hemingway's apparently objective, impersonal manner a scene or incident of danger which you have experienced or witnessed. Suggestions:

A swimmer's predicament   Heedless child
Car wreck   An unwanted trip
Motorcycle close call   Unexpected visitor
"Unloaded" gun   Sudden cowardice
A walk at night   Unwilling witness

2. Describe by means of an illustrative example your concept of one of these:

The courageous person   A real friend
The thoughtful person   The ideal relative
A good neighbor   The good citizen

3. In 500 concise words, explain forcefully your views on one of the following often heard statements:

Suicide is the coward's way out.   I'll try anything once.
Cowards die a thousand deaths.   Ignorance is bliss.
Follow the crowd.   The world owes me a living.
You never know until you try.   It's no skin off my nose.

THE FUNCTION
OF STYLE:
ERNEST HEMINGWAY

WRIGHT MORRIS

Before I go on with this short history, let me make a general observation—
the test of a first-rate intelligence is the ability to hold two opposed ideas
in the mind at the same time, and still retain the ability to function. One
should, for example, be able to see that things are hopeless and yet be
determined to make them otherwise.

—F. Scott Fitzgerald, *The Crack-Up*

"ALL modern literature," Hemingway stated in *The Green Hills of Africa*,
"comes from one book by Mark Twain called *Huckleberry Finn*." In such
a comment there is an uncanny amount of truth, but it is a characteristically
revealing, oversimplified observation. What the master is saying is, "I began
with Huckleberry Finn." It was perhaps inspired in order to settle the dust on
that tiresome quarrel with Gertrude Stein—who claimed that she gave birth
to Ernest—but, as he indicates, it was Twain who got in the first, and the
last lick.

In the essentials, Ernest Hemingway, born in Illinois, is a latter-day
Huckleberry Finn. His "Big Two-Hearted River" is a latter-day retreat into
the wilderness. The differences are precisely those that time would have made,
what time would have done to both Huck and the territory ahead. He would

Reprinted from *The Territory Ahead* by Wright Morris. New York: Harcourt, Brace &
World, 1957 by permission of the author.

have learned, at a very early age, that there was no such animal. His life would have begun with disenchantment rather than enchantment: he would be the first of that new breed of young men who knew too much, who knew more than their fathers would admit to knowing.

The boy who witnessed the death in the Michigan woods came out of the woods a man no longer subject to change. He had had it. But it took time to learn *what* he had had. The nature of this disenchantment is described with classic finality in the stories and sketches of *In Our Time*. The man who emerged lived and wrote by the values forged in his fiction. Both the writer and his work, that is, resisted change. A process of "seasoning," rather than development, links the disillusion of *In Our Time* with the resolution of *The Old Man and the Sea*. The facts are the same. You can't win. In the long run, life will beat you. First the big fish eat the little ones, then the little fish eat the big ones. But a brave and simple man can win a bit of the laurel, nevertheless. In never giving up, win or lose, he enjoys a final triumph over death itself.

With this wisdom, dramatized in a tale that is a lucid model of his craft, few modern men will care to argue. It seems true to life, and we know it is true to Hemingway. It is what he has been saying, and how he has been living, since he stepped, just forty years ago, to the edge of the wilderness and did not like at all what he saw. To that shock of recognition he has been consistent. In his life and his art he has been his own man. His craft has cast a spell that both inspires and takes a yearly toll. In attempting to come to terms with this man—or, as I choose to believe, this *style*—we are essentially concerned with coming to terms with his age, with the fact that he is largely responsible for it. His style—like the clear water that flows at the heart of all of his fiction—sounds the note of enchantment to the very disenchantment it anticipates. The reader grasps, immediately, that this man is not so tough as he looks. Quite the contrary, he looks and sounds so tough because his heart is so soft. Behind the armor of his prose, the shell of his exile, lurks our old friend Huck Finn, American dreamer, the clean-cut boy who just wishes Aunt Sally would leave him alone, who wants nothing more, nor less, than a clearing of his own in the wilderness. The dream itself he left unchanged, he merely moved to a smaller river, but he brought to it a style that revealed the dream to itself. There was no need to cry "O lost, lost—lost!" in the voice of Tom Wolfe, since the style had absorbed the state of disenchantment: the style was it. It was not merely the man, nor a handful of crafty exiles, but the age itself, the old moon of enchantment with the new moon of disenchantment in its arms.

When the young man Hemingway came to the edge of the clearing, when he saw what man had left in the place of nature, he found it something more than an unpleasant shock. He found it unacceptable. In that early judgment he has never wavered. It is expressed with finality in his exile. In this feeling, and in his exile, he is not alone, but being an artist he has been able to give his judgment a singular permanence. As the style of Faulkner grew out of his rage—out of the impotence of his rage—the style of Hemingway grew out of the depth and nuance of his disenchantment. Only a man who had believed, with a child's purity of faith, in some haunting dream of life, in its vistas of promise, is capable of forging his disillusion into a work of art. It is love of life that Hemingway's judgment of life reveals. Between the lines of his prose, between the passage and the reader, there is often that far sound of running water, a pine-scented breeze that blows from a cleaner and finer world. It is this air that makes the sight of so many corpses bearable. Invariably it is there—a higher order than the one we see before us in operation—as if the legend of the past were stamped, like a signature, on his brow. We have never had a more resolute moralist. A dream of the good life haunts the scene of all the bad life he so memorably observes, and when under his spell it is the dream of the good life that we possess. For such an artist, should there be anything but praise? Could there be anything conceivably impotent about such a style? It is when we come to brood on his consistency—on the man who does not change, or seem aware of it—that we see that the author, as well as the reader, has been under a spell, the same spell—the spell of a style. The consistency lies in what the style will permit him to think, to feel, and to say.

Every writer who is sufficiently self-aware to know what he is doing, and how he does it, sooner or later is confronted with the *dictates* of style. If he *has* a style, it is the style that dictates what he says. *What* he says, of course, is *how* he says it, and when we say that the style is the man we have testified to this property. The writer who develops, as a man and a writer, cannot be self-contained in a style, however memorable and charming, that has served its purpose. The style must change, or the writer must adapt himself to it. This is notably true of the writers whose style is the most highly personalized, and distinctive: the most distinctive stylist of this order in our time is Hemingway. He *is* a style. He has never departed from it. Tentative departures—in *For Whom the Bell Tolls,* for example—have appeared as flaws in the marble, rather than as symptoms of development. It is the nature of Hemingway's style to prohibit development. When he remains within it, he sounds *like himself.* When he attempts to escape, we do not know what he sounds like. Neither does he. It is a lesson he has taken to heart. *The Old Man and the Sea* is a two-way fable, that of an old man who has mastered a fish, and that of an aging writer who bows to the mastery of his style. Within these stylistic commitments he sounds all right. He does *not* sound, however, like he did more than thirty years earlier, when this style, and these commitments, were being forged. *The Old Man and the Sea* is an act of will; within the terms of this will it is a moving achievement, but as an act of the imagination it is dead. The style, not the creative mind, dictates the range and nature of the experience, selects the cast, and determines what is permissible. Here again the Spanish language—the simplifying agent —is used to reduce the complexities, in the manner of that memorable night of love and conversation in the sleeping bag. This technique, on occasion, leads to revelation, but as a rule it is merely reduction. The apparent simplicity lies in the style, rather than in the nature of the material, but Hemingway takes pains to build up a consistently simple scene. Man, fish, and Joe DiMaggio are attuned to the demands of the simple epic; complexities, human complexities, are reduced to a minimum. Complicated types enter Hemingway's world only to lose their complications. Man must appear simple, subject to simple corruptions, so that NATURE, writ large, will appear complex. The restoration of Nature—the Nature undefiled of the "Big Two-Hearted River"— would seem to be the passion behind Hemingway's reduction of man. It is why his disillusion, limited to man, is still grained with hope. Man is a mess, but Nature will prevail. It is the sea that triumphs, the sea and the sky against which man's puny drama is enacted, but they are not used, as in Hardy, to dwarf man to insignificance; rather, they remind him, in the complex way Hemingway will not permit his characters, of the paradise lost that might still be regained, that green breast of the world Huck Finn preserved in the territory ahead.

This scale of values—Man finitely simple, and Nature infinitely complex —is the Hemingway palette and the key to the scale of his style. He is never reduced to tampering with personalities. A Cézanne-like simplicity of scene is built up with the touches of a master, and the great effects are achieved with a sublime economy. At these moments style and substance are of one piece, each growing from the other, and one cannot imagine that life could exist except as described. We think only of what is there, and not, as in the less successful moments, of all of the elements of experience that are not.

The Hemingway economy, his sublime economy, is one thing when dictated by the imagination, but another when merely by the mechanical blue pencil of his style. These two slices of life, superficially, will look the same. Both will have the authority of his craft. There is no litmus test that the reader can apply to distinguish between the prose, the economy of the prose, of *The Sun Also Rises* and *Across the River and into the Trees*. Both books are *written*. But only one has been creatively imagined. In the absence of the shaping imagination Hemingway can always rely on his *craft,* and he is one of the great craftsmen of the age. The proof of this, ironically enough, is less in the books that were intensely imagined than in the books that were primarily an act of will. Here it is craft, and craft alone, that sustains both the reader and the writer, and it is what we mean, what we feel to be true, in observing that the author has fallen under his own spell. Indeed he has. And the spell is almost enough. The response of a new generation to *The Old Man and the Sea* was evidence of how much an artist might achieve through pure technique.

This technique, this celebrated style, was born full-fledged—whatever the line of descent—and in nearly forty years it has undergone no visible change. Neither has the life it portrays, since the style and the slice of life are the same. In the interests of this style things remain as they are, they do not change. It is a lens of the finest precision; it records, accurately, the author's field of vision, but the price of the performance is that the *field* must remain the same. Time—in the sense of development—must stand still. The timeless quality of the Hemingway snapshot is truly timeless—growth and change have been removed. The illusion of things as they are is raised to a point that has seldom been equaled; a frieze-like sense of permanence enshrines the Big Two-Hearted River and its world-wide tributaries. This woodland stream, symbolic of all that is undefiled in both man and nature, rises at the source of Hemingway's young manhood and flows through his life and his work to the sea. Clear water, clear fast-moving water, links the exile, on a weekend in Spain, with the Big Two-Hearted River back in Michigan. From different streams the fisherman pulls the same trout. Good fish and running water serve him as the means of coming to terms with life.

As Thoreau went to Walden for the *facts,* Hemingway went to the Michigan woods and the bullfight. In the grain of both men was a passionate desire for reality—be it life or death. Both men feared only one thing: being cheated of life. The *big* cheat, for both men, was the world of Aunt Sally, and only in the woods could one see life cleanly, in the wilderness of nature, or, for Hemingway, in the *nature* of war. But one began in the wilderness.

> He sat on the logs, smoking, drying in the sun, the sun warm on his back, the river shallow ahead entering the woods, curving into the woods, shallows, light glittering, big water-smooth rocks, cedars along the bank and white birches, the logs warm in the sun, smooth to sit on, without bark, gray to the touch; slowly the feeling of disappointment left him. It went away slowly, the feeling of disappointment that came sharply after the thrill that made his shoulders ache. It was all right now.

Any man who has ever tried to write will feel in this passage the line-taut passion of a man who would die rather than cheat you with a cliché. It is *this* that is moving—rather than what he tells us. We feel, in this prose, the man's passion for the truth. We hang on every word, as he intends, secure in the feeling that the word will support us. There is no thin ice in this style. We have our hands on experience. We are in possession of the facts.

On the Big Two-Hearted River the artist cut his teeth, but it is not till his exile that he clamps down with them. He waits, appropriately, till his exiles do a little fishing. It is in Spain, that the trout in the Big Two-Hearted River get their bite.

> While I had him on, several trout had jumped at the falls. As soon as I baited up and dropped in again I hooked another and brought him in the same way. In a little while I had six. They were all about the same size. I laid them out,

side by side, all their heads pointing the same way, and looked at them. They were beautifully colored and firm and hard from the cold water. It was a hot day, so I slit them all and shucked out the insides, gills and all, and tossed them over across the river. I took the trout ashore, washed them in the cold, smoothly heavy water above the dam, and then picked some ferns and packed them all in the bag, three trout on a layer of ferns, then another layer of ferns, then three more trout, and then covered them with ferns. They looked nice in the ferns, and now the bag was bulky, and I put it in the shade of the tree.

This is like a summing up and a prophecy. After the sad goings on of the lost generation, we have plunged, in this stream, back to clean reality, beautifully colored and firm and hard, like the trout. That is nature. That is the nature of life. Bulls are sometimes good, sometimes bad, but only man is vile. In returning to nature it is possible for man to cleanse himself.

It is in keeping with this style that man should undergo a progressive brutalization, and nature a progressive refinement and serenity; that man, who should speak for himself, fails to do so, and that nature, who cannot, should become articulate. The river that flows through *The Sun Also Rises,* reflecting what is lost in the lost generation, is a clearer and more incorruptible stream than the one that flows through *In Our Time.* The Spanish stream has been *tested.* The trout are firm immortal trout. They lie before our eyes, all their heads pointing in the same direction, like the timeless fish in one of the paintings of Braque. Technique has snatched them from the river of life and made them into art. . . . He is still, like his master Mark Twain, a boy at heart. While we pause to read what he has to say he is already off for the territory ahead before the world, or Aunt Sally, tries to civilize him. He can't stand it.

COMMENTARY

Wright Morris singles out for us two significant facts about style. Through an analysis of Ernest Hemingway's works, he shows us, first, that the kind of person a writer is dictates the way he writes and, second, that in time he may become a slave to the characteristic attitudes and techniques that once gave him great originality. According to this vision of style, the literary work bares the nature of the man who wrote it; he has written what he essentially *is.* The book mirrors the man in his attitudes and values regarding the world of society and nature that surrounds him.

In the course of his remarks, Morris makes another significant comment about style. "*What* he says, of course," referring to Hemingway, "is *how* he says it." In other words, thought is intimately related to expression. Thought, in fact, is expression. And expression is acquired techniques, which evolve through deliberate choice.

If we look closely at the style of Wright Morris in this essay we may find that it reveals at least something of the nature of this penetrating critic of American life and literature. Certainly his language tells us that he has a good ear for American idioms, for expressions untranslatable and uniquely American. Here are a few of them: "to settle the dust," "got in the first and the *last* lick," "there was no such animal," "in the long run, life will beat you," and "the clean-cut boy."

Hemingway's style, as we saw, is deceptively simple and direct, although concrete and extremely specific. Morris' style, on the contrary, is not what one would call simple. For one thing, he is extremely fond of figurative expressions, particularly metaphors, as we can see in the following: "In order to settle the dust on that tiresome quarrel . . . ," "The man who emerged lived and wrote by the values forged in his fiction," "In the long run, life will beat you. First the big fish eat the little ones, then the little fish eat the big ones. But a brave and simple man can win a bit of the laurel, nevertheless." Morris compares Hemingway's style to clear, flowing water. "His style," he writes, "like the clear water that flows at the heart of all his fiction. . . ." And he continues to use this figurative comparison throughout the essay, summarizing at the end: "The river that flows through *The Sun Also Rises,* reflecting what is lost in the lost generation, is a clearer and more incorruptible stream than the one that flows through *In Our Time.* The Spanish stream has been *tested.* The trout are firm immortal trout. They lie before our eyes, all their heads pointing in the same direction, like the timeless fish in one of the paintings of Braque. Technique has snatched them from the river of life and made them into art. . . ." The metaphors follow each other in such rapid succession, at times, that the image becomes a trifle confused.

Another aspect of Morris' style is its allusiveness. He makes a certain demand upon his readers, expecting them to be conversant with Cézanne, Braque, Gertrude Stein, Thomas Hardy, Milton (note the comments about *Paradise Lost* and *Paradise Regained*), Thoreau and Walden Pond, Thomas Wolfe, Mark Twain (the world of Aunt Sally), Faulkner—even the superstition in the Scottish ballad Sir Patrick Spens (the reference to the old moon with the new moon in its arms).

From his insistence when talking about Hemingway that "Both the writer and his work . . . resisted change," we can infer that Morris believes a writer should welcome change. Our question naturally is "what kind of change?" Morris would seem to accept any kind as long as it enlarges the artist's understanding of the complexities of human life and nature, and enables the artist to grow in vision, to "creatively imagine."

Since you have already read at least one Hemingway sample, you have some basis on which to judge the validity of Morris' criticism. Also in the study sections coming up you will find additional clues to the relationship between Wright Morris the man and his own particular style. Do your own thinking on these two related matters of Morris on Hemingway and you on Morris and Hemingway and the "commentaries" on them. What you learn about this relationship between the character of the writer and his techniques through the study of a representative work will help you in your own efforts to become a better writer. That relationship involves all the issues involved in the criticism of any literary effort.

WHAT DOES IT SAY?

1. By saying that Hemingway's comment on *Huckleberry Finn* is "a characteristically revealing, oversimplified observation," does Morris imply that Hemingway is given to making such statements? If so, what do they tell us of Hemingway as a thinker?

2. What are two implications of the statement "I began with Huckleberry Finn"?

3. What images does "a latter-day Huck Finn" suggest to you?

4. What, in context, is the difference between "seasoning" and "development"?

5. Can you name two features of Hemingway's "craft" that have "cast a spell" over many modern authors?

6. What are "the *dictates* of style"? Are they to be feared?

7. How can Morris condemn *The Old Man and the Sea*, Hemingway's last novel, as "a moving achievement, but as an act of the imagination it is dead"?

8. Morris maintains that Hemingway's "scale of values" is the "key to the scale of his style." What does *scale* mean here?

WHAT DO YOU THINK?

1. How valid do you think F. Scott Fitzgerald's "test of a first-rate intelligence" is? Show how Morris applies this "test" to Hemingway's works in order to describe their basic style.

2. Write an essay applying the Fitzgerald "test" to Wright Morris, as he reveals himself in this critical essay, or in one of his own novels, such as *The Field of Vision*.

3. Have you read *Huckleberry Finn*? What is there in this famous novel that could make Hemingway admit—in the words of Morris—"I began with Huckleberry Finn"?

4. Huckleberry Finn had little education. Write a sketch of the "modern Huckleberry Finn" as Morris imagines he would be. .

5. On the basis of Morris' summaries of Hemingway's outlook on life in the third paragraph, for example, limit one of the following general topics and write a brief essay on your topic:
   a) Hemingway is right.
   b) Hemingway is always oversimplifying.
   c) Morris is oversimplifying Hemingway.
   d) Everybody relies on oversimplifying things.

6. Is your concept of "the good life" at all like that of Hemingway's? Using your imagination, describe the version of "the good life" you would want for yourself and everyone else.

THE NOVELIST
OR THE HISTORIAN?

CHARLES ALVA HOYT

MUCH HAS been made, in the unprecedented hullabaloo that surrounded the publication of *In Cold Blood,* of that book's inaugurating a "new literary genre." It is an estimate with which the author concurs. In an interview in *The New York Times Book Review* Truman Capote advanced his case for "a serious new art form: the 'nonfiction novel,' as I thought of it." He was careful to disavow the statement—attributed to him, and subsequently cried up in certain quarters—that "reporting is now more interesting than fiction." "What I think," he said, "is that reporting can be made *as* interesting as fiction, and done *as* artistically—underlining those two 'as'es."

What Mr. Capote thinks he has discovered is already known to the world by a different name: history. History is the art of telling the truth, selectively (so that the reader may not strangle on vast accumulations of data) and gracefully (so that the reader will want to read in the first place). That is what Mr. Capote has done. If it is objected that history is usually concerned with larger issues, reflect what the similar ordeal of a 15th century family might be worth today to the historian, if he were lucky enough to find it written in such careful and well-authenticated detail.

Journalism is a branch of history. There is no use adding "journalism as its best," or "responsible journalism"; if journalism often strays from objective truth, why so do the other branches of history. For every corrupt newspaper article there is a history text trying to prove that Hitler was sent to

Reprinted from the Columbia University *Forum,* Vol. 9, Number 53. Copyright 1966 by the Trustees of Columbia University in the City of New York.

Germany by God, or the United States of America into Mexico by Manifest Destiny. On the other hand, intelligent newspaper reporting is one of the chief sources for the academic historian, and always will be.

Mr. Capote is a brilliant writer, and we are fortunate that he has turned his gifts, for a time at least, to the field of history. It is not, however, particularly remarkable that he has done so. Contemporary historiography has attracted a large number of such writers, men and women who are well qualified to serve the tastes of our time. For just as the eighteenth century found its representative historian in Gibbon, so the twentieth finds its own in Bruce Catton or—though some might disagree—Barbara Tuchman. The eighteenth century's taste in historical writing included a certain elevation, ironic urbanity, style worked to a high polish. Ours seems to prefer intimacy, informality, and color.

But in all ages it has been recognized that history, like the novel, must entertain. Like the novel it must explore motives, dwell upon personalities, descend to gossip. As Hazlitt said, "All that does not lay open the fine network of the heart and brain of men, that does not make us see deeper into the soul, is but the apparatus and machinery of history-painting, and no more to it than the frame is to the picture."

What Mr. Capote wants to do for his history, I take it, is what the novel can do for its subject matter: present it so compellingly that it escapes its relatively narrow base into universal significance. That is a commendable ambition in the historian, who is far more than the novelist committed to specifics. It is in terms of this problem that I apprehend Aristotle's dictum that poetry is truer than history. Even so, the best historians have always been able to present their facts so creatively and suggestively as to make small incidents serve great generalizations. Thus Fletcher Pratt, on the aftermath of the Battle of The Wilderness:

> At Chancellorsville House there is a three-corner. The road to the left led back across the Rappahannock, back to the Potomac, out of that grim wood to fortifications, comfort and safety; that on the right led past the rebel front, deeper than ever into the perilous and uncertain Wilderness. As the defeated troops came slogging down to the turn, the dispirited soldiers saw dimly a man in an old blue coat sitting horseback at the crossroads with a cigar in his mouth. He silently motioned the guides of each regiment down the right-hand road. Grant.
>
> They stared a moment—and then the slanting lines of steel took the road to terror and death, upborne on an uncontrollable wave of cheering. "That night the men were happy."
>
> They could never be beaten now.
>
> —Short History of the Civil War.

Mr. Capote's book, I believe, may then be seen as a welcome development in a well-established trend in contemporary writing, not as an innovation.

An outstanding example of modern historiography or, if you prefer, great journalism, it is to be considered not a reproach to the novel, but perhaps its debtor.

COMMENTARY

"What is good style in the writing of history?" might well be the subtitle of Charles Alva Hoyt's well-reasoned essay, and after having read it you probably are not surprised to discover that the writing skills and attitudes that make a well-written history enjoyable reading are also the same ones that we have found at work in the other essays of this book.

But before going into any specific details regarding that "ideal" style for historiographers (writers of history), let us lay out in syllogistic form Hoyt's basic logic in appraising what Truman Capote has accomplished in his best-seller, *In Cold Blood*:

Major premise: Everyone who has written a factual narrative has thereby written a history.
Minor premise: Truman Capote has written a factual narrative.
Conclusion: Truman Capote has written a history.

We can sum up Hoyt's argument also in this fashion: Capote has written a journalistic narrative, but journalism is a branch of history; therefore, Capote has written a history. If this conclusion is valid, then Capote is wrong in thinking he has created "a serious new art form: the 'nonfiction novel'."

Hoyt's main concern, however, is not with Capote but rather with the excellent writing style of historiographers like Bruce Catton and Barbara Tuchman, and what these have in common with the novelist. Hoyt quotes a passage from another contemporary, Fletcher Pratt, to show an example of this desirable style. Its main features arise from purposes and techniques that novelists also share; namely, to "explore motives, dwell upon personalities, descend to gossip" and to give important incidents "universal significance." What gives the historiographer the edge over the novelist, says Hoyt, is his being more "committed to specifics" than is the novelist.

By "specifics" Hoyt means concrete, picture-making or fact-supporting details. The lesson here is obvious. If factual, specific details make history interesting to read, you can always find the same kind of details in your subject to make your writing interesting. Also, if a good historian can endow a special incident with "universal significance," like that of the soldiers meeting Grant at the Chancellorsville House crossroads, you, too, can borrow that technique to give light and substance to your work. What is "good style" then, in the writing of history requires the same techniques of effective writing that we have been examining and experimenting with all along.

Again, what seems required is a lively curiosity about things and people, some imagination, and a keen desire to clarify and dramatize in organized language what one has discovered is strange, surprising, or important. These personal qualities—attainable by almost anyone who really wants them—teamed with writing skill will make any style readable and generally interesting, if not brilliant.

Hoyt is writing literary criticism, not history, as was Morris. In contrast to Morris' highly figurative language, Hoyt writes in almost literal terms at all times. In commenting upon Hemingway, Morris wrote: "The apparent simplicity lies in the style, rather than in the nature of the material." The same might be said of Hoyt. As much a literary critic as Morris, since he is dealing with a popular novelist and the inaugurating of what he calls a "new literary genre," the "nonfiction novel," Hoyt could have been, as far as his subject is concerned, as metaphorical as Morris. He chose, rather, to eschew figures almost completely. Morris writes of Hemingway:

> We hang on every word, as he intends, secure in the feeling that the word will support us. There is no thin ice in this style. We have our hands on experience.

Hoyt writes of Capote:

> History is the art of telling the truth, selectively (so that the reader may not strangle on vast accumulations of data) and gracefully (so that the reader will want to read in the first place). That is what Mr. Capote has done.

Except for the metaphor "strangle" Hoyt's language is completely literal. A comparison of the styles of the two men (Morris and Hoyt) is illuminating. What is the effect secured by the style of each? Try reaching a conclusion about the advantages and disadvantages, or, gains or losses attendant upon the use of figurative language as revealed by the style of these two essays.

WHAT DOES IT SAY?

1. How adequate as a definition is Hoyt's on *history*: "History is the art of telling the truth, selectively . . . and gracefully . . ."?

2. What qualities of ideal reporting are implied in the expressions "journalism at its best" and "responsible journalism"?

3. What is meant by "Manifest Destiny" as a justification for a country's aggressive acts and policies?

4. In the following quotation define the words in italics: "The eighteenth century's *taste* in historical writing included a certain *elevation, ironic urbanity*, style worked to a *high polish*."

5. "Mr. Capote is a brilliant writer," says Hoyt. What does *brilliant* mean in this context?

6. What faults would a "corrupt newspaper article" have?

7. Restate in your own terms what you think the quotation from Hazlitt means.

8. In the context of the final sentence what is the meaning of *reproach* and *debtor*?

WHAT DO YOU THINK?

1. Restrict the scope of one of the following topics, and write a meaningful description or report of your subject as if you were observing it through the senses of a history-minded journalist. The topics are divided into two categories of general subject matter.

Campus Topics	*Home and City Topics*
Dress fashions (male, female)	City bus travel
Current slang	City sanitation
Manners (good, bad)	Window-shopping downtown
Views on religion	Parental behavior regarding:
Favorite foods (dislikes)	music
Week-end behavior patterns	dating
Treatment of athletes	spending money
Dormitory visitation	marriage

2. In the light of the distinctions and parallels made in Hoyt's essay, write an analysis of either John Updike's "Eclipse" or Ernest Hemingway's "Death in the Afternoon" as having historical value.

3. Do you agree that "history, like the novel, must entertain"? If so, write an essay analyzing the entertaining features of your favorite historical work (not a novel!).

THE THEATRE
OF EDWARD ALBEE

ALAN PRYCE-JONES

ONLY SIX YEARS ago, what was generally known of Edward Albee could have been written on a postcard. The first of his plays to be performed in New York, off Broadway, opened in January 1960. It was *The Zoo Story*, and it attracted startled attention to a young man, lately turned thirty, of obvious talent.

Some people hated *The Zoo Story*, but nobody overlooked it. Yet in a way it was Albee himself, rather than his play, which held their attention. He aroused curiosity. His background, for instance, appealed to a nation of romantics. The adopted son of rich parents, given every facility for a conventional success in life, he was said to have given it all up in order to try his luck after his own fashion. In appearance he had somewhat the air of a changeling, even a fallen angel: dark, discontented, rather hostile. No, perhaps on second thoughts not so much a changeling as a fierce young cuckoo in search of a nest to outrage.

Now, with three full-length plays behind him—five, if you count his adaptations of Carson McCuller's *Ballad of the Sad Café* and James Purdy's *Malcolm*—it is possible to round out a little that first impression.

Not that Albee is the kind of playwright on whom a label can be stuck. He is not a Harold Pinter or an Arnold Wesker, an Arden or an Osborne. You cannot fit him into the Theatre of the Absurd, or into any other kind of theatre: you cannot pigeon-hole him as a political satirist, or yet another victim of that dull obsession, the inability of human beings to communicate with one another. Each of his plays enfolds a statement of a different kind: not always a ringing statement—far from it—but something like a message sealed up in a bottle and tossed into the ocean, to be found far off by an unsuspecting native.

Take his latest play, *A Delicate Balance,* now playing on Broadway. It is unlike anything he has so far written, both in style and in content. Until now, a mark of his writing has been the sharp naturalism of his speech. Even when the effect he aims at is poetic rather than dialectical—say, in *The American Dream*—he has used strictly the language of every day. In *A Delicate Balance* the process is inverted. The speech becomes highly mannered, in order to convey a set of prose statements from which poetry has been emptied. That these statements are often obscure is irrelevant: part of Albee's purpose is to make his audience dig them out for itself.

It is a curious process to watch. Go to a matinée at the Martin Beck Theatre and you will find a large house packed with the kind of lady who frequents a Wednesday afternoon in the New York theatre: ladies with vast heads of hair touched up to the colours of sunset over the Nile, ladies shaped like an immense doughnut swathed in fur, ladies in chattering groups up for the day from suburbs like Yonkers and New Rochelle. They listen with care, and laugh at the jokes. But what on earth do they make of Albee's intention? What do they carry home with them in their Ford Galaxies?

They will have seen a middle-aged couple ensconced in a lovely home: the drinks tray, stage left, in constant use; the sofa inviting; the panelling spruce. In a way, Tobias and Agnes—the couple—are very much like the audience watching them, living out what Thoreau called their lives of "quiet desperation." Agnes wonders if she may not be going mad. As a daily cross to bear they have living with them Agnes's sister Claire, who drinks a bit; and the desperation increases when their daughter Julia suddenly comes home after the failure of her latest marriage—only to find that home is not home any more.

For a neighbouring couple, Harry and Edna, are occupying her room. They have arrived in a panic. But what kind of panic? We don't know. They don't know. Sitting in their own home they became frightened, and so they turn for refuge to their best friends.

That is all. There is no further action unless you equate action with subtraction. After the first hour the play is a long diminuendo. Agnes will not go mad. The frightened couple will eventually leave. The lovely home will return to its normal tedium, interspersed with moments of hangover. *A Delicate Balance* will turn out to have been about the brief moment of displacement while Harry and Edna are calling the normality of their friends and the security of their house into question.

The first thing to notice in this is that Albee has written an extremely American play. In terms of Paris or London it would be unimaginable. Mysterious fear is not an uncommon subject in the theatre: Harold Pinter has used it effectively more than once. But Albee's fear is not only mysterious: it is, so to speak, a white fear, entirely colourless, a fear with no overtones of menace, or guilt, or anything else. When Henry James, in *The Turn of the Screw*, insisted that the atmosphere of terror he was invoking would be the more powerful for its imprecision, he at least gave it a kind of moral potency. Whereas the fear which drove Harry and Edna out of their house was just a fear, as a headache is just a headache: it was a force, but a blind one.

I do not suggest that American households are often, or ever, in the grip of such unreasonable panic. But I think that the notion of continual insecurity is familiar to a surprising number of such households. Fear of losing a wife or a lover, a job or an income, fear of failure, of not getting ahead of the Joneses—such fears are a strong motive force in the Great Society. Nibbling their chocolates, the ladies from Yonkers in the audience will have felt a sympathy with Harry and Edna which their sisters from Dorking or Chantilly might find it hard to understand.

Then there is the matter of Albee's technical skill. He shows it by managing to hold the attention for three acts with the minimum of incident to help him. True, the daughter Julia has a hysterical fit, but it takes place mainly offstage. True, Claire, her aunt, brisks up the even flow of strictly grammatical dialogue by reaching for her accordion or pouring down yet another brandy and soda. True, there is an ironic pleasure in watching the various responses of two couples to an easily comprehensible dilemma—that of how to treat unwanted guests, and how to be treated. Can shelter be claimed as a right if the hosts are old and true friends? Or is it a privilege? Is the host happy to help his friends in need, or is he likely to feel put upon? Such problems may not be strictly dramatic, but Albee makes them so by skilful variations of rhythm and tempo, and by some wintry word-play which, if it is not exactly wit, at any rate raises a laugh. If nothing happens, the spectacle on stage is never boring, only, at times, a trifle slow. And I think that slowness is deliberate. Domestic life, after all, *is* slow at times; and one of the technical problems solved by Albee is to stress that fact without allowing his audience to be bored by it.

He also shows something more like a tender heart in this play than in his earlier work. Not very like a tender heart, I admit; but at least in control of the destructive demon which rages through *Who's Afraid of Virginia Woolf?*

His weakness, I suspect, is a certain shortness of wind. For my taste, his most successful plays have been the early one-acters, notably *The Zoo Story*. In this, with two characters only, he turns farce inside out, so that it becomes something half-way between melodrama and tragedy; and the modulation, towards the end of the play, by which this suddenly happens seems to me one of the most effective surprises in the modern theatre.

But when he writes a full-length play I am conscious that it is only his skill which stops me becoming restive. For are they not really one-acters drawn out to more than their natural length? Even *Virginia Woolf* would be strengthened by compression, and the weakest of the full-length plays, *Tiny Alice,* is hardly more than a sequence of scenes, some highly effective, some disconcertingly opaque. It is barely a play at all.

What has made Albee a popular success is the violence of his response to the world of conventional people. His appeal has been to the masochistic element in society, the desire for self-immolation which makes even quite normal citizens delight in recognizing themselves in parody or caricature. *A Delicate Balance,* however, suggests that he is not going to be content with repeating earlier attitudes. Had Claire carried her brandy glass into the world of *Who's Afraid of Virginia Woolf?* or *The American Dream,* she would have been severely punished for doing so. As it is, Albee leaves her alone; he even allows us to become fond of her, to welcome her clowning rather as we welcome the entrances of the Fool in *King Lear.*

And there is another thing to notice in this play: that Albee has repressed a natural tendency to depict one sex in terms of the other. One of the better American critics, John Simon, writing of *Virginia Woolf* when it appeared four years ago, having noticed that the structure of the play "resembles too closely that of O'Neill's *Long Day's Journey into Night,*" and that what he calls the "equivocating little flicker of hope at the end" stems from Tennessee Williams, speaks also of what, thinking no doubt of Proust, he calls "Albertine strategy." He is wondering, I suppose, whether the two couples in the play might not make better sense if they were presented as four men.

This ambiguity is not present in *A Delicate Balance.* If anything, the characters, with the exception of Claire, are reduced to the stature of mere vehicles for speech and gesture, like the characters in Greek classical drama. Albee has repressed his own knowingness, his tendency to, as it were, wink at the corruption of humanity; this time he is neither sardonic nor punitive, he simply presents a situation with no comment and as clear a focus as he can adjust.

It looks as though he were turning away from his original world of night-mare comedy and reaching towards a soberer theatre of ideas. Only, what exactly *are* the ideas? It may be possible to find a parallel in the work of other writers whose first impulse, as young men, was to round on society, but who later, even if they never overcame a fundamental dislike of the human race, put themselves at the service of a constructive discipline.

There is no indication that he will adopt any of the positions commonly taken up by writers who are essentially moralists. There is not much of the

Marxist or the Catholic about his work, still less of the anarchist. But I can imagine him exploring areas of human relationship with the courage and more than the theatrical skill, of, say, Jean Genet.

At any rate, his art has continually developed during the eight years since he began writing plays. Now, at two years short of forty, he remains a writer of rare promise as well as considerable performance.

COMMENTARY

Now, after excursions into the styles of novelists and historians, we have come to Alan Pryce-Jones's analysis of the style of modern American drama as represented by the plays of Edward Albee. As an essay written to entertain as well as to inform, this one succeeds because, like the others, it offers an abundance of factual detail and manages to suggest that some of the incidents it describes are of "universal significance."

After three paragraphs of introduction, the essay focuses attention on Albee's *A Delicate Balance*, which is "unlike anything he has so far written, both in style and content." By *content*, we may presume, is meant the "plot," or the whole pattern of action. The question, however, of the meaning of *style* as it is distinguished from *content* is not so easily answered. Without trying to divorce the two terms completely, Pryce-Jones makes some clear distinctions between them on the basis of his impressions after seeing the play, and by making comparisons.

The first aspect he considers distinctive of the style of *A Delicate Balance* is its "highly mannered" speech "in order to convey a set of prose statements from which poetry has been emptied." As the sentence following this judgment clarifies, *speech* here means the lines written for the actors—the "script" or text of the play—as well as the manner in which the lines were spoken. This speech differs from the "naturalism" of the "every day" language characteristic of his previous plays.

As in the other literary genres, style in drama appears to be a composite of the very personal outlook, temperament, and experience of a writer. And again the "good" style is the one true to the nature of the world as the writer sees it in its truest light. We can conclude that developing a style is a matter of integrity, courage, growth in understanding, and a command of the language in order to make what one has to say credible and entertaining.

As a dramatic critic Pryce-Jones reveals a mastery of sentence structure that serves him well. Note the skill with which he phrases his ideas in the two opening paragraphs. The first sentence—a periodic one—comes to a strong climax with the words "written on a postcard." The two following show an effective control of rhythmic structure in their phrasing. Compare them, for instance, with the following version: "*The Zoo Story*, which was the first play of his that was performed in New York, opened off Broadway in January 1960. It attracted startled attention to this young man who had just turned thirty and who was obviously talented." The sentence which opens the second paragraph is balanced to emphasize the contrast in ideas. And then, shortly after, comes the succession of short, wiry sentences and phrases: "He aroused curiosity. His background, for instance, appealed to a nation of romantics. The adopted son of rich parents, given every facility for conventional success in life. . . ."

Again, although he is not writing narrative, Pryce-Jones is as specific and concrete in his details, upon occasion, as is Updike or Hemingway. Note how he presents the matinée spectators: "ladies with vast heads of hair touched up to the colours of sunset over the Nile, ladies shaped like an immense doughnut swathed in fur, ladies in chattering groups up for the day from suburbs like Yonkers and New Rochelle." And they do not drive home in "automobiles," but in "Ford Galaxies." Once more we can see how an effective style, made up of well-chosen words and a mastery of sentence rhythm, can allow a writer to say what he wants to say because of his intense feelings on the subject.

WHAT DOES IT SAY?

1. Pryce-Jones calls the United States "a nation of romantics." What does *romantics* mean, and what historic American traits and practices can possibly justify his typing us as such?

2. Explain in simpler terms what is meant by saying Albee had "the air of a changeling, even a fallen angel" but was more of "a fierce young cuckoo in search of a nest to outrage."

3. Again we see by allusions the kind of backgrounds a general reader is expected to have. What are some of the features of the Theatre of the Absurd? Who are Pinter, Wesker, Arden, Osborne, O'Neill, Tennessee Williams, Proust, and Genet?

4. Pryce-Jones has a flair for colorful language. Select five examples that brighten his style.

5. What mixture of emotions do you associate with the term "unreasonable panic" that Pryce-Jones regards as present in some degree in American households?

6. Distinguish between *farce, melodrama, tragedy,* and *nightmare comedy.*

7. What are the significant differences alluded to in saying of Albee "there is not much of the Marxist or the Catholic about his work, still less of the anarchist"?

8. What does a tendency to "wink at the corruption of humanity" imply about the moral attitudes of an author?

WHAT DO YOU THINK?

1. Do you agree that "Domestic life, after all, is slow at times"? If so, describe a typical day of such "domestic life," but at the same time try to suggest what tensions or conflicts creating "unreasonable panic" underlie this "slowness." Suggestions:

Another day for golf	Who used the car last?
Laundry and cleaning time again	It was a nice party
A day too hot to breathe	Where have you been?
More, more rain	What's for dinner?
Who turned up the furnace?	Do I have to go?
Money again?	There's always the telephone

2. If you have read or seen *The Zoo Story*, explain why you liked or disliked it. Note especially its style.

3. Discuss the style of the following excerpt from a review of Albee's *A Delicate Balance* in comparison with that of Pryce-Jones:

The play begins. The wisps of subterranean smoke arise. A hint of suicide here, of dipsomania there, of inability to give or receive love. There is much talk; and very hifalutin subjunctivated talk, too, from the opening line on, for this isn't one of those hardboiled-dialogue plays; these people speak literature. Ma apostrophises the rising sun and all the sunrises man has witnessed in his long unhappy history. Pa discourses epigrammatically on the subject of epigrams. And Sis describes sexual intercourse as getting one's "pudenda stuffed"—even the dirty talk is arcane in this play.

To be sure, there were some chunks of gilded rhetoric in *Tiny Alice* between a cardinal and the devil, but now Albee has gone all out and crammed it in the mouths of babes. Babes perorating on the dullness of life in suburbia, to boot. The result is a set of characters so incredible and remote that when the expected volcanoes go off they go off on the moon somewhere.

Also, the awaited revelations themselves are not first-rate, which is strange, because it would seem there could be no end to the shocks which can be invented by this method. On the contrary. After only two or three plays, Albee appears to have dragged out all his choicest skeletons, and only the lees is left in his vault to brag of. The prize of writing in Victorian rhetoric seems sought as consolation. There is a moment in the first act where Pa confesses murdering a pet cat because the cat had ceased to love him. This is a mighty small skeleton to haunt a play. Yet for all the subsequent rattling, nothing much bigger falls out of the closet.—(Ed Fisher, "Broadway: Ashes to Ashes," *Spectator*, December 9, 1966, p. 754.)

ON MODERN ART—
HAVE WE
BEEN HAD?

LESTER D. LONGMAN

I THINK it is important to point out just now that in addition to those who say so openly, there are many artists, museum men, professors, teachers of art and art critics who now privately question the views they have held supporting abstract expressionism, action painting and neodadaism in art.

It is quite true that "we have been had." But it would be hard to say that anyone is at fault. We did it to ourselves, usually with the utmost sincerity, by convincing ourselves that we were being original and contemporaneous and that this is all that really counts.

Perhaps a brief description of the current scene in the world of art would be useful. Up until the second World War the development of the various arts in our century was in the healthy direction of liberating the artist from the stifling bonds of moribund tradition and opening up the whole of art history as an unlimited reservoir of ideas to stimulate the artist's creative imagination. Theoretically, the artist should then have been free to be himself; and a major exhibition should then have featured art in the most diverse styles, each work reflecting the personal gifts, interests, and convictions of its maker. *But this is not what happened.* After the war most roads were blocked, leaving only one broad freeway down which *all* artists have had to

Reprinted from *Oberlin Alumni Magazine*, February 1962, by permission of author and publisher.

travel if they would be sophisticated and respectable, if they would win a prize or even get their work accepted, if they would have it sold by leading dealers, purchased by museums, or discussed in art journals. This highway is marked "abstract expressionism," which includes as variations such anti-art phenomena as "action painting," "neodadaism," "junk culture," and the "art of assemblage."

While this is often called *avant-garde* art, which implies that it is the expression of a minority of individualistic and divergent fringe artists, it is on the contrary the all-pervasive conventional art of the respectable *cognoscenti* in all quarters, from which we can only deduce that our intellectual leaders have become temperamental conformists. To judge by the absurd fruits of their labor, they have also lost faith in God, in man, in reason, and in the future of the human race, and so have forfeited their power for constructive leadership in the realms of moral and social values. Not that all of them are fully aware of their plight and of the implications of their ideological conventions. Lionel Trilling's remark is applicable to our new academy of intellectuals, that "an ideology is not acquired by thought, but by breathing the haunted air."

Those who are not familiar with the current art world may be interested in examples of this respectable elite art. We can all enjoy them, of course, by temporarily suspending disbelief in the conventional premises on which they are based. There are painters who, by means of dripping or smearing techniques of applying paint to canvas, claim to be creating exciting space relationships and who are sometimes called "the push-pull painters" or "the space cadets." Some call themselves "action painters," the import of this term being that the value is in the action itself, of which the physical painting is but the lifeless document. They may paint very rapidly. Tsingos, for example, once completed twenty oil paintings in one evening, although only two were described as masterpieces. Kujawski paints ten pictures simultaneously. Mathieu has painted a whole exhibition in a day and sometimes paints while dancing or riding a bicycle. Sondorborg titles his paintings by the time it took to paint them, varying from fifteen minutes to three-quarters of an hour. Newman paints huge pictures with one or two thin vertical stripes. Yves Klein paints huge pictures with a roller such as one uses to paint a kitchen wall. They are solid cobalt blue and sell for from three to ten thousand dollars each. He calls his art "a voyage through the void of the immaterial," and says, "The true painter is the one who creates nothing visible." Klein also paints what he calls "draggings" or the "living paint brush," by smearing paint on nude girls and then dragging them over the heavy paper used for a canvas. The price for a typical "dragging" is $2,500. His prices are said to have risen fourfold in the past two years. All this neodadaism is a lucrative folly, as many of the artists will admit. One abstract expressionist painter has confessed that he laughs all the way to the bank. But most of the critics and professors and museum curators take it all very seriously. Were this not so, the absurd in art would go unnoticed and its exploitation would be impossible.

Fontana, a highly respected Italian artist, takes a knife or nail and cuts, tears, or pokes holes in the canvas, and such pictures sell for $1,000 each. Xanti Schawinsky puts paint on his shoes and dances on the canvas. He also puts paint on the tires of a small automobile and drives it over large canvases to make works of art. New York University cooperated in the car-track paintings by blocking off Greene Street for his use.

Robert Rauschenberg, the neo-dada leader of the American so-called "Junk School," or more recently the "Art of Assemblage," and whose works are shown in the most respectable museums, does such things as hang on the museum wall as a work of art his bedclothes smeared with paint. Another of his works of art is a stuffed goat with an old automobile tire around it. Cesar takes old cars, crushes them with giant presses and exhibits them as art, and several museums have purchased them. Jean Tinguely made as a work of art a junk machine which ceremoniously and ritualistically destroyed itself in the garden of the Museum of Modern Art in New York, before an assembled crowd of egregious arbiters of polite taste and high priests of our cult of futility. In October 1961 the Museum of Modern Art presented a large exhibition of 252 junk constructions, newly christened as the "art, non-art, and anti-art of assemblage," which traveled during 1962 to museums in Dallas and San Francisco. The Clert Gallery in Paris put on an exhibit of junk culture, "La Culture du Débris," and to dramatize it ordered two truck-loads of junk, which the junk man dumped in the gallery in such a way as to leave just enough room for people to walk through it.

In New York, Allan Kaprow, whose wisdom and dignity are guaranteed by a professorship at Rutgers University, is the leader of a school called "Happenings." An example of this combination of art and theater would be as follows: Hang refuse materials on the walls of a room and tattered pieces of canvas in front of them. Strew the room with debris from slums, such as old bottles, chicken wire and garbage. Hang some old bed springs from the ceiling and put up signs with absurd remarks, such as "Dirt is deep and very beautiful." Then, for the "happening," have a voice counting continuously in German, a machine making retching noises, a beatnik girl repeatedly stabbing a dummy, and a man pouring paint over his own head. Burn sulphur to make the audience in the room go into paroxysms of coughing.

In the other fine arts there are, of course, similar, if less offensive, manifestations of a taste for the irrational, the formless, the absurd, the accidental, the shocking and repulsive, the anti-aesthetic and anti-moral. In the novel, there is the "Literature of the Object" and in the cinema the "Nouvelle Vague." Much poetry is obscure gibberish. In the "anti-plays" or "plays of despair" of Ionesco, Gelber, Albee, Genet, and others, life is presented as devoid of meaning and purpose, and all our spiritual premises and securities are blatantly challenged as though to trumpet and proclaim a universal moral cataclysm. There is *"musique concrète"* or "tapesichord music," "electronic music," and John Cage's "music of the prepared piano" and his composition called 4'33", which is four minutes and thirty-three seconds of silence with composer seated at the piano. This compares favorably with an exhibition of "paintings" held some years ago, which consisted of a number of completely blank canvases.

It would appear from these few examples that we are in an age which has fallen in love with disorder, an age of anxiety and despair, of existentialist nausea and self-pity, of parasitic cynicism and moral degeneration. We are obsessed with the tortured conviction of the emptiness, futility, and boredom of life.

We can all understand this *avant-garde* art and can recognize its causes, but to understand it and to explain it is not to justify it. Our bourgeois world is not so hopeless as the conformist intellectuals would have us believe; nor is it so decadent as the artists who are denouncing its decadence. They pretend in their art and in their manifestoes to be taking the temperature of a sick world, but they are more accurately exhibiting the degree of their own fever. The real subject matter of the abstract art of today is the state of the artist's own soul. The arts in our time are dying of their own eccentric excesses and of their modish anemia, and are likely to live in the future only as curiosities for scholars. Our intellectual elite lack not only faith and hope, but also courage. They say, "I paint, therefore I am," or *"Après nous le déluge,"* or *"Gefühl, Gefühl ist Alles,"* content to have lost their moral anchor, handcuffed by ideological conformity, and driven by the emotions of resignation and defeat.

What we need are independent minds, courageous dissenters, in this era of inquisition against the heresy of reform. A saner view of the state of the world and of man's hope would also be a truer view. Let the intellectuals of the world arise; they have nothing to lose but their ideological chains. And let them take as their text these words of André Malraux: "A man becomes truly a man only when in quest of what is most exalted in him. True arts and cultures relate man to duration, sometimes to eternity, and make of him something other than the most favored denizen of a universe founded on absurdity."

COMMENTARY

Analysis and judgment of any composition, whether it be a literary one or a work of fine art such as a painting or a sculpture, always involve consideration of content and style. It matters little what other names we give these fundamentals—"object" and "design," "subject" and "treatment," and so forth—the qualities they represent are always present in any discussion of a creative work. *Style* and its synonyms are expressive of the personal values, insights, imagination, and techniques that produced the work. What then does Lester D. Longman say of style in "modern art"?

Longman attacks by name many modern artists and their works. In his unhappiness with all *avant-garde* art, he seems to make no distinctions between content and style and rejects everyone and everything connected with it, including the critics and the museum purchasers who praise these symbols of "moral degeneration." His essay—it is almost a diatribe!—cites for attack one after the other the artists and their "schools" such as "abstract expressionism" and "junk culture." His thesis maintains that all forms of *avant-garde* painting, sculpture, literature, and music smack of charlatanism and have destroyed the freedom of development the arts should enjoy. He insists modern artists and their supporters "have also lost faith in God, in man, in reason, and in the future of the human race." He urges both in his introduction and his conclusion the rise of a "new intellectual elite" who will have courage and faith enough to revolt against the "ideological chains" that have enslaved the arts since World War II.

Such a universal condemnation must raise questions in the minds of his readers, as surely it has in yours. Do none of these art works of the past twenty years or more have any true value? Are none of the names cited to be credited with insights and "social values" equal to those of the pre-War artists? Are both the "content" and "style," for example, of a stuffed goat wearing a rubber tire around its neck or a play by Albee or Ionesco equally worthless? It appears that only artists who have the kind of personal and social views that Longman advocates can produce works deserving of recognition.

His is the view of an extremist, one that permits no compromise, no tolerance of existing "wrongs," or charity for the "wrong-doers." Yet this intensity of conviction gives his detail-filled protest a distinctive style. If it is evangelical in tone and purpose, it has also marshalled a considerable number of factual instances to support its plea for a turn to a new kind of art based, however, on traditional values.

WHAT DOES IT SAY?

1. Which, if any, of the specific examples of artists at work explains the nature of the following schools of art objected to by Longman: "abstract expressionism," "action painting," "neo-dadaism," "junk culture," "art of assemblage," "happenings"?

2. What do *cognoscenti* have to do with "an ideology"?

3. How does "the irrational" differ from "the absurd"?

4. What kind of "nausea" is *existential nausea*?

5. Point out three examples of the kind of art works that Longman terms products of a "parasitic cynicism." What does the phrase mean?

6. Translate *"Après nous le deluge"* and *"Gefühl, Gefühl ist Alles."* How appropriate are these expressions?

7. Explain the meaning of all the terms in this statement from the final paragraph: "What we need are independent minds, courageous dissenters, in this era of inquisition against the heresy of reform."

8. Interpret this Malraux quotation appearing in the final sentence: "A man becomes truly a man only when in quest of what is most exalted in him. True arts and cultures relate man to duration, sometimes to eternity, and make of him something other than the most favored denizen of a universe founded on absurdity."

WHAT DO YOU THINK?

1. If you have not recently visited a show of "modern art," visit such an exhibition in a museum or gallery, and then write a 500-word essay expressing, with ample detail, your approval or disapproval of one of the following statements about such art.
   a) Pop art is "an assemblage in which a real lawnmower leans against a painted canvas" or "a disembodied female breast . . . looms, big as a mountain, over a diminutive seashore."
   b) ". . . There seems to be no criteria, no opposition, not even an insistence on the artist's uniqueness or individuality—the very claim that used to animate artistic revolutions."
   c) "More and more people are beginning to feel that the current state of art, as Robert Frost said of free verse, is like playing tennis without a net."
   d) "What then is art? . . ." Says Sherman Lee, director of the Cleveland Museum of Art: "It is an expression of individual sensibilities. A neon Coca-Cola sign is in a very real sense a piece of art. The fact that anyone could make it is more or less beside the point. The fact is that no one else did make it."
   e) What is art? According to the Museum of Modern Art's Alfred Barr, "It is folly to say what is art. Works can become art by fiat—sometimes by the fiat of one man. And it can be art for a while and then not art."
   f) According to Sir John Rothenstein, former director of the Tate Gallery, "Art derives from the intention of the artist. But time is the only impeccable judge."

g) Art "critics are now saying more and more about less and less."

h) "There is no place in art for life . . . the one thing to say about art is its breathlessness, lifelessness, deathlessness, contentlessness, formlessness, spacelessness, and timelessness."—*Time* Essay, "What Is Art Today?" *Time,* January 27, 1967, pp. 24–25.

2. Write an analysis of what you consider to be the *style* of an artist whose works give you pleasure.

3. From your observations or acquaintance with some form of art or artists, write a detailed definition with examples of the meaning of *talent*. Explain also how talent can be recognized and evaluated.

Index
of Authors
and Titles

Index of Authors and Titles *

* Titles are italicized.

249